#Share

#Share

How to Mobilize Social Word of Mouth (sWOM)

Natalie T. Wood and Caroline K. Muñoz

BUSINESS EXPERT PRESS

#Share: How to Mobilize Social Word of Mouth (sWOM)

Copyright © Business Expert Press, LLC, 2017.

First published in 2017 by
Business Expert Press, LLC
222 East 46th Street, New York, NY 10017
www.businessexpertpress.com

ISBN-13: 978-1-63157-441-2 (paperback)
ISBN-13: 978-1-63157-442-9 (e-book)

Business Expert Press Digital and Social Media Marketing and Advertising Collection

Collection ISSN: 2333-8822 (print)
Collection ISSN: 2333-8830 (electronic)

Cover and interior design by Exeter Premedia Services Private Ltd., Chennai, India

First edition: 2017

10 9 8 7 6 5 4 3 2 1

Printed in the United States of America.

To Timothy, Conor, Ronan, and Ava,
who sometimes share too much.

To J, M, S, and my mother.
Thanks for your patience.

Abstract

Each day, millions of consumers venture online to search and exchange product information, seek out, and share opinions. Electronic word-of-mouth (eWOM) communication has been shown to influence consumer actions across a variety of industries (King, Racherla, and Bush 2014). A significant portion of eWOM occurs on social media platforms. Whether it is a status update of an upcoming vacation on Facebook, a picture of a laundry room makeover on Pinterest, or a YouTube video discussing the features on the new iPhone, consumers are turning to a variety of social platforms to make everyday purchasing decisions easier for themselves and others. Indeed, social word of mouth (sWOM)—a subset of eWOM—has incredible reach with the potential to influence over 2 billion active social media consumers.

The purpose of this book is to examine the influence of sWOM and provide guidance on how to operationalize its growing power. Our goal in writing this book was to bring together industry best practices and academic research to help you construct social media content that speaks with your brand voice, stimulates engagement, inspires consumers to share (#share), and that complies with industry and federal guidelines. Each chapter highlights a key area of sWOM that will further your understanding of the topic and provides actionable information to assist you in mobilizing positive sWOM for your company.

Keywords

Brand Advocates, Brand Ambassadors, Brand Endorsers, Consumer Reviews, eWOM, Facebook, Google+, Influencers, Instagram, Pinterest, Social Influence, Social Media Marketing, Social Media Policy, Social Media Regulations, sWOM, Twitter, Viral Marketing, WOMM, Word of mouth marketing, YouTube

Contents

Preface

Social media is, in many ways, akin to the wild, Wild West—lawless, crazy, messy, and sometimes, a little brutal. If you agree, feel some sympathy for us who attempt to teach this topic. Without question, social media is a fascinating subject, and let's face it, it's not going anywhere. So, let's take the horse by the reins, follow the regulatory laws, develop some order, and learn more about how you can use social media in your company. But, before we get carried away, we should warn you—this book is not a "Complete Guide to Social Media" (there are plenty of books that have tackled that monster). This book focuses on what lies at both the heart and soul of social media: what motivates consumers to update their Facebook status, retweet an interesting piece of news, and pin things that they will probably never make (Hello, Bourbon Brown Sugar Maple Bacon Candy!). This book focuses on a topic that is under-represented on digital and physical bookshelves. This book focuses on the topic of social sharing (#Share).

Everyday consumers are drawn to social media to share their opinions, ideas, purchases, events, recent finds, and much more with their social networks. They also use social media to find information to help them make their purchase decisions. Logically, companies are drawn to social media to reach and engage with their consumers. However, for many companies, trying to engage with consumers on social media is extremely challenging. The sheer volume of tweets, status updates, pins, and videos that consumers are exposed to every day is staggering—it is like drinking from a fire hose. Companies are increasingly frustrated that despite all their hard work, their social media efforts appear to produce little results. It is not easy getting people to like your Facebook page, retweet your news alert, comment on your video, and it is even more difficult to get them to discuss and share your posts with others.

When consumers share, they are engaging in word of mouth (WOM). One form of WOM is electronic WOM (eWOM). There is a wealth of books and websites that discuss the importance of eWOM and how to use it for business purposes. Yet, there is a big empty spot (at the time of writing this book) on bookshelves on the topic of social WOM (sWOM). Certainly, there are similarities between eWOM and sWOM; however, we suggest that we should view sWOM as a subset of eWOM. We believe that there are differences—differences that warrant a closer look. And, that is what we aim to do.

In this book, we discuss the importance of understanding the social consumer—who he is, what social media accounts he or she uses, why he or she uses them, what content he or she wants to engage with, and more importantly, what makes him or her want to share his or her opinion and your company message with others. We advocate that to be successful with engaging consumers in sWOM it needs to be a companywide effort. That is, your company needs to become a social business in which communicating and sharing on social media is a part of your company's DNA. Going back to our Wild West analogy, we highlight the various federal and industry regulations supporting sWOM and discuss the importance of developing a social media policy. From here, we delve into how to create content that resonates with your consumers—content that engages them, which they feel compelled to discuss and share. We examine how to craft engaging textual stories and highlight the power of visuals. We also discuss how you can harness the powers of persuasion to encourage your consumers to share, retweet, comment, and the like. Throughout all of this, we offer examples of companies who are already succeeding in this area and provide you with resources to help your company succeed.

CHAPTER 1

Social Word of Mouth Marketing (sWOM)

Caroline Munoz @CarineMunoz 5s

My name is Caroline and I am a Diet Coke addict #shareacoke

Figure 1.1 An example of social sharing on Twitter

Source: Courtesy of C. Munoz.

Too personal? A tweet can say a lot. And a tweet with a hashtag and an image not only communicates more, but is also much more likely to be shared. The screenshot in Figure 1.1 embodies many topics that this book will explore: the role of storytelling, the persuasive power of images, emotional appeals, personalization, and social sharing. It also marks the beginning a positive story—which is where all good social media campaigns (and books) should begin.

In the summer of 2014, Coca-Cola launched the personalized, "Share a Coke" campaign. Twenty oz. bottles of Coca-Cola, Diet Coke, and Coke Zero were adorned with 250 of the most popular American names for millennials and teens. Consumers were prompted to share their photos of the personalized bottles using #Shareacoke on social media. They could visit shareacoke.com to create, then share virtual, personalized bottles on Instagram, Facebook, Tumblr, and Twitter. They could also be featured on Coke billboards by using #Shareacoke (Hitz 2014). Consumers were drawn to soda bottles that were emblazoned with not only their name, but also the names of their family and friends. Coca-Cola's bottle personalization was putting into action something that Dale Carnegie taught us long before—"A person's name is to that person, the sweetest, most important sound in any language." So, naturally, consumers wanted to share their name discovery on Twitter, Facebook, and Instagram.

Over the course of the campaign, consumers shared their experiences via the #Shareacoke hashtag over 250,000 times (Deye 2015). During the 2014 campaign cycle, more than 353,000 bottles were disseminated virtually (Tadena 2014). Geo-tagging and sales were correlated, and sure enough, there was a significant relationship between social sharing and sales (Deye 2015). By all accounts, the campaign was a sales success; Coke saw sales growth of more than 30 percent in one week (Deye 2015). Part of this success was certainly attributed to the power of social word of mouth (sWOM) marketing.

---

84 percent of consumers worldwide trust recommendations from family and friends more than any other type of advertising (Nielsen 2013).

Why Word of Mouth Marketing?

You are reading this book because you get it. Word of mouth (WOM) marketing is powerful—it impacts not only product preferences and purchasing decisions, but it serves to mold consumer expectations and even post-purchase product attitudes (Kimmel and Kitchen 2014). The beauty of branded WOM marketing communication is that it is a natural, normal part of our everyday conversations. In fact, 2.4 billion conversations each day involve brands (Google; KellerFay Group 2016). The ample number of conversations related to products and services is attributable to the fact that we need and actively seek out input from family and friends before we make a purchase. A 2016 study from the referral company Ambassador found that 82 percent of the respondents surveyed sought out recommendations before making a purchase (Patton 2016). One of the reasons that family and friends' recommendations matter so much is that they are simply trusted more—84 percent of consumers worldwide trust recommendations from family and friends more than any other type of advertising (Nielsen 2013).

Marketing executives (64 percent surveyed) agree that WOM marketing is the most effective type of marketing (Whitler 2014). The creation and membership roll of WOMMA (Word of Mouth Marketing Association) who are devoted to "representing and improving the WOM marketing industry" underscores the importance of WOM. Outside of an implicit understanding that people seem to prefer the opinions of others over a TV advertisement, billboard, or branded website, on what information are marketers basing these beliefs? Can we quantify the effect of WOM?

In 2014, WOMMA along with six major brands commissioned a study to determine the ROI on WOM marketing (WOMMA 2014). This was the first major study addressing not only the differing category impact of WOM, but also its role in the overall marketing mix. Not surprisingly, the results reinforce many established beliefs about WOM's level of importance.

- $6 trillion of annual consumer spending is driven by word of mouth (i.e., on average 13 percent of consumer sales).
- WOM's impact on sales is greater for products that consumers are more involved with (i.e., more expensive, higher-risk).
- Most of the impact of WOM (two-thirds) is through offline conversations, whereas a third is through online WOM.
- WOM, directly and indirectly, impacts business performance. For example, it can drive traffic to website or search engines, which can then impact performance measures.
- WOM can amplify paid media (e.g., advertising) by as much as 15 percent. The value of one offline WOM impression can be 5 to 200 times more effective than a paid advertising impression.
- Two weeks after exposure, online WOM (85–95 percent) has a quicker impact than offline WOM (65–80 percent) and traditional media—TV (30–60 percent).

Are these numbers compelling enough?

If you were paying attention, you would have noticed that according to these statistics, offline WOM appears to matter much more. Wharton Professor and author of *Contagious*, Jonah Berger, also suggests that we are spending much too much time and effort on looking at online WOM (Berger 2013). Research supports Berger's statement—a 2011 study from the Keller Fay Group found that only 7 percent of all brand-related WOM conversations occur online (Belicove 2011), with 94 percent of brand impressions happening offline (Google; KellerFay Group 2016). Berger suggests that this overestimation of online WOM occurs because we can easily see the conversation and we spend a lot of time online. And, we do spend a lot of time online; global online users spend more than six hours per day online (Mander 2015) with *50 minutes* (on average) devoted solely to Facebook properties (i.e., Facebook, Instagram, and Messenger) (Stewart 2016). In the United States, 73 percent of consumers are online every day, 42 percent are on the Internet multiple times a day and 21 percent reporting an almost "constant" online presence (Perrin 2015). Without question, offline brand-related WOM matters more. But is online brand-related WOM limited to only 7 percent?

The truth is offline and online WOM are not like oil and water; they can and do mix. The 2014 WOMMA study illustrates that offline and online work together to, directly and indirectly, impact business performance. Consumers today move seamlessly between online and offline communication, making it increasingly difficult for us to pinpoint whether the message that we saw came to us in-person or via social media. And, the 7 percent?—that is from a study completed in 2011 (aka 35 years ago in Internet dog years). To offer some perspective, in September 2011, Snapchat launched and Instagram only had 10 million users. Smartphone adoption of American adults was at 35 percent (Smith 2011). Things are different in 2016. Instagram now boasts over 500 million monthly active users (Instagram 2015), and by the time you read this, smartphone adoption will be close to if not greater than 80 percent (comScore 2016).

Socializing online is seamlessly integrated into our offline lives. For today's consumers, particularly those from a younger generation, there is no offline or online socializing, it is simply socializing. Even when we are supposedly offline, we are drawn back through a symphony of chirps and beeps alerting us to an online conversation we should be responding to. We are being normalized to believe that we should upload images of our food, family outings, and post about positive and negative consumer experiences. Consumer e-commerce websites, such as Amazon, are providing more opportunities for not only consumer comments, but also allowing individuals to upload images and videos showcasing their recent purchase. Consumer feedback or input is essential in the purchase of the product. This feedback is becoming increasingly visual. Take for instance, the online rental dress company—Rent the Runway. On the primary product screen for each dress, Rent the Runway shares photographs taken by their consumers wearing the rented dress. The company encourages consumers to review the dress and provide personal information such as their height, weight, bust, body type, age, size worn, usual size, and event occasion. For any one dress, there could be well over 100 photos highlighting not only the fit, but "how others wore it," illustrating how to accessorize and wear one's hair with the dress.

With the advent and ubiquity of smartphones, image and video creation is easy and uploading almost instantaneous. In 2015, consumers uploaded 700 million photos per day to cross-platform mobile messenger WhatsApp, 350 million to Facebook, and 70 million to Instagram. Relative to the number of users, Snapchat had the most photos shared with 8,796 per second (Morrison 2015). Video uploads are also incredibly high—up to 400 hours of video is uploaded each minute to YouTube (Brouwer 2015). Video consumption is even greater—eight billion views or 100 million hours of video watched is viewed each day on Facebook (Constine 2015a; Constine 2015b). And, if industry reports are accurate, consumers collectively watch close to five billion YouTube videos each day, totaling over three billion viewing hours per month (Statistic Brain 2016).

Marketers also seek to further blend online and offline worlds. Television and print ads are prompting consumers to go online and watch, follow, and like. Traditional televised news programs routinely integrate social media conversations and "what's trending" segments. While old and new media continue to become more integrated, the line is also blurring between types of online media. *Owned media* (e.g., company website, blog), *earned media* (e.g., shares, reviews, reposts), and *paid media* (e.g., sponsored posts, tweets) are becoming fused. For example, finance website The Penny Hoarder (owned media) pays guest bloggers (paid media). The Dunkin Donuts website (owned media) has a rotating consumer social media feed of consumer content curated from Twitter and Instagram posts (shared media), which include the hashtag #DDPerksLove. Fashion-orientated discount store, Marshalls, has a very prominent, dedicated section of the website (owned media)—dubbed #MarshallsSurprise—devoted to displaying consumer (and ambassador) images from Instagram and Twitter accounts (earned and paid media). While Dunkin Donuts and Marshalls simply take a gallery approach to integrating social media, furniture store Pier 1 Imports takes it a step further, integrating social WOM to direct purchases. On the Pier 1 store website, under the heading, "#Pier1love," there is a curated list of photos taken from consumers' Instagram accounts. When you click on each Instagram image, it enlarges, and consumers are asked to "Shop This Look." A Pier 1 store item taken from the displayed Instagram picture is then pictured separately and linked to the retail landing page for purchase. Another approach that creatively blends earned and owned media are branded Snapchat lenses and Facebook filters. Taco Bell turned consumers' heads on Snapchat into large tacos on Cinco de Mayo (with 224 million views by May 5, 2016), while IronMan Masks covering individuals faces using Facebook filters resulted in over 8 million views by March 9, 2016 (Meeker 2016). So, why are marketers exerting this level of interest in both shaping and spreading sWOM? You know the answer—many consumers are more likely to purchase a product after seeing it shared on social media via a friend or family member (Patton 2016). WOM marketing matters. So let's explore it together.

Traditional WOM and Electronic WOM (eWOM)

Without question, WOM marketing is powerful and perhaps is one of the most persuasive factors in the consumer decision-making process. The focus on WOM marketing has grown exponentially and with it, related marketing constructs intended to increase its potency: influencers, referral programs, brand ambassadors, viral marketing, seeding campaigns, and brand communities (Kimmel and Kitchen 2014). A growing number of companies have been created to capitalize on the power and potential of WOM. But what exactly is it and how does word of mouth extend to the Internet?

WOM marketing is not new—but rather our appreciation, evolving technology, and growing number of firms and resources devoted to the topic is what has changed. The WOMMA trade association defines WOM marketing as "any business action that earns a customer recommendation." Academically, numerous definitions have been put forward that are typically more complicated than industry's (see Kimmel and Kitchen 2013 for a review). For example, "word of mouth is the interpersonal communication between two or more individuals, such as members of a reference group or a customer and a salesperson" (Kim, Han, and Lee 2011, 276). Or "in a post-purchase context, consumer word-of-mouth transmissions consist of informal communications directed at other consumers about the ownership, usage or characteristics of particular goods and services and/or their sellers" (Westbrook 1987, 261). Both definitions focus on the activity or the result of the activity (i.e., similar to WOMMAs) (Kimmel and Kitchen 2013). As some of these definitions indicate, WOM communication can be either instigated by consumers *organically* or when marketers are involved the messages become *amplified*. Organic WOM refers to when consumers, without being prompted by marketers, discuss their product experiences. Whereas, amplified WOM refers to marketing efforts to encourage consumers to amplify the WOM. This can include reaching out to influentials to spread the word, carefully crafting messages so that that consumers want to share them and that are easy to be shared, creating buzz, and using referral programs. Later in this chapter, we will argue that we need to give more attention to the third type of WOM communication—*collaborative*. Collaborative can be thought of as a combination of both organic and amplified—a message that is jointly created and shared by marketers and consumers who have an interest in a product.

On the surface, WOM appears to be simple. It involves the communicator, message, and receiver. However, the WOM process is impacted by a host of contributing factors. What are the attributes of the communicator—in particular, credibility? What is motivating the communicator and receiver in creating or looking for the message? How much knowledge does the receiver have about the product? How important is the product to them? How strong is the connection between the communicator and the receiver? What is the message valence—positive, negative, neutral? What is the mode and delivery of communication? As you can see, it gets complicated. And, one of the more recent complexities is understanding whether or not what we know about traditional offline WOM translates to the Internet (eWOM)—is it "old wine in new bottles"? (Hint: it's not).

eWOM

Over a decade ago, scholars sought to differentiate eWOM from traditional WOM, defining it as, "any positive or negative statements made by potential, actual, or former customers about a product or company, which is made available to a multitude of people and institutions via the Internet" (Hennig-Thurau et al. 2004, 39). Unlike traditional WOM, which is communicated verbally, eWOM is transmitted through a variety of electronic communication channels: discussion boards, corporate websites, blogs, e-mails, chat rooms or instant messaging, social media, review websites, and newsgroups. There are numerous differences, outside of modality, between WOM and eWOM (Cheung and Thadani 2012; Chu and Kim 2011):

- **The messenger/source:** In traditional WOM, the receiver of the message is acquainted with the individual communicating it—the messenger or source. Even if the individual is somewhat of a stranger, there is a context and cues that will help discern the messenger's credibility. In eWOM, the consumer may not be acquainted with the individual. This complicates the credibility of the message and authenticity of the messenger.

- **Many messengers and many receivers:** In "real-life," WOM occurs as a one-on-one conversation between friends or in a small gathering, whereas, eWOM can be akin to one individual (or many) screaming into a packed stadium full of people that is continually turning over with new spectators.

- **Message/opinion transmitter:** In traditional WOM, there is the opinion giver and receiver. However, eWOM provides a new role—that of the message or opinion transmitter. The transmitter may be the opinion giver, receiver, or someone new. As opposed to traditional WOM where distortion is likely to occur when and if the message is shared (think "game of telephone"), in eWOM, the message can be transmitted with a higher degree of accuracy.

- **Limited privacy:** WOM conversations occur in person typically between two individuals or in a small group. In contrast, eWOM messages can be shared immediately, repeatedly, and with 100 percent accuracy to the Internet world. Messages can be accessible to the masses.

- **Asynchronous (not in real-time) communication:** WOM communications are typically synchronous. eWOM is primarily asynchronous—conversation occurs over a period that, in some cases, can span years.

- **Messages are enduring:** Unlike face-to-face conversations, which quickly fade from our memories, online communication endures, sticking around long after that initial exchange.

- **Measurable/observable:** The Internet allows us to track, observe, measure online conversations through a host of online analytic tools and measures (i.e., Constant Contact, Hootsuite). This simply is not possible (to this degree) in traditional WOM (yet).

- **The speed of communication diffusion:** eWOM can spread at an exponential speed. Conversation is not limited to water cooler banter, but can spread across the globe in a matter of seconds. This is particularly true within social media.

- **More communication with weak ties:** Within an online environment, there is more exposure to what is known as "weak ties." The term "weak ties" refers to "contacts with people where your relationship is based on superficial experiences or very few connections" (Tuten and Solomon 2015, 92). For example, a casual acquaintance or a friend of a friend. In traditional WOM communication, we frequently receive messages from friends and family ("strong ties"). While communication with "strong ties" certainly occurs online, there is more exposure and interaction with "weak ties"—strangers and online only acquaintances. At least one study found that online weak ties were more persuasive than strong ties when selecting college courses and professors (Steffes and Burgee 2009).

sWOM Defined and Explained

When the Internet was first launched, electronic content was created by the few but consumed by the masses. Consumers could only read content; they could not create it (the Web 1.0 era). At the turn of the millennium, there was a gradual shift to create a Web where Internet users were not only consumers, but also creators of Web content. The Web became a place where consumers could create, engage, and collaborate with each other (the Web 2.0 era). At first, electronic communication modalities consisted primarily of online discussion forums (e.g., Yahoo! Groups), boycott websites (e.g., walmartsucks.org), and the most popular of all, opinion websites (e.g., epinions.com) (Hennig-Thurau et al. 2004). Now it includes a vast array of social platforms with varying degrees of media richness. But is WOM communication delivered via Facebook, the same as those posted to a chat room, or message sent via an e-mail? Similarly, to the delineation of eWOM from traditional WOM, we believe that WOM communication via social media (sWOM) also deserves a more nuanced look. Specifically, we view social word of mouth (sWOM) as a subset of eWOM. We are not the first to propose reexamining and segmenting eWOM. Researchers Wang and Rodgers (2010) recognized the limitations of the earlier eWOM definition. They point out that conversations are not just positive or negative—many include mixed reviews and include neutral information (Wang and Rodgers 2010). They also acknowledge the relationship between user-generated content (UGC) or consumer-generated content (CGC) (i.e., Internet content created and posted online by consumers) and eWOM, viewing eWOM as a type of UGC. Wang and Rodgers (2010) suggest that eWOM should be broken down further into two categories: informational-orientated contexts (i.e., online feedback systems and consumer review websites) and emotionally oriented contexts (i.e., discussion boards and social networking sites). Both of these typologies do not encompass all forms of electronic communication (i.e., e-mail and chat rooms or instant messaging).

In many respects, it almost sounds silly and redundant to call it sWOM. Yes, the essence of WOM is about being social. However, we argue there is a distinct difference between WOM communication via social media and other eWOM tools, such as Instant Communication (IM) chat rooms, e-mail communication, review websites and newsgroups.

- **Personal accounts:** In the case of eWOM, a large majority of information is shared on a company or third-party accounts. For example, a consumer writing a restaurant review on Yelp or a product review on Amazon, a concerned citizen posting a comment on a news website, or complaining about a malfunctioning product in a customer service forum. In contrast, a large percentage of sWOM is posted to and shared from a consumer's personal account. The recipients of sWOM are more likely to be connected to the poster (strong or weak ties) than are the readers of posts that appear on the company or a third-party account. This fact alone may increase the credibility, and therefore the persuasiveness of the message.

- **Audience:** When a consumer posts a comment to his or her personal social media account, it has the potential to be seen by a wider assortment of consumers. In contrast, eWOM's reach may be limited to those consumers who have an interest in the topic or product being discussed. For example, product reviews on Amazon are seen only by those consumers viewing the product, whereas a larger audience may see a product review posted on Facebook. Granted a consumer's Facebook friends may not have an interest in the product mentioned. However, the fact that they are exposed to the posting may have some level of influence at a later point in time.

- **Defined messenger:** Within social media, a user's communication is connected to their profile. Profile information typically consists of an image and multiple descriptors. A descriptor can be as short as a sentence (e.g., Twitter) or as lengthy as a resume (e.g., LinkedIn). E-mail, newsgroups, review websites and chat rooms will typically only provide a username and user address. User descriptors are an important step in building credibility and trustworthiness in WOM communications.

- **Communication direction:** Social media platforms allow for one-to-one, one-to-many, and many-to-many forms of communication between the message communicator and receiver(s) (Figure 1.2). In other words, conversations can be between individuals (e.g., private direct messages on Twitter), one-to-many (e.g., tweet to a network), but also many-to-many, where a message is created and discussed within a network (e.g., tweet using a hashtag). sWOM encompasses three communication directions, whereas traditional WOM and eWOM are limited to one or two directions.

- **Highly accessible and searchable:** Unless a user has established privacy settings, social media posts can quickly be found through searches on social media platforms, major search engines, and specialized social media monitoring tools (e.g., Hootsuite, TweetDeck). In contrast, chat rooms or IM and e-mail and are not publically searchable. It should also be noted that an increasing number of social media platforms are becoming synchronous and transient through the use of video and expiring content (i.e., Snapchat and Periscope).

Scope of sWOM

sWOM Scope		Select Examples
One-to-One (Private) Bi-Directional communication Visible only to sender and receiver Highly tailored message		Twitter: Direct Message Facebook: Messenger LinkedIn: Message Snapchat: Share with one friend
One-to-Many (Public) Bi-directional and possibly multi-directional communication Visible to anyone with access to the page Less tailored message		Twitter: Tweet to network Facebook: Status update Snapchat: Share with many friends YouTube: Public Video Blog: Blog entry
Many-to-Many (Public) Multi-directional communication Visible to anyone with access to the page Least tailored message		Twitter: Status update with popular hashtag Facebook:/LinkedIn Participation in group discussion Pinterest: Post to collaborative board

Figure 1.2 Scope of sWOM

- **Faster scalability:** Chat rooms or IM, e-mails, and news-groups do not have the potential reach of various social media venues such as Twitter and Facebook. While an e-mail certainly has the potential to be sent far and wide, its dissemination does not match the speed and out-of-network connections that social media can. You also do not see entire TV shows and regular news segments devoted to trending e-mail.

- **Saturated, information overload:** Many social media platforms (e.g., Facebook, Twitter) provide users with an abundance of information each time they log in. On social media, marketers face fierce competition for consumer's attention (Daugherty and Hoffman 2014). To further complicate this issue, the active lifespan of a social media post can be very short, as it becomes buried in the sea of newly created content. On a website, a product review can live forever, but on social media, the life of a message can be fleeting. The median lifespan of a tweet is a matter of minutes, and a Facebook post will get the vast majority of its impressions in the first few hours after posting (Ayres 2016).

- **Communication occurs in a mediated environment:** Communication within social media occurs, primarily, through their social media platform. While many platforms (e.g., Facebook, Twitter) allow for direct communications via an internal mail system, the content that is shown or is more prominently displayed is readily controlled by the platform's algorithm. Popular user posts and trending news and information, which can be commented upon, is not fully under consumers' control.

- **More visual:** Social media is becoming an increasingly visual medium. Facebook's acquisition of Instagram, the ease with which you can incorporate images and video into a tweet, and the popularity of Pinterest, Instagram, and Snapchat all speak to consumers' ability and desire to incorporate imagery into their communication. Older forms of electronic communication, such as e-mail, are not as visually oriented.

- **Co-creation:** Social media content is frequently co-created between consumers and between marketers and consumers (and vice versa). This is often referred to as collaborative content. Marketers can inspire conversations or the creation and sharing of images through a variety of initiatives such as contests and hashtag campaigns. Sometimes, these conversations generate a positive result, other times consumers can, intentionally or unintentionally, take them in a negative direction. There are many examples of where hashtags have become "bashtags." In 2012, McDonalds adopted the hashtag #McDStories to encourage consumers to share their happy McDonald's stories. Unfortunately, consumers used the hashtag to relay a host of unflattering restaurant experiences. In 2014, the hashtag #myNYPD sought to encourage positive images of police officers and instead received, over one day, almost 102,000 tweets addressing various civil rights violations (Swann 2014). In some cases, marketers have also taken over existing consumer hashtags with negative consequences. In one example, Digiorno Pizza used the hashtag #WhyIStayed and included the answer—"I had Pizza." Unfortunately, the hashtag was already associated with domestic violence (cringe!). Needless to say, they quickly deleted the message and profusely apologized, but not before it received wide media attention (Griner 2014). But there are examples of positive consequences—DDB New York used the established #FirstWorldProblems meme for their highly successful WATERisLife viral video ad campaign. The campaign featured impoverished Haitians reading various "problems" (i.e., "I hate it when my house is so big, I need two wireless routers") (Payne and Friedman 2012).

sWOM communication is any visual or textual post about a company or their product offering that is either created independently by a consumer, created by a company, or created by a consumer in collaboration with a company and publically shared on a personal or company social media account.

We define sWOM communication as any visual or textual post about a company or their product offering that is either created independently by a consumer, created by a company, or created by a consumer in collaboration with a company and publically shared on a personal or company social media account. This definition is broader than other WOM or eWOM definitions, in that it considers not just opinions regarding the traditional products that a company sells, but also the *content* that the company disseminates via social media. The stories that brands tell via social media are part of the product and contribute to its brand equity. This idea is similar to what consulting company McKinsey has called a "consequential" type of WOM marketing, "which occurs when consumers directly exposed to traditional marketing campaigns pass on messages about them or brands they publicize" (Bughin, Doogan, and Vetvik 2010). Social media has provided countless ways to distribute a wide variety of information that consumers deem valuable enough to share. Whether a social media post includes an e-book, white paper, product photography, how-to video, recipe, or even a joke, the act of sharing itself is an endorsement or recommendation. And, while a consumer may not be directly discussing the traditional product offerings of a company, they are still disseminating and conversing about a company's offering in the form of their digital assets. This act of sharing in the social media space can be as simple as forwarding information on (i.e., retweet or share), personalizing information that is created by someone else, writing product- or brand-related comments, or creating product- or brand-related content and posting it (i.e., video, photograph, etc.). The other aspect of this definition that we need to highlight and explore is the intersection between consumers and company in the social media environment (Figure 1.3). Increasingly, consumers and companies are co-creating content in both planned and organic ways.

As illustrated in Figure 1.3, sWOM communications can include one-to-one (e.g., direct message on Twitter), one-to-many (e.g., Facebook status update), or many-to-many (e.g., the use of a popular hashtag) messages. Communication can originate from a consumer, a company, or both parties can collaborate (the 3 Cs). Consumer content is content that is created by a consumer without any involvement from a company—organic content. Examples include sharing an experience on Facebook,

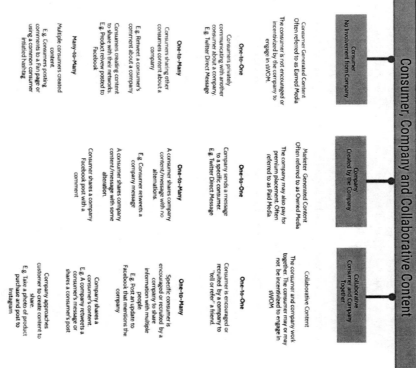

sWOM Typology
Consumer, Company and Collaborative Content

Consumer — No Involvement from Company

Company — Created by the Company

Collaborative — Consumer and Company Together

Consumer Generated Content
Often referred to as Earned Media
The consumer is not encouraged or incentivized by the company to engage in sWOM

One-to-One
Consumers privately communicating with another consumer about a company.
E.g. Twitter Direct Message

One-to-Many
Consumers sharing other consumers content about a company.
E.g. Retweet a consumer's comment about a company

Many-to-Many
Consumers creating content to share with their networks.
E.g. Product review posted to Facebook

Multiple consumers created content.
E.g. Consumers posting comments to a Fan page or using a common consumer initiated hashtag

Marketer Generated Content
Often referred to as Owned Media
The company may also pay for premium placement. Often referred to as Paid Media

One-to-One
Company sends a message to a specific consumer.
E.g. Twitter Direct Message

One-to-Many
A consumer shares company content/message with no alternatives.
E.g. Consumer retweets a company message

A consumer shares company content/message with some alteration.

Consumer shares a company Facebook post with a comment.

Collaborative Content
The consumer and company work together. The consumer may or may not be incentivized to engage in sWOM

One-to-One
Consumer is encouraged or recruited by a company to "tell or refer" a friend.

One-to-Many
Specific consumer is encouraged or recruited by a company to share information with multiple people.
E.g. Post an update to Facebook that mentions the company

Company shares a consumer's content.
E.g. A company retweets a consumer's message or shares a consumer's post

Company approaches customer to create content to share.
E.g. Take a photo of product purchase and post to Instagram

Figure 1.3 sWOM Typology

creating a video for YouTube, or Instagramming a photo of a recent purchase. This is commonly referred to as earned media because there is no cost to the company. Company-generated communication refers to content created and posted by the company's marketing department. The company shares this communication with one or more consumers in the hope that they will engage with the content through liking, sharing, retweeting, and commenting, thereby amplifying the communication. This is commonly referred to as paid media, particularly if the company has paid to promote the communication (e.g., promoted tweet). Outside of consumer-generated and company-generated content, there is a middle ground; a combination of both organic and amplified WOM efforts—collaborative. In this instance, consumers and companies are working together to create and share information. For example, a company may invite consumers to upload photos of their purchase with a hashtag. The Dunkin Donuts and Marshall's examples offered earlier in this chapter are examples of collaborative communications. Collaborative communication has seen significant growth in recent years, thanks in part, to high smartphone adoption rates (Tode 2015). Stores are now thoughtfully integrating social media within consumers' in-store experience. Consumers are not only prompted via signage to not only "follow," "like," "Check-In," and review retail venues, but also to contribute to social media conversations via a preselected and promoted hashtag. Some stores, like Target and Victoria Secret, are even crafting in-store photo-ops. See Figure 1.4 for an example. Both campaigns encourage users to take a photo and use their hashtag (#targetdog, #vstease, #vsgift). Victoria Secret went a step further by rewarding their consumers with a "sexy surprise" (after they showed an associate that they shared their branded selfie). Signage is also becoming more dynamic, as retail is slowly starting to embrace digital signage. Perhaps, displaying consumer tweets and posts related to brands will become commonplace within stores. Companies can create contests that require consumers to create content to be shared. Another example of collaboration communications is when companies hire social influencers to tweet positive statements about the company. Depending on the strategy, collaborative communication can be a combination of earned, paid, and owned media.

Regardless of whether the sWOM is consumer- or company-generated, or whether it is a collaborative effort, some forms of sWOM require more effort than others. Retweeting takes much less effort than generating a new post. Generating a new status update takes less work than creating a video and posting it on YouTube. The amount of effort required of the consumer is closely tied to consumer engagement. The topic of engagement is covered in Chapter 2, so we will not be discussing it here. But for now, suffice to say that marketers need to ensure that they account for varying levels of engagement and pay more attention to consumers participating in higher level engagement forms of sWOM.

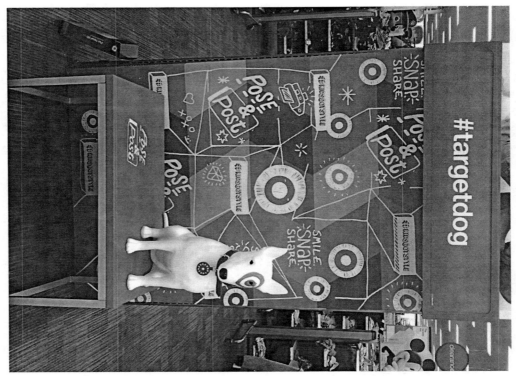

Figure 1.4 #targetdog

Source: Courtesy of C. Munoz.

Importance of sWOM

The importance of sWOM for marketers can be summarized in two key facts. First, almost everyone who is online is using a social network (Mander 2016b). While usage rates may vary dramatically between consumer segments, social media is touching and impacting the lives of most consumers. Second, sWOM influences each stage in the consumer decision-making process and can impact sales. Similar to WOM and eWOM, sWOM serves as an important information source in the pre-purchase research process. The GlobalWebIndex survey found that social networks are used by over 30 percent of online users in their product research. Social networks and mobile apps were even more popular in product searches for younger consumers (Mander 2016a). Simply put, consumers are increasingly turning to social networks and consumer reviews to hear their friends' (and strangers') opinions on products, view pictures depicting how the product "really" looks, and find new uses and applications through videos. However, the extent to which they rely on social media in their investigations depends heavily on the type of product they are considering purchasing (Bughin 2015). Outside of facilitating product research, sWOM is leading to sales. Management consulting company McKinsey found that approximately 26 percent of purchases across 30 different product categories were influenced by social recommendations (Bughin 2015). A 2013 survey found that four in ten social media users make a purchase (online or offline in approximately equal amounts) of a product after sharing or favoriting it on Twitter, Facebook, or Pinterest. The purchase is also occurring within a week after sharing or favoriting the item (Samuel et al. 2013). Given the increasing rates of online shopping and the growing number of technologies that integrate shopping options directly into social media posts, it is not unreasonable to expect that sWOM's direct sales influence will continue to increase.

Outside of being instrumental in product research and influencing sales, sWOM communication has other benefits. Let's look at some examples of how sWOM communication has made a difference:

- **Generate awareness or buzz:** sWOM can draw attention to or create brand awareness with individual consumers (and groups) that normally would not be exposed. Home improvement retailer Lowe's "Fix in Six" Vine video series creatively and quickly (in six seconds) solves a multitude of household problems. With almost 64 million loops (views) seen primarily by a millennial audience, Lowes has garnered awareness with consumers that would not normally be exposed to Lowe's marketing messages (Beer 2015).

- **Increase social media engagement:** Popular WOM content via social media can quickly increase a brand's engagement, likes or number of followers on social media. Cadbury decided to honor (and elicit engagement) from their nearly one million fans of their UK Facebook page by creating a giant Facebook "like" thumb out of Cadbury milk chocolate. The result was over 40,000 new Facebook likes (in two days) and an increase of 35 percent for active fans (Bazu 2013).

- **Inspire new product ideas and resurrect old ones:** There is truth to TED Talk's slogan—"Ideas Worth Spreading." Good ideas do catch on, and smart marketers look to popular sWOM messages for product inspiration. Popular organically created hashtags such as #BringBackCrystalPepsi helped inspire Pepsi to re-release this 1990's clear soda in 2016 (Mitchell 2015; PepsiCo 2016). Whereas, other companies ask consumers directly to come up with new product ideas. Take, for instance, Lay's "Do Us A Flavor" contest, which asked consumers to come up with new potato chip flavors, and encouraged fans to vote via social media. The flavor winner received $1 million, and consumers' taste buds were treated to exotic flavors such as Southern Biscuits and Gravy (2015 winner), Wasabi Ginger (2014), and Cheesy Garlic Bread (2013).

- **Increase consumer satisfaction:** It goes without saying that you need to monitor social media conversations about your brand. Some companies take it a step further and ask consumers for their input in a continuing effort to improve their product(s). Starbuck's website and related hashtag #mystarbucksidea ask consumers for ways that they can improve. While this hashtag certainly helped to create new product ideas, the open forum also allows Starbucks to craft a better overall experience, thereby increasing customer satisfaction. Companies such as Nike and JetBlue have satisfaction.

also created dedicated Twitter handles to address consumer comments and questions. This has allowed them to provide, especially in the case of JetBlue, real-time support, and frankly, happiness. Take for instance, the story of JetBlue customer who tweeted that he was going to board his 100th flight with them that year. Without knowing his name or flight (but looking up his handle and then tracking him down), they met him at his arrival gate with a banner and cupcakes (Kolowich 2014). Heck, we would have been satisfied with a retweet!

- **Raise awareness of a nonprofit cause:** A growing number of nonprofits have been using sWOM to increase awareness for their cause and inspire donations. An interesting example can be found with UNICEF's creative use of a Pinterest board. Instead of creating an image board filled with aspirational products, they created a page for a fictional, poor 13-year-old girl from Sierra Leone. Under the heading, "Really want these," they included life's essentials (i.e., a picture of rice, soap, shoes, etc.). In the first few days of the campaign, the page was seen by over a million people and repinned thousands of times (Weapon7 2012).

Our Journey Ahead

This book is not an introductory "how-to" book on social media. It is assuming that you have already gotten your feet wet (or drenched) in the topic. Instead, the purpose of this book is to examine the influence of sWOM and provide guidance on how to operationalize its growing power. Our goal in writing this book is to bring together industry best practices and academic research to illustrate how much sWOM matters. It should also help you construct social media posts that will be both shared and conform to regulatory guidelines. Each chapter highlights a key area of sWOM that will further your understanding of the topic and provide actionable information to increase the likelihood of creating your own your sharable sWOM marketing successes:

The Social Consumer

The social consumer examines individuals who use social media to inform their product decisions and also share product-related information and opinions with others. This chapter explores who they are, the different roles they play (i.e., social listener, social sharer, and social influencer), and their motivations to share.

The Social Business

In most companies, social media usage begins in the marketing department, but it should not end there. Social media can add value in other ways including, offering strategic insights, identifying problems, crowd-sourcing ideas for new products and services, improving customer service, recruiting new employees, and empowering employees to spread positive sWOM. In this chapter, we discuss the importance of becoming a social business. We review the stages of social business development and how social tools can be integrated to become part of your company's DNA.

Legal and Regulatory Issues

There is a very fine line between encouraging and incentivizing consumers and employees to engage in sWOM about your brand—a line that *may* have legal implications for your company. In this chapter, we examine "material connections"—relationships that exist between a company and an endorser of your brand—and the guidelines that must be followed to ensure that consumers are not being deceived by information they learn and recommendations they receive on social media.

Social Media Policy

As your company begins to integrate social media into more business functional areas and as more employees use it, your company's liability exposure increases. The first step to mitigating risk is to develop and implement a social media policy. In this chapter, we will examine the importance of having a well-developed social media policy, the process of creating a policy and appropriate content.

Storytelling

Social media posts need to tell a story and marketers need to learn to be good storytellers. This chapter explores how to construct shareable stories concentrating on not only textual content, but also the importance of visual communication in all your marketing efforts.

Social Influence

To be successful in social media and to encourage sWOM, your company needs to be influential. In this chapter, we explore six principles of persuasion as they apply to social media.

Social Sharing Applied

In our final chapter, we present some best practices encouraging positive sWOM. We examine the important components of a company's social media presence and offer platform-specific recommendations for LinkedIn, Facebook, Twitter, YouTube, Pinterest, and Instagram.

Special Notes: We have, on occasion, included statistics to emphasize a particular point. At the time of writing, these were the most current statistics. These statistics may not be current today. As such, we ask that you try not to focus too much on the actual numbers, instead, pay attention to the trends and patterns to guide your social endeavors.

Those who work in the business-to-business (B2B) market typically refer to the buyer of products or services as customers. In the business-to-consumer (B2C) market, we often refer to the end users as consumers. For consistency purposes, we have chosen to use "consumer" throughout this book when referring to buyers in a B2B or B2C market. The term *customer* is used when discussing customer service activities.

References

Ayres, S. 2016. "Shocking New Data about the Lifespan of Your Facebook Posts." Post Planner. Retrieved from www.postplanner.com/lifespan-of-facebook-posts/ (accessed June 22, 2016).

Bazu, A. 2013. "Cadbury's 'Thanks a Million' campaign: The Sweet Taste of Success." *UCD Graduate Business School Blog.* Retrieved from http://ucdblogs.ucd.ie/digitalmarketingstrategy/cadburys-thanks-million-campaign-sweet-taste-success/

Beer, J. 2015. "How Lowe's Brought Social Savvy and a Sense of Humor to Home Improvement." *Fast Company,* July. Retrieved from www.fastcocreate.com/3048021/behind-the-brand/how-lowes-brought-social-savvy-and-a-sense-of-humor-to-home-improvement

Belicove, M. 2011. "Measuring Offline Vs. Online Word-of-Mouth Marketing." *Entrepreneur,* November. Retrieved from www.entrepreneur.com/article/220776

Berger, J. 2013. *Contagious.* New York, NY: Simon and Schuster.

Brouwer, B. 2015. "YouTube Now Gets Over 400 Hours of Content Uploaded Every Minute." *Tubefilter.* Retrieved from www.tubefilter.com/2015/07/26/youtube-400-hours-content-every-minute/

Bughin, J. 2015. "Getting a Sharper Picture of Social Media's Influence." *McKinsey Quarterly.* Retrieved from www.mckinsey.com/business-functions/marketing-and-sales/our-insights/getting-a-sharper-picture-of-social-medias-influence

Bughin, J., D. Jonathan, and V. Ole. 2010. "A New Way to Measure Word-Of-Mouth Marketing." *McKinsey Quarterly.* Retrieved from www.mckinsey.com/business-functions/marketing-and-sales/our-insights/a-new-way-to-measure-word-of-mouth-marketing

Cheung, C.M.K., and D.R. Thadani. 2012. "The Impact of Electronic Word-of-Mouth Communication: A Literature Analysis and Integrative Model." *Decision Support Systems* 54, no. 1, pp. 461–70. doi: 10.1016/j.dss.2012.06.008

Chu, S.C., and Y. Kim. 2011. "Determinents of Consumer Engagement in Electronic Word-Of-Mouth (eWOM) in Social Networking Sites." *International Journal of Advertising* 30, no. 1, pp. 47–75.

comScore. 2016. "comScore Reports February 2016 U.S. Smartphone Subscriber Market Share—comScore, Inc." Retrieved from www.comscore.com/Insights/Rankings/comScore-Reports-February-2016-US-Smartphone-Subscriber-Market-Share

Constine, J. 2015a. "Facebook Hits 100M Hours of Video Watching, 1 B Users on Groups, 80M on Fb Lite." *Tech Crunch.* Retrieved from https://techcrunch.com/2016/01/27/facebook-grows/

Constine, J. 2015b. "Facebook Hits 8 Billion Daily Video Views Double from 4 Billion in April." *Tech Crunch*. Retrieved from https://techcrunch.com/2015/11/04/facebook-video-views/

Daugherty, T., and E. Hoffman. 2014. "eWOM and the Importance of Capturing Consumer Attention within Social Media." *Journal of Marketing Communications* 20, no. 1–2, pp. 82–102. doi:10.1080/13527266.2013.797764

Deye, J. 2015. "#ShareACoke and the Personalized Brand Experience." *Marketing Insights*. Retrieved from www.ama.org/publications/eNewsletters/MarketingInsightsNewsletter/Pages/shareacoke-and-the-personalized-brand-experience.aspx

Google; KellerFay Group. 2016. "Word of Mouth (WOM)." Retrieved from https://ssl.gstatic.com/think/docs/word-of-mouth-and-the-internet_infographics.pdf (accessed May 28, 2016).

Griner, D. 2014. "DiGiorno Is Really, Really Sorry About Its Tweet Accidentally Making Light of Domestic Violence." *AdWeek*. Retrieved from www.adweek.com/adfreak/digiorno-really-really-sorry-about-its-tweet-accidentally-making-light-domestic-violence-159998

Hennig-Thurau, T., K.P. Gwinner, G. Walsh, and D.D. Gremler. 2004. "Electronic Word-Of-Mouth Via Consumer-Opinion Platforms: What Motivates Consumers to Articulate Themselves on the Internet?" *Journal of Interactive Marketing (John Wiley & Sons)* 18, no. 1, pp. 38–52. doi:10.1002/dir.10073

Hitz, L. 2014. "Simply Summer Social Awards Contestant #3 | Simply Measured." *The Simply Measured Blog*. Retrieved from http://simplymeasured.com/blog/simply-summer-social-awards-contestant-3-cocacolas-shareacoke-campaign/#sm.00018n9uis1172fifrc4xqq28xm0f

Instagram. 2015. "Press Page." *Instagram*. Retrieved from www.instagram.com/press/

Kim, W.G., J.S. Han, and E. Lee. 2011. "Effects of Relationship Marketing on Repeat Purchase and Word of Mouth." *Journal of Hospitality & Tourism Research* 25, no. 3, pp. 272–88. doi:10.1177/109634800102500303

Kimmel, A.J., and P.J. Kitchen. 2014. "Introduction: Word of Mouth and Social Media." *Journal of Marketing Communications* 20, no. 1–2, pp. 2–4. Retrieved from http://ovidsp.ovid.com/ovidweb.cgi?T=JS&PAGE=reference&D=psyc11&NEWS=N&AN=2013-45151-002

Kimmel, A.J., and P.J. Kitchen. 2013. "WOM and Social Media: Presaging Future Directions for Research and Practice." *Journal of Marketing Communications* 20, no. 1–2, pp. 1–16. doi:10.1080/13527266.2013.797730

Kolowich, L. 2014. "Delighting People in 140 Characters: An Inside Look at JetBlue's Customer Service Success." *Hubspot Blog*. Retrieved from http://blog.hubspot.com/marketing/jetblue-customer-service-twitter#sm.00018n9uis1172fifrc4xqq28xm0f

Mander, J. 2015. "Daily Time Spent on Social Networks Rises to 1.72 Hours." *Global Web Index*. Retrieved from www.globalwebindex.net/blog/daily-time-spent-on-social-networks-rises-to-1-72-hours

Mander, J. 2016a. "40% of 16–24s Use Social Media to Research Products." *GlobalWebIndex*. Retrieved from www.globalwebindex.net/blog/40-of-16-24s-use-social-media-to-research-products

Mander, J. 2016b. "97% Visiting Social Networks." *GlobalWebIndex*. Retrieved from www.globalwebindex.net/blog/97-visiting-social-networks

Meeker, M. 2016. "Internet Trends 2016—Code Conference." Retrieved from www.kpcb.com/internet-trends

Mitchell, E. 2015. "Pepsi Makes the Most of Viral #BringBackCrystal PepsiCampaign." *Adweek*. Retrieved from www.adweek.com/prnewser/pepsi-makes-the-most-of-viral-bringbackcrystalpepsi-campaign/115132

Morrison, K. 2015. "How Many Photos Are Uploaded to Snapchat Every Second." *Adweek*. Retrieved from www.adweek.com/socialtimes/how-many-photos-are-uploaded-to-snapchat-every-second/621488

Nielsen. 2013. "Under the Influence: Consumer Trust in Advertising." Retrieved from www.nielsen.com/us/en/insights/news/2013/under-the-influence-consumer-trust-in-advertising.html

Patton, T. 2016. "8 Statistics That Will Change the Way You Think about Referral Marketing." *Ambassador Blog*. Retrieved from http://app.mbb.io/e/np3/57

Payne, E., and C. Friedman. 2012. "Viral Ad Campaign Hits #FirstWorld Problems." *CNN*. Retrieved from www.cnn.com/2012/10/23/tech/ad-campaign-twist/

PepsiCo. 2016. "Celebrate the 90s with Crystal Pepsi—Iconic Clear Cola to Hit Shelves This Summer." *PepsiCo Press Release*. Retrieved from www.pepsico.com/live/pressrelease/celebrate-the-90s-with-crystal-pepsi---iconic-clear-cola-to-hit-shelves-this-su06292016

Perrin, A. 2015. "One-Fifth of Americans Report Going Online 'Almost Constantly.'" Retrieved from www.pewresearch.org/fact-tank/2015/12/08/one-fifth-of-americans-report-going-online-almost-constantly/

Samuel, A., L. Lam, D. Sevitt, and C. Loh. 2013. "From Social to Sale," 1–28. Retrieved from www.visioncritical.com/resources/social2sale/

Smith, A. 2011. "Smartphone Adoption and Usage." Retrieved from www.pewinternet.org/2011/07/11/smartphone-adoption-and-usage/

Statistic Brain. 2016. "YouTube Company Statistics." Retrieved from www.statisticbrain.com/youtube-statistics/

Steffes, E.M., and L.E. Burgee. 2009. "Social Ties and Online Word of Mouth." *Internet Research* 19, no. 1, pp. 42–59.

Stewart, J.B. 2016. "Facebook Has 50 Minutes of Your Time Each Day. It Wants More." *The New York Times*. Retrieved from www.nytimes.com/2016/05/06/business/facebook-bends-the-rules-of-audience-engagement-to-its-advantage.html?_r=0

Swann, P. 2014. "NYPD Blues: When a Hashtag Becomes a Bashtag." *Public Relations Society of America*. Retrieved from www.prsa.org/Intelligence/TheStrategist/Articles/view/10711/1096/NYPD_Blues_When_a_Hashtag_Becomes_a_Bashtag#.V3PelvkrKM8

Tadena, N. 2014. "Coke's Personalized Marketing Campaign Gains Online Buzz—CMO Today—WSJ." *The Wall Street Journal*, July 15. Retrieved from http://blogs.wsj.com/cmo/2014/07/15/cokes-personalized-marketing-campaign-gains-online-buzz/

Tode, C. 2015. "Retailers Adapt Social Media for Real-World, In-Store Sales Impact." *Mobile Commerce Daily*, August 10. Retrieved from www.mobilecommercedaily.com/retailers-adapt-social-media-for-real-world-in-store-sales-impact

Tuten, T., and M.R. Solomon. 2015. *Social Media Marketing*. Thousand Oaks, CA: Sage Publications.

Wang, Y., and S. Rodgers. 2010. "Electronic Word of Mouth and Consumer Generated Content: From Concept to Application." In *Handbook of Research on Digital Media and Advertising: User Generated Content Consumption*, ed. M. Eastin, 212–31. New York, NY: Information Science Reference. doi:10.4018/978-1-60566-792-8.ch011

Weapon7. 2012. "UNICEF Pinterest Case Study." Retrieved from www.youtube.com/watch?v=Vq7Hz9YpDeA

Westbrook, R.A. 1987. "Product/Consumption-Based Affective Responses and Postpurchase Processes." *Journal of Marketing Research* 24, pp. 258–71. doi:10.2307/3151636

Whitler, K. 2014. "Why Word of Mouth Marketing Is the Most Important Social Media." *Forbes*. Retrieved from www.forbes.com/sites/kimberlywhitler/2014/07/17/why-word-of-mouth-marketing-is-the-most-important-social-media/#3443d9c37a77

WOMMA. 2014. "Return on Word of Mouth." Retrieved from https://womma.org/wp-content/uploads/2015/09/STUDY-WOMMA-Return-on-WOM-Executive-Summary.pdf

CHAPTER 2

The Social Consumer: The Who, What, Why, and How Behind Sharing

It may feel like everyone (and their grandmother) spends their entire day liking, tweeting, and creating snaps—yet, that is not the reality. Everyone is not spending extensive time on social media and those who are do not use every social media platform. Overtime, consumers change their social media platform preferences and behavior. Just because a consumer group is using a platform today offers no guarantee that they will be using the same platform tomorrow. Indeed, social media is a fluid and evolving space. Many of the changes that occur in social media can be attributed to technological advancements and perhaps, more importantly, consumer behavior. The future of social media platforms, such as Facebook and Instagram, and the manner in which consumers use them to both connect with companies and engage in sWOM is dependent on each platform's ability to meet consumer needs. Therefore, to be successful in your social media efforts, it is crucial to understand social media consumer behavior. So, who is the social consumer and why should we care?

What Is a Social Consumer?

A social consumer is an individual who uses social media to both identify and share product-related information (i.e., articles and opinions) that assists their own or others' consumption decision-making process. A social consumer may use Facebook to checkout a friend's new outfit, LinkedIn to establish the credibility of a local home improvement company, Twitter to keep abreast of breaking industry news, YouTube to learn how to build a bookcase from Lowes, and Pinterest to bookmark future purchases. In other words, consumers are using social media to help them identify, evaluate, and use products and services. They are both viewing and engaging in communication with their personal networks and businesses. In addition, they are sharing information and offering their opinion on products, thereby potentially influencing the behavior of others. This chapter will explore the demographic and behavioral differences behind these consumers, with specific emphasis on a subset of social consumers—social influencers.

Who Are Social Consumers?

Globally, 2.3 billion individuals or one in three people are active social media users, with roughly 2 billion accessing their social media accounts from a mobile device (Kemp 2016). The heaviest users of social media, specifically social networking sites (SNS), are the young (e.g., 2015: 90 percent of 18–29-year-olds); however, older consumers are adopting SNS at an increasing rate. Between 2010 and 2015 usage among those aged 65 and over more than tripled (11 percent to 35 percent) (Perrin 2015). Adoption rates are also tied to education and income. Consumers with a higher level of education and income are the most likely to use social media (Perrin 2015). Historically in the United States it was women who boasted the highest use of social media. Today, the gender gap has narrowed. In 2015, 68 percent of women online used SNS, compared to 62 percent of men (Perrin 2015). However, gender differences do exist for specific social media platforms. To illustrate, Pinterest, Instagram, and Facebook are more frequently used by women. Pinterest is used almost three times more by women than men. YouTube, Twitter, Tumblr, and LinkedIn have comparable adoption rates for both genders, whereas online forums (i.e., Reddit, Digg) are more popular with men (Anderson 2015b; Blattberg 2015). Even though YouTube adoption rates are similar, men spend up to 44 percent more time on the entertainment platform per month than women (Blattberg 2015).

Social media platforms adoption rates also vary by race and ethnicity. A 2015 study by Pew Research Center revealed that while Facebook is the most popular platforms across racial or ethnic lines, with comparable rates of usage, other platforms saw significant differences. For example,

> 2.3 billion individuals or 1 in 3 people are active social media users.

Instagram has higher usage rates with Hispanics and blacks, compared to white online users. Pinterest is significantly less popular with black online users. LinkedIn is equally adopted by whites and blacks, while Latinos usage is significantly less in comparison. Twitter usage is relatively equal between blacks (27 percent) and Hispanics (25 percent), with whites using it slightly less (21 percent) (Krogstad 2015; Duggan 2015).

Figure 2.1 outlines the number of active users for each platform along with a brief demographic overview of the typical user.

Major Social Media Platforms Active Users and Demographic Overview

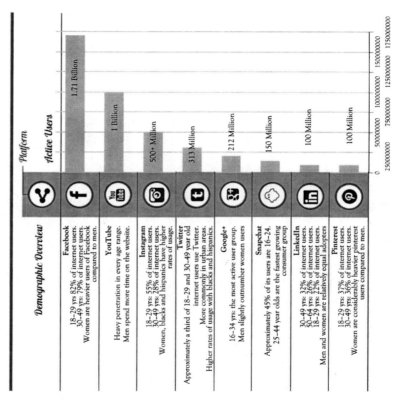

Figure 2.1 *Major social media platforms adoption rates and demographic overview*

Source: Facebook (Duggan 2015), YouTube (Blartberg 2015), Instagram (Duggan 2015), Twitter: (Duggan 2015), Google+ (Delzio 2015), Snapchat (Frier 2016; Young 2016), LinkedIn (Duggan 2015; Weber 2015), Pinterest (Duggan 2015; Griffith 2015; Lafferty 2015).

Consumers across the globe have adopted an average of eight different social media platforms. In the United States adoption rates are slightly lower, with the average consumer using six different platforms (Global-WebIndex 2016). If consumers are limiting their social media usage to just one platform, chances are it is Facebook. As for the frequency of use, Facebook, Instagram, and Twitter lend themselves to more active daily use. Pinterest and LinkedIn are more likely to be used on a weekly or less basis (Duggan et al. 2015).

How Do Social Consumers Access Social Media?

In 2016, smartphone adoption rates (72 percent) were almost as high as computers (75 percent). Adoption rates for tablets were at 42 percent (Google 2016). Young adults have even higher adoption rates—86 percent of 18–29-year-olds and 83 percent of 30–49-year-olds own a smartphone (Anderson 2015c). But, smartphones aren't just for adults; in 2015, three in every four U.S. teenagers owned a smartphone (Lenhart 2015). Outside of age, smartphone ownership in the United States is somewhat equally divided between men and women, but skewed toward younger, college-educated consumers earning higher incomes. Minorities (i.e., blacks and Hispanics) have slightly higher ownership rates when compared to whites (Anderson 2015a). For 15 percent of smartphone consumers, their smartphone is their primary, if not only, means to access the Internet (Smith 2015).

Outside of simple access, it appears that consumers are spending considerably more time using social media on their smartphone compared to their desktop or laptop computers. Pew Research found that 89 percent of smartphone users accessed the Internet and 75 percent used SNS from their phones (Smith 2015). Yet, this is not true for every platform. Some platforms, such as Instagram and Snapchat lend themselves to mobile usages, whereas consumers prefer to browse YouTube videos and check LinkedIn from a desktop. Facebook, Google+, and Pinterest are equally accessed from both desktop and mobile devices (Adobe 2015).

When we look at social sharing behavior (e.g., retweeting, liking, commenting, and sharing), mobile may have the upper hand. To illustrate, a 2015 study by social data and engagement platform ShareThis found that when consumers share online information, it is typically through a mobile device. Social sharing accounts for 20 percent of activity on smart-phones, 13 percent on tablets, and 6.7 percent on desktops (ShareThis 2015). So, which social media platform generates the most amount of sharing? The answer is Facebook, which accounts for at least 81 percent of shares (Haslam 2015). The second most popular sharing platform is Pinterest (Delzio 2015).

Levels of Engagement and Social Consumer Roles

Social media satisfies a variety of purposes—it allows us to stay in touch with friends, network with professionals, stay current with news or events, provides entertainment, but it also provides us with the opportunity to share our opinions simultaneously with a large number of consumers and to engage with brands. Social consumers play a variety of roles that impact the consumer decision-making process: social listeners, social sharers, and social influencers. Before we delve into these roles, let's first examine the levels of engagement possible within social media.

Charlene Li, CEO and Principal Analyst at Altimeter Group, research, developed an engagement pyramid (Figure 2.2). The engagement

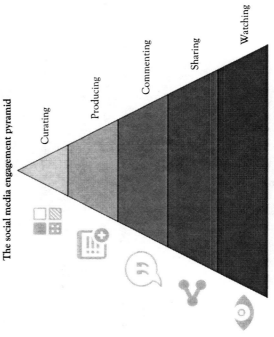

The social media engagement pyramid

Figure 2.2 The social media engagement pyramid

Source: Adapted from Li (2010).

pyramid depicts various levels of engagement that social consumers and social employees can have within social media. It reveals that a substantial number of consumers and employees are engaged at the lower levels. For example, in the United States, 80 percent of consumers surveyed in 2010 were watchers and 61 percent were sharers (Li 2010).

The *Watching* segment's engagement is limited to watching (or listening) to social media. In academic and industry research, these are commonly referred to as Lurkers (Gong, Lim, and Zhu 2015). They are passive observers to tweets, Instagram posts, articles that they see on Facebook, and videos they watch on YouTube. They are neither sharing nor interacting, but simply consuming information. Industry experts originally claimed that as much as 90 percent of social media were classified as Lurkers (Nielsen 2006). Others have since claimed that this number maybe inflated (Vision Critical 2014; Dembosky 2012). But regardless of the actual number, all agree that the majority of consumers are simply watching. The second level is *Sharing*. At this level, consumers become more engaged—they are not only listening and digesting information, but they are also frequent sharers of information. They retweet and share content produced by other individuals and companies' content. *Commenting* is the next level, where consumers craft and share their opinions. Their opinions are not private, but rather part of a larger public dialog. Arguably, the next two steps take a considerable jump up in the engagement level when compared to commenting. In *Producing*, consumers create fresh new content (e.g., YouTube videos, Facebook posts) to share with others. The last level of engagement, *Curation*, is only accomplished by a small number of consumers. These individuals are very active on social media, sorting through content and sharing only the most relevant data with their networks. They make it easy for consumers to find what is important and relevant, and for that reason, they are seen as trusted advisors (Li 2010). As a company, you don't want all of your consumers to simply watch (or listen) to your social media content. If all they do is watch, then their level of influence is low. Instead, you should strive to develop content that moves some of consumers up to higher levels of the engagement pyramid.

The three roles of social listeners, social sharers, and social influencers are related to engagement—although they are somewhat broader constructs (Figure 2.3).

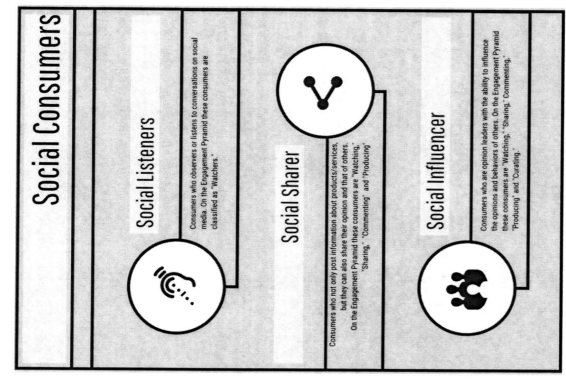

Social Consumers

Social Listeners

Consumers who observers or listens to conversations on social media. On the Engagement Pyramid these consumers are classified as "Watchers."

Social Sharer

Consumers who not only post information about products/services, but they can also share their opinion and that of others. On the Engagement Pyramid these consumers are "Watching," "Sharing," "Commenting," and "Producing"

Social Influencer

Consumers who are opinion leaders with the ability to influence the opinions and behaviors of others. On the Engagement Pyramid these consumers are "Watching," "Sharing," "Commenting," "Producing," and "Curating."

Figure 2.3 Social consumers

Social Listeners

A social listener, as the name implies, is an individual who observes or listens to conversations on social media. They participate in the "watching" level of engagement. This individual may be in a passive or active shopping mode. A passive shopping mode is when "information and advice [that consumer[s] need to make a purchase comes to them unsolicited" (Belch and Belch 2014, 131). Consumers are continually collecting information that may come from a Facebook post, a tweet that they happen to glance at, or a pin that they came across when they were looking for a great guacamole recipe. Although consumers may not be interested in purchasing the product at that time, the fact that they have read the post allows them to accumulate knowledge that maybe helpful to them in the future or which they can share with others. For example, reading a review of a restaurant posted by a friend and then later sharing this information with another friend who is looking for a new place to eat. In truth, consumers are constantly in this passive stage—unknowingly accumulating knowledge for future use.

In the active shopping mode, consumers are "purposefully seeking information and/or assistance so [consumers] can make informed purchase decisions with confidence" (Belch and Belch 2014, 131). This hunt for product information often leads consumers to social media. A study undertaken by Forrester Research revealed that the average U.S. adult uses social media to both "discover" and "explore" new products (Fleming 2016). One study found that 23 percent consumers surveyed were reading ratings at least once a week and 27 percent a couple of times a month. GlobalWebIndex found that almost 25 percent of Facebook users surveyed were motivated to use the popular platform to "research/find products to buy" (Buckle 2016b). Younger consumers are more likely to use social media in their product search than are older consumers—more than 40 percent of 16–24-years-old are using social networks, such as Facebook, to help them make decisions. While age is certainly important, gender may play a bigger role in the likelihood of using social media to inform purchases. A 2014 study from the Society for New Communications Research found that women (31 percent) were considerably more likely than men (15 percent) to use social media in their purchasing decisions. For 66 percent of those surveyed, ratings were the first or second most important information source of information when purchasing from an unfamiliar company (DiMauro and Bulmer 2014).

When Do They Listen?

Let's face it; we are not always receptive to other people's advice. Sometimes, we simply don't care that Sally loves her new car, found a new recipe on Pinterest, or looks fabulous in those Instagramed shoes. But, there are other times where we are not only interested, but are more receptive to these social recommendations to assist us in our purchase. We are certainly more receptive when we are in the active shopping mode—but there are other factors that make us more likely to listen to sWOM?

Academic research on traditional WOM and eWOM, coupled with industry studies addressing social media, has identified a number of conditions when social consumers are more likely to seek out and are receptive to social recommendations and information:

- Purchasing a product for the first time or little experience within the product category (Bughin 2015; Gilly et al. 1998).
- High involvement purchase (e.g., higher level of risk associated with purchase) (Beatty and Smith 1987).
- Younger consumers (18–34-year-olds) (Mixon 2016).
- Americans with more than $100,000 yearly household income (Mixon 2016).
- When the message is personalized and effectively targeted (Bughin 2015).
- For specific types of product categories (i.e., 40 to 50 percent of consumers used social recommendations when selecting travel and investment services) (Bughin 2015).
- Consumers who use a search engine in researching a product are also more likely to use social media in their pre-purchase investigation (Bughin 2015).
- When the recommendation is received from a highly credible source (Park and Lee 2009; Gilly et al. 1998).
- Influence is stronger when the "tie strength" is strong. In other words, your relationship or connection with the recommender is robust (i.e., friends or family) (Brown and Reingen 1987).

Social Sharers

Not all social media users share information. In fact, the act of social sharing is relatively uncommon (Haslam 2015). Yet, many of us do share, retweet, and comment. Social sharers are consumers who not only post information about products or services via social media, but they can also share their opinion and that of others. These consumers are sharing, commenting, and producing. One study indicated that 24 percent of individuals shared content online at least once a month (DiMauro and Bulmer 2014), and often, this content comes from a social influencer—an individual who is recognized as an expert in a particular area. A study sponsored by Twitter and Annalect found that 20 percent of the consumers surveyed have shared content they saw from an influencer (Swant 2016). Their level of engagement on social media can include not only sharing, but also commenting and even creating content.

There are two types of social sharing: implicit sharing—that relates to products (e.g., sharing a news article involving a product or endorsing a company through a "like") and explicit sharing—sharing that includes a discussion about a product (e.g., creating a post that explicitly discusses a product). Both types are influential. A 2015 Adobe Study of European social media users (UK, France, Germany, Sweden, and Netherlands) found that implicit (i.e., follows or likes) and explicit endorsement (i.e., mentions) varied by platform, with endorsements more prevalent on Facebook and Instagram compared to Google+ and Snapchat (Figure 2.4). Interestingly, 18–24-year-olds depended considerably more on the visually oriented platform Instagram (72 percent) than the average social media user (Watt 2016).

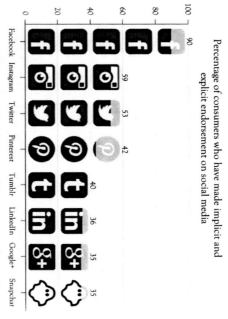

Percentage of consumers who have made implicit and explicit endorsement on social media

Figure 2.4 Percentage of consumers who have made implicit and explicit endorsements on social media

Source: Watt (2016).

Implicit sharing can come in many forms. It can be simply retweeting a news article without providing a personalized comment or providing a simple brand endorsement. In other words, the endorsement is implied. A "like" on Facebook or Instagram, a "favorite" on Twitter and a "follow" on Facebook are some of the many examples of quick implicit brand endorsements. This form of endorsement is very common perhaps, in part, to the ease at which a consumer can communicate their support. For example, "liking" a product requires less effort than a writing a comment. A global study of social media users found that 84 percent of those surveyed "liked" or followed a brand (eMarketer 2015).

Explicit brand endorsements are more involved. They can be textual, visual, or both. Textual endorsements include personalized messages, comments, or hashtags, which may be attached to an existing piece of communication. For example, retweeting an article and including a comment and a hashtag. Hashtags can be a fast and effective way of endorsing a product (e.g., #ShareaCoke, #WantAnR8, #ShareYourEars, #PepsiPerfect). Consumers can also embed their product endorsements through visual communication. For instance, a consumer may model their new Gucci sunglasses on Instagram or pin an image of a Pottery Barn couch they are planning to purchase to their personal decorating board on Pinterest. They can also do all three—post a picture with a comment and a hashtag. This type of sharing represents a higher level of engagement, it requires more time and effort, but may be more influential.

Some of the most involved product discussions on social media are those which describe a consumer's experience with a product. Both positive and negative brand experiences are commonly shared via social media (eMarketer 2015). A 2015 survey by Social@Ogilvy found that 58 percent of respondents shared both good and bad brand experiences. The product discussions may contain textual descriptions of a product's strengths and weaknesses, but they may also include images and video. These visual modes of communication are powerful in their ability to influence (Chapter 6). The inclusion of hashtags can increase the likelihood of the post being discovered in a search. The most popular platforms for sharing product recommendations are YouTube and Facebook (Adobe 2015). Both of these platforms make it easy to create devoted fan pages and channels to specific brands.

Why Do We Share?

There are many reasons behind why we share within social media. Some studies have addressed this question broadly, whereas others have examined sharing behavior within specific social media platforms. Understanding what drives consumers to push the "retweet" or "share" button directly impacts the type of content and conversation you hope to have with your target market.

In 2011, the *New York Times* conducted a comprehensive U.S.-based study examining the motivations behind social media sharing. The "Psychology of Sharing" study involved ethnographies, focus groups, and a survey of 2,500 social sharers across a variety of social media platforms. The researchers identified five separate motivations for sharing: "to bring valuable and entertaining content to others; to define ourselves to others; to grow and nourish our relationships; self-fulfillment; and to get the word out about causes or brands" (*The New York Times* 2011). Underlining each of these motives was the importance of relationships. In addition, the study identified "six personas of online sharers" (*The New York Times* 2011):

- Altruists: Individuals motivated to share information by a sense of helping others. These people are described as helpful, reliable, thoughtful, and connected.

- Careerists: For these individuals, sharing is concentrated on information related to career and reputation enhancement.

- Hipsters: Hipsters share to express their identity. They are creative, young, on the cutting-edge, and popular.

- Boomerangs: For boomerangs, sharing is linked to validation. These individuals are seeking feedback from others.

- Connectors: For these individuals, sharing is linked to making, planning, and connecting to their offline lives (e.g., sharing a deal for a brunch with friends).

- Selectives: Selectives are not frequent sharers, but they are thoughtful. They only share when the information is relevant or useful to others.

Other studies examining consumers motivation to use social media revealed similar results. For instance, the 2013 Ipsos study of 12,420 global online "sharers" in 24 countries revealed that consumers are motivated "to share interesting things" (61 percent), important things (43 percent), funny things (43 percent), "to let others know what I believe in and who I really am" (37 percent), and recommending a product (30 percent) were the most popular motivations (Ipsos 2013). These echo some of the motivating factors behind altruists, hipsters, and selectives personas. Outside of the global averages, the study revealed some interesting cross-cultural differences. To illustrate, Turkey reported "shares important things" as a much higher motivating factor (67 percent vs. the 43 percent global average) in sharing. Japanese consumers are less likely to use social media "to let others know what I believe in and who I am really am" than other countries (19 percent vs. 37 percent global average) (Ipsos 2013). Having an extended conversation of country or cultural differences is beyond the scope of this book—however, it emphasizes that marketers must also consider the innate cultural differences that occur both within and between our global borders.

Both of these studies reveal somewhat similar themes—consumers are sharing information that can bring value to other people's lives. For information to be shared, it needs to be interesting, funny, or unique. We share information out of a desire to help others (e.g., alturists). We also share information to help form our identities (e.g., hipsters). Through social media, we project to others what we want to believe and want others to believe about us.

So, which persona or personas does your target market fall into? Are they hipsters? Careerists? Both? What motivates your consumers? This New York Times sharing typology may be helpful in guiding your content planning and marketing message. However, it would be helpful for you to conduct an analysis of your target market sharing behavior on your social media platforms and perform primary research exploring their specific sharing motivations. More on this in Chapter 3.

Thus far, we have talked about general sharing motives, but what motivates us to engage with brands online and share information about our product experiences? To begin, there are a number of reasons why consumers "like" and follow a brand. The top reasons are to hear about products and offers, provide direct feedback, to interact with the company, be entertained, and to show an association with the organization (eMarketer 2015). Academic studies addressing traditional WOM (although still applicable for sWOM) have identified a number of factors that increase the likelihood of sharing product experiences. Briefly, consumers often post about products when they are very satisfied or very dissatisfied (Bowman and Narayandas 2001; Anderson 1998) when the product is new (Richins and Bloch 1986; Bone 1992), when there is high product involvement (i.e., the product is relevant to consumers) (Richins and Bloch 1986), and when the consumer is highly involved in the marketplace (i.e., market mavens) (Slama and Tashcian 1985).

Marketers need to understand sharing behavior so that they may identify the type of content that is most likely to be shared on each social media platform. Unfortunately, the act of sharing does not mean that that individual will be influential. A social consumer can post a rave review about a product, but what if that consumer has only a handful of followers and what if they never see the review? In this case, the social sharer may have limited influence on the behavior of others. For that reason, it is important the companies seek out social influencers.

Social Influencers

There are a relatively small number of social consumers that have a disproportionately large amount of social influence when it comes to sWOM. One study by McKinsey found that 5 percent of "power influencers" in the shoes and clothing product category were responsible for 45 percent of product recommendations (Bughin 2015). In this book, we will refer to these "power influencers" as social influencers. In the marketing world, they are commonly referred to as opinion leaders. Influencers (or opinion leaders) typically focus their expertise in a specific area (i.e., fashion, food, exercise). Social influencers, those who influence the opinions and behaviors of others are engaged at all levels—they share, comment, produce, and curate. Their recommendations are surprisingly powerful. A joint study by Twitter and Annalect found that recommendations from influencers on Twitter were relied upon almost as much as recommendations from friends (56 percent relied on friends vs. 49 percent for influencers). Forty percent of those surveyed admitted to purchasing a product as a result of an influencer's recommendation (Swant 2016).

Marketers recognize the importance and value of these influencers, which is why formal influencer campaigns, and the agencies that support them, have become commonplace. A 2015 study found that 84 percent of worldwide marketing/communications professionals had plans to employ at least one influencer campaign in the upcoming year, and 81 percent of those companies that had previously conducted an influencer campaign believed it to be effective (Augure 2015). Influencer programs are seen as effective at fulfilling three objectives: building brand awareness, generating sales lead, and increasing consumer loyalty.

Social influencers come in many shapes and forms, with varying levels of influence. They can provide companies with completely informal, organic support (or non-support). Alternatively, their role can also be much more formal, with input and compensation provided by the company. Following are some of the most common types of social influencer categories, categorized as paid and unpaid.

Paid Influencers

Paid Social Influencers

These are everyday consumers, brand fans, and/or experts who are incentivized for their product-related sWOM posts. They typically have large social media followings. These compensated efforts last for a relatively short period of time and are dedicated to a specific marketing campaign (Sussman 2015). Paid social influencers can become self-built stars because of their social media activities. Through social media, they become credible subject matter experts (e.g., fashion, cosmetics). Social influencers may not have as many followers as a celebrity, and therefore may not generate as much exposure for a brand, but their followers are more concentrated allowing for more targeted marketing (Hitz 2016). Research confirms that consumers trust social influencers almost as much as they do their friends (Hitz 2016). As a social influencer's following grows, so too does her fee for social media word of mouth endorsements. Some social influencers now command as much as celebrities for their social posts. To illustrate, social media Vine darling Logan Paul is said to make over $100,000 per sponsored video post (Chen 2016a). Jaw-dropping—but he may be worth it! Mr. Paul's paid social media postings were credited for 25,000 Dunkin' Donuts gift card purchases (32 percent of the month's total) (Stanley 2016). Even social influencer dogs (yes, we are serious) are getting into the act and can receive $2,000–$10,000 per sponsored Instagram post (Birkner 2016). Now that is something to woof at.

Brand Ambassadors

Brand ambassadors are everyday consumers, brand fans, experts that enter into a long-term relationship to endorse a product. Brand ambassadors are frequently paid to represent the brand (Sussman 2015). Instead of paying for a one-off post or a series of posts for a dedicated marketing campaign, brand ambassadors become the spokespeople for a brand. An ambassador is someone that is passionate about your brand and who is already aligned (through their organic social media posts) with the brand's values and messaging. Their brand relationship is apparent throughout social channels. Brands can pay them on a retainer basis and often will give them special access to brand information (Sussman 2015).

Celebrities

"Traditional" celebrities, those whose stardom was originally gained outside of the social media sphere, can also become powerful influencers for brands. Social media analytics firm, D'Marie suggests that celebrities such as Kendall Jenner and Selena Gomez can provide a firm 12 times the return on investment (ROI) compared to "average digital marketing efforts." With a price tag of $230,000 per social media for Jenner and Gomez to post across social media platforms—that is quite a return (Heine 2015).

Unpaid Influencers

Everyday Consumers

Businesses may not need big names and famous faces when they have loyal, happy, and social savvy consumers to help spread the word on Facebook, Twitter, Instagram, and other popular platforms. Every day consumers and brand fans can organically post and also be encouraged to spread sWOM.

Case Study: The Laughing Chewbacca

Candace Payne is a 37-year-old stay-at-home mother of two from Grand Prairie, Texas. On May 19, 2016, Payne decided to share the details of her successful shopping spree at the Kohl's department store. Sitting in her car in the store parking lot, Payne recorded and posted to her Facebook page a video in which she, with unbridled excitement, shows off her find of the day—a battery-operated mask of the Star Wars character, Chewbacca. For approximately 2 minutes of the 4-minute video, Payne demonstrates to her friends how the mask works. Within 24 hours, the video was viewed 54 million times (Whitten 2016). Six days later, it had amassed over 145 million views and was reported through multiple news outlets. Payne even appeared with Star Wars producer J.J. Abrams on James Corden's "Carpool Karaoke" skit on CBS. Payne's uncontrollable, infectious laugh was a huge hit and so too was the mask. Within three days of the video being posted, the mask sold out on Kohls.com, Target.com, and Walmart.com (*USA Today* 2016). In the words of the great Hans Solo to Chewbacca, "Laugh it up, Fuzzball!" Overnight Payne evolved from being an everyday mom on social media to that of a social influencer.

A simple example of encouraging a consumer to share her experience on Facebook or post a picture of her recent purchase on Instagram is through store signage (Figure 2.5).

Figure 2.5 Share a coke

Brand Advocates

Brand advocates can be considered "super fans" or "brand loyalists" who are not incentivized or compensated for their posts. Their love of the brand is organically infused within their social media posts and the brand itself may be an extension of their identity (i.e., they mention the brand in their bio, social media profile image, or even have a brand tattoo).

Experts

Experts (at least in this typology) are those consumers who acquired their expertise outside of the social media sphere in RL (real life). They accumulated their credibility through industry experience, academic degrees, or "real-life" experience. Social media is simply a communication outlet that they use to share their knowledge. According to the 2016 Global Edelman Trust Barometer, technical experts (67 percent) and academic experts (64 percent) garner considerably more trust than an employee (52 percent), CEO (49 percent), or government official (35 percent) (Edelman 2016).

Social Influence Marketing Programs

The diversity of online influencer types warrants a variety of marketing programs. Some of these programs capitalize on the social influence of everyday consumers (i.e., referral programs), whereas others focus on paid social influencers. Sponsored social programs—those that focus on paid social influencers—are becoming more common and are almost as widely used as more traditional display advertising tactics, such as online display (Halverson Group 2015). The following section explores both referral and influencer programs.

Referral Programs

Referral programs drive purchase conversion. They can also be considered another form of paid media. In a nutshell, it comes down to having individuals taking an action based on friends or family's opinion on a product (ReferralCandy 2016). Certainly, this process occurs organically when consumers are reading opinions from their friends and family on Twitter or Facebook, but increasingly, companies are coordinating their referral efforts, many of which directly involve social media. For example, ride-sharing company Uber has routinely relied on consumers inviting their networks via Twitter, Facebook, blogs, and e-mail to ride with Uber. Current and new users both get $20 credit #Uberlove! They also use referrals to recruit drivers. Uber's referral program works first and foremost because people are genuinely happy with the service. Second, Uber has made it very easy to share by integrating a number of "share" options via the smartphone app (i.e., share on Facebook, tweet, text, and e-mail). Third, they offer an incentive for both the referrer and the referee—a double win.

The request for a referral can occur in a number of ways—although not all of them involve social media. Often, companies provide a link on the website's home page "invite a friend, get X." After clicking on the link, users are given more details on the incentive and provided with a number of sharing options. It can also be built into the purchase or order screen. If you have a great product, why limit your referral requests to one page— include a referral button on every page. Outside of having a great product, referrals need enticing incentives. As the Uber example illustrated, double incentives (for the referrer and the referee) worked well. You can also use a credit system referral program—for X number of referrals an individual can earn points, which can lead to a fixed dollar amount off their next purchase or even a specific prize. Another option would reward referrers with a specific percent of the dollar value of a friend's purchase. Figure 2.6 outlines the keys to successful referral program (adapted from Veerasamy n.d.).

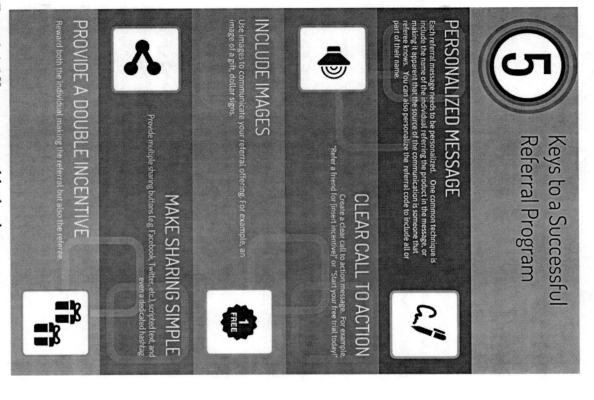

5

Keys to a Successful Referral Program

PERSONALIZED MESSAGE

Each referral message needs to be personalized. One common technique is include the name of the individual referring the product in the message, or making it apparent that the source of the communication is someone that referee knows. You can also personalize the referral code to include alt or part of their name.

INCLUDE IMAGES

Use images to communicate your referral offering. For example, an image of a gift, dollar signs.

CLEAR CALL TO ACTION

Create a clear call to action message. For example, "Refer a friend for [insert incentive]" or "Start your free trial today"

MAKE SHARING SIMPLE

Provide multiple sharing buttons (e.g. Facebook, Twitter, etc.), scripted text, and even a dedicated hashtag.

PROVIDE A DOUBLE INCENTIVE

Reward both the individual making the referral but also the referee.

Figure 2.6 5 Keys to a successful referral program

Influencer Programs

The importance of identifying and creating relationships with influencers is well established. In truth, identifying "the right" influencers is one of the hardest tasks. Companies such as Klear who provide global influencers across platforms and interest areas can, for a fee, offer you access to their influencer library. However, a good and less expensive place to start is to create a profile of what you consider to be the ideal influencer (e.g., age, gender, location) and then try to find a match. Monitor social media and follow hashtag conversations that your ideal influencers would be participating in. Set up a Google search for your brand and see who is talking about it. You can also use monitoring tools such as Hootsuite and Social Mention to track brand-related conversations (Matthews 2013). In the appendix of this book, we offer some suggestions of websites and services that can assist in identifying influencers.

Identifying a potential influencer is only the first step in establishing an influencer program. Next, you need to understand the extent of the social influence that the individual possesses. Thankfully, there are a number of social influence analytic tools that allow you to measure an individual's level of social influence (Klout, Brandwatch, and so on). The most well-known social influence tool is, perhaps, Klout. Klout is a third-party application that ranks social media users on a scale of 1–100 based on their social media influence level. The average Klout score is 40 and a very high score of 63 would put you in the top 5 percent (Klout 2013). While the algorithm is unknown and dynamic, Klout does look at the frequency of posts, along with the number of followers, likes, retweets, and shares an individual receives to determine their level of influence.

When selecting your influencers pay attention to their social influence score and don't use the influencer's number of followers as your only deciding factor. You also need to pay attention to the level of engagement that they have with social media. Content quality is also an important consideration in your selection (Halverson Group 2015). You will want to make sure that the quality of their content and their communication style is consistent with your brand and intended message. The best influencer programs give influencers the freedom to make their own content, so you need to ensure that you have a good fit. While some brands go after the big social media fish (e.g., Keds and Taylor Swift and her 74,900,000+ Facebook followers), individuals with smaller follower counts can also be influential (and sometimes even more influential) (Chen 2016b). Micro-influencers, those with followings between 10,000–100,000 are being considered more frequently for campaigns. The term "power middle influencers" social media users that have followers between 100,000 and 200,000 has also been put forward to further segment the social influencer category (Chen 2016b).

Marketers can obviously choose from a wide selection of social platforms, but they also have a number of choices on the type of content they sponsor. IZEA's 2015 State of Sponsored Social study revealed that the most popular sponsored social elements were sponsored Facebook status update (60 percent), followed by brand "like" (56 percent), brand "follow" (48 percent), sponsored tweets (40 percent), and sponsored blog posts (32 percent). Sponsored pins (7 percent) and sponsored Vines (5 percent) were some of the least popular social elements (Halverson Group 2015).

Structuring Influencers Programs

Marketers need to approach a relationship with a potential influencer just like a new budding friendship. Personalize your e-mail, meet them in person. Know what they like, their interests, their posting style. Marketers really need to sell their brand to the influencer—explain why it is a good fit for them, why the influencer's audience would find the brand discussion interesting or relevant (Halverson Group 2015).

Collaboration is the key when working with an influencer. Marketers need to meet with influencers and provide them with sample content and a general outline of their story—but influencers need to have input, "skin in the game"—because it is *their playground* you are asking your brand to play on. In truth, the reason why you are approaching an influencer is that you want to capitalize on their preexisting consumer relationships. You are also relying on their communication and content expertise within specific social media platforms (Maoz 2016a).

Following is a list of items adapted from Klear's influencer informational guidelines (Maoz 2016b):

- Company and product overview: If an influencer isn't already familiar with brand, they should be told about the company and the product.

- Campaign overview: They should be given a description of the campaign, its objectives, and the theme.

- Creative: Outline the key messaging points you are looking for, highlight great examples of posts the influencer has previously done, and identify other social media posts that are consistent with the creative approach you would like to see.

- Social media platforms: Identify which platforms you would like (ideally) to see the influencer post on.

- Content volume and disclosure: Identify the preferred number and frequency of posting. Also, explicitly state your method of disclosure.

While creative freedom is good, it is important to create explicit guidelines and a firm contract that states your goals and expectations (Maoz 2016a). Specifying frequency is an important first step in having some control. More than once a week and two or three times of month are the most common sponsored posting durations (Halverson Group 2015).

Incentives matter when encouraging consumers to discuss your product via social media. Eighty-eight percent of the U.S. consumers and 95 percent of the 18–34-year-olds surveyed indicated they would like an incentive to share. The incentive of choice: money (Mixon 2016). Free products, discounts or coupons, free services, gift cards, and trips or travel are other desired forms of compensation (Halverson Group 2015). There are legal and regulatory issues that companies must consider when engaging in incentivized or paid relationships with consumers. Chapter 4 examines this in detail.

The last consideration you need to make when launching a sWOM campaign is seeding. The process of seeding is just as it sounds—carefully selecting multiple people or influencers (seeds) to distribute your content or product with the hope that it will grow and flourish. The end result is not only exposure to your content or product, but, hopefully, conversions (i.e., product sales). Academic research proposes that seeding programs benefit marketers through market expansion and consumer acceleration.

In other words, consumers that wouldn't normally purchase the product do and consumers that would normally have purchased it do so at an earlier time (Libai, Muller, and Peres 2013). The question is of course, who do you pick? Seeding programs are more effective when they target social influencers as opposed to randomly selecting consumers (Hinz et al. 2011). These social influencers can be broken into three seeding groups (Libai, Muller, and Peres 2013):

- Hubs: Individuals that are well-connected (Goldenberg et al. 2009).

- Experts/Persuaders: These individuals are effective not for their audience size, but for their ability to persuade. This is drawn from their subject expertise.

- Bridge: These individuals bridge different social networks—they are connected to many different groups of consumers. Their power is in their ability to spread information outside to new groups of consumers (Hinz et al. 2011).

The good news is that all of the work that companies invest in social influencer campaigns can pay off. One 2016 study of Twitter users found that 47 percent of the consumers purchased a product based on the recommendation of social influencers (Swant 2016). When Twitter users saw tweets from brands, their purchase intent increased 2.7 times, but when they saw tweets from both the brand and social influencers, purchase intent increased to 5.2 times (Swant 2016). Now that is something to tweet about!

The writing is on the (Facebook) wall, or in this case, the screen—we love social media. For every 3 minutes we spent online in 2016, 1 minute was on a social platform (Buckle 2016a). Aided by mobile devices, social media provides us with the opportunity to engage with brands and share our opinions with the masses. It also has the potential to change the way we do business.

References

Adobe. 2015. "Social Intelligence Report: Adobe Digital Index Q2 2015." www.cmo.com/content/dam/CMO_Other/ADI/ADI_Mobilegeddon/Q2-2015-Social-Intelligence-Report.pdf

Anderson, E. 1998. "Customer Satisfaction and Word of Mouth." *Journal of Service Research* 1, no. 1, pp. 5–17.

Anderson, M. 2015a. "6 Facts About Americans and Their Smartphones." www.pewresearch.org/fact-tank/2015/04/01/6-facts-about-americans-and-their-smartphones/

Anderson, M. 2015b. "Men Catch Up with Women on Overall Social Media Use." www.pewresearch.org/fact-tank/2015/08/28/men-catch-up-with-women-on-overall-social-media-use/

Anderson, M. 2015c. "Technology Device Ownership: 2015." www.pewinternet.org/2015/10/29/technology-device-ownership-2015/

Augure. 2015. "State of Influencer Engagement in 2015." www.augure.com/resources/whitepapers/influencer-engagement-report?download=19053

Beatty, S., and S. Smith. 1987. "External Search Efforts: An Investigation Across Several Product Categories." *Journal of Consumer Research* 14, no. 1, pp. 83–95.

Belch, G., and M. Belch. 2014. "The Role of New and Traditional Media in the Rapidly Changing Marketing Communications Environment." *International Journal on Strategic Innovation Marketing* 1, no. 3, pp. 130–36.

Birkner, C. 2016. "Why Internet-Famous Dogs Are Fetching So Much Love From Brands." *Adweek*. www.adweek.com/news/advertising-branding/why-internet-famous-dogs-are-fetching-so-much-love-brands-173339

Blatberg, E. 2015. "The Demographics of YouTube, in 5 Charts." *Digiday*. http://digiday.com/platforms/demographics-youtube-5-charts/

Bone, P. 1992. "Determines of Word-of-Mouth Communications During Product Consumption." In *Advances in Consumer Research*, eds. J.F. Sherry and B. Sternthal, 572–83. Provo, UT: Association for Consumer Research. www.acrwebsite.org/search/view-conference-proceedings.aspx?ld=7359

Bowman, D., and D. Narayandas. 2001. "Managing Customer-Initiated Contacts with Manufacturers: The Impact of Share of Category Requirments and Word-of-Mouth Behavior." *Journal of Marketing Research* 38, no. 3, pp. 281–95.

Brown, J.J., and P.H. Reingen. 1987. "Social Ties and Word-of-Mouth Referral Behavior." *Journal of Consumer Research* 14, no. 3, pp. 350–62. http://search.ebscohost.com/login.aspx?direct=true&db=bth&AN=4657957&site=ehost-live

Buckle, C. 2016a. "2 Hours Per Day Spent on Social Media and Messaging." *Global Web Index.* www.globalwebindex.net/blog/2-hours-per-day-spent-on-social-media-messaging

Buckle, C. 2016b. "Top 10 Reasons for Using Social Media Among Facebookers." *Global Web Index.* www.globalwebindex.net/blog/top-10-reasons-for-using-social-media-among-facebookers

Bughin, J. 2015. "Getting a Sharper Picture of Social Media's Influence." *McKinsey Quarterly.* www.mckinsey.com/business-functions/marketing-and-sales/our-insights/getting-a-sharper-picture-of-social-medias-influence

Chen, Y. 2016a. "Inside the Rocky, Love-Hate Relationship Between Marketers and 'Influencers.'" *Digiday UK.* http://digiday.com/brands/inside-rocky-love-hate-relationship-marketers-influencers/

Chen, Y. 2016b. "The Rise of 'Micro-Influencers' on Instagram." *Digiday UK.* http://digiday.com/agencies/micro-influencers/

Delzio, S. 2015. "New Research Reveals Instagram Users Like to Shop: Social Media Examiner." *Social Media Examiner.* www.socialmediaexaminer.com/instagram-users-like-to-shop/

Dembosky. April 2012. "In the West We're Mostly Social Media 'Lurkers.'" *The Globe and Mail.* www.theglobeandmail.com/technology/digital-culture/social-web/in-the-west-were-mostly-social-media-lurkers/article1357516/

DiMauro, V., and D. Bulmer. 2014. "The Social Consumer Study." www.slideshare.net/vdimauro/the-social-consumer-study

Duggan, M. 2015. "The Demographics of Social Media Users." www.pewinternet.org/2015/08/19/the-demographics-of-social-media-users/

Duggan, M., N. Ellison, C. Lampe, A. Lenhart, and M. Madden. 2015. "Social Media Update 2014." www.pewinternet.org/2015/01/09/social-media-update-2014/

Edelman. 2016. "2016 Edelman Trust Barometer: Global Report." www.edelman.com/insights/intellectual-property/2016-edelman-trust-barometer/global-results/

eMarketer. 2015. "Social Promoters More Likely Than Sharers to Actively Engage Directly with Brands." www.emarketer.com/Article/Social-Promoters-Power-Brand-Engagement/1012758

Fleming, G. 2016. "The Data Digest: Forrester's Social Technographics 2016." *Data Insights Professionals Blog.* http://blogs.forrester.com/category/social_technographics

Frier, S. 2016. "Snapchat User 'Stories' Fuel 10 Billion Daily Video Views." *Bloomberg.* Retrieved from www.bloomberg.com/news/articles/2016-04-28/snapchat-user-content-fuels-jump-to-10-billion-daily-video-views

Gilly, M., J.L. Graham, M. Wolfinbarger, and L. Yale. 1998. "A Dyadic Study of Interpersonal Information Search." *The Journal of the Academy of Marketing Science* 26, no. 2, pp. 83–100.

GlobalWebIndex. 2016. "GWI Social Q3: 2106." http://insight.globalwebindex. net/social

Goldenberg, J., H. Sangman, D.R. Lehmann, and J. Weon Hong. March 2009. "The Role of Hubs in the Adoption Process." *Journal of Marketing* 73, no. 2, pp. 1–13.

Gong, W., E.P. Lim, and F. Zhu. 2015. "Characterizing Silent Users in Social Media Communities." *Proceedings of the Ninth International AAAI Conference on Web and Social Media*, pp. 140–49.

Google. 2016. "The Online and Multiscreen World." *Consumer Barometer with Google.* www.consumerbarometer.com/en/insights/?countryCode=US

Griffith, E. September 2015. "Pinterest Hits 100 Million Users." *Fortune.* Retrieved from http://fortune.com/2015/09/17/pinterest-hits-100-million-users/

Halverson Group. 2015. "IZEA'S 2015 State of Sponsored Social Study." www. clearslide.com/v/latmd5

Haslam, Ed. 2015. "The Second Generation of Sharing," *Adweek.* www. adweek.com/socialtimes/sharethis-ed-haslam-guest-post/632742?utm_ source=Website&utm_medium=NewsPage&utm_term=Adweek+Article& utm_content=Second+Generation+of+Sharing&utm_campaign=website+ tracking

Heine, C. 2015. "These 4 Celebrity Influencers Can Charge $230,000 for a Single Brand Post." *Adweek,* December 4. www.adweek.com/news/technology/ these-5-celebrity-influencers-can-charge-230000-every-time-they-post-brand-168466

Hinz, O., B. Skiera, C. Barrot, and J.U. Becker. May 2011. "Seeding Strategies for Viral Marketing: An Empirical Comparison." *Journal of Marketing* 75, no. 6, pp. 55–71.

Hitz, L. 2016. "The Influencers vs. Celebrities: The Critical Differences." *The Simply Measured Blog.* http://simplymeasured.com/blog/influencers-vs-celebrities-the-critical-differences/#sm.00018n9uis1172fifrc4xqq28xm0f

Ipsos. 2013. "Global 'Sharers' on Social Media Sites Seek to Share Interesting (61%), Important (43%) and Funny (43%) Things." www.ipsos-na.com/ news-polls/pressrelease.aspx?id=6239

Kemp, S. 2016. "Digital in 2016." http://wearesocial.com/uk/special-reports/ digital-in-2016

Klout. 2013. "What Is the Average Klout Score?" http://support.klout.com/ customer/en/portal/articles/679109-what-is-the-average-klout-score-

Krogstad, J.M. 2015. "Social Media Preferences Vary by Race and Ethnicity." *Pew Research Center.* www.pewresearch.org/fact-tank/2015/02/03/social-media-preferences-vary-by-race-and-ethnicity/

Lafferty, J. 2015. "Pinterest Hits 100 Million User Mileston." *Adweek.* Retrieved from www.adweek.com/socialtimes/pinterest-hits-100-million-user-milestone/626896

Lenhart, A. 2015. "73% of Teens Have Access to a Smartphone; 15% Have Only a Basic Phone." *Teens, Social Media and Technology Overview*. www.pewinternet.org/2015/04/09/teens-social-media-technology-2015/pi_2015-04-09_teensandtech_06/

Li, C. 2016. "The Engagement Pyramid." *Social Media Models*.

Li, C. 2010. *Open Leadership: How Social Technology Can Transform the Way You Lead*. New York: John Wiley & Sons, Inc.

Libai, B., E. Muller, and R. Peres. 2013. "Decomposing the Value of Word-of-Mouth Seeding Programs: Acceleration Versus Expansion." *Journal of Marketing Research* 50, no. 2, pp. 161–76.

Maoz, Y. 2016a. "First Steps for Healthy Influencer Relationships." *Klear Blog*. http://klear.com/blog/first-steps-with-influencers/?utm_source=newsletter

Maoz, Y. 2016b. "Marketing Brief Template for An Influencer Campaign." *Klear Blog*. http://klear.com/blog/influencer-brief-template/?utm_source=newsletter

Matthews, K. 2013. "The Definitive Guide to Influencer Targeting." *Kissmetrics Blog*. https://blog.kissmetrics.com/guide-to-influencer-targeting/

Mixon, I. 2016. "8 Statistics That Will Change the Way You Think About Referral Marketing." *Ambassador*. http://app.mhb.io/e/npo3/57

Nielsen, J. 2006. *The 90-9-1 Rule for Participation Inequality in Social Media and Online Communities*. California: Nielsen Norman Group.

Park, C., and T.M. Lee. 2009. "Information Direction, Website Reputation and the eWOM Effect: A Moderating Role of Product Type." *Journal of Business Research* 62, no. 1, pp. 61–67.

Perrin, A. 2015. "Social Media Usage: 2005–2015." www.pewinternet. org/2015/10/08/social-networking-usage-2005-2015/

ReferralCandy. 2016. "Referral vs. Affiliate Marketing: What's the Difference? [Infographic]." www.referralcandy.com/blog/referral-vs-affiliate-marketing-whats-difference-infographic/ (accessed September 7, 2016).

Richins, M., and P. Bloch. 1986. "After the New Wears Off: The Temporal Context of Product Involvement." *Journal of Consumer Research* 13, no. 2, pp. 280–85.

ShareThis. 2015. "Q1 2015 Consumer Sharing Trends Report." www.slideshare. net/sharethis/q12015-cstr-sharethis

Slama, M., and A. Tashcian. 1985. "Selected Socioeconomic and Demographic Characteristics Associated with Purchasing Involvement." *Journal of Marketing* 49, pp. 72–82.

Smith, A. 2015. "U.S. Smartphone Use in 2015." www.pewinternet.org/ 2015/04/01/us-smartphone-use-in-2015/

Stanley, T.L. 2016. "How Vine's Hunky Goofball Logan Paul Plans to Become Mainstream Superstar." *Adweek.* www.adweek.com/news/advertising-branding/how-vines-hunky-goofball-logan-paul-plans-become-mainstream-superstar-169152

Sussman, B. 2015. "Influencer vs. Ambassadors: Stop the Confusion." *Entreprenuer.* www.entrepreneur.com/article/249947

Swant, M. 2016. "Twitter Says Users Now Trust Influencers Nearly as Much as Their Friends." *Adweek.* www.adweek.com/news/technology/twitter-says-users-now-trust-influencers-nearly-much-their-friends-171367

The New York Times. 2011. "The Psychology of Sharing." http://nytmarketing. whsites.net/mediakit/pos/

USA Today. 2016. "Chewbacca Masks Selling Fast after Video." May.

Vision Critical. 2014. "New Vision Critical Report Identifies Major Gaps in Social Media Data Companies Use to Analyze Customer Behavior." www. visioncritical.com/news-events/new-vision-critical-report-identifies-major-gaps-social-media-data-companies-use-analyze/

Watt, N. 2016. "ADI: Best of The Best Brands Driving Social Media Success." *CMO.* www.cmo.com/adobe-digital-insights/articles/2016/7/18/adi-best-of-the-bestdriving-social-media-success-.html#gs.b90iG=k

Weber, H. 2015. "LinkedIn Now Has 400M Users, But Only 25% of Them Use It Monthly." Retrieved September 3, 2016, from http://venturebeat. com/2015/10/29/linkedin-now-has-400m-users-but-only-25-of-them-use-it-monthly/

Whitten, S. 2016. "Where to Find the Chewbacca Mask." *CNBC.* www.cnbc. com/2016/05/20/where-to-find-the-chewbacca-mask.html

Young, K. 2016. "Snapchat Is Getting Older." Retrieved August 30, 2016, from www.globalwebindex.net/blog/snapchat-is-getting-older

CHAPTER 3

Social Business: It's Not Just About Marketing

Technology has significantly transformed the business landscape over the last century. It has impacted not only how products and services are produced, marketed, and distributed, but also how businesses communicate, build, and maintain a relationship with their consumers. Numerous technological advancements have strengthened and furthered businesses ability to grow and expand. For example, the Remington typewriter occupied a dominant presence in the workplace through most of the 1900s, and by the 1960s, the telephone displaced the traditional letter as the primary method of communication (Polt 1995; Dillerm 2015). The 1980s marked the beginning of the modern technology era with the introduction of the first personal computer (i.e., Apple's Macintosh), brick-size cellular phones, and the fax machine (Novell 2013). By the turn of the millennium, the rate of technological advancements exploded. The Internet led the charge. The Web made companies more accessible, e-mail became a popular communication tool, the first smartphone was released, we could send text and photo messages, and e-commerce changed forever the way we shop (Dillerm 2015; Williams 2012). Apple's iPhone introduction, coupled with high consumer adoption rates of smartphones, further propelled the usage of social media and launched the era of the social consumer. Today, technology is fully integrated into all aspects of our daily lives. We live, work, and play in a digital world.

Historically, businesses held the majority of the power in the marketplace. Companies decided what to produce, when and where to release it, and how consumers would purchase and consume it. This is no longer true; today consumers sit in the driver's seat. Social media has given consumers a loud voice. They are now able to widely broadcast what they want, how, when, and where they want it. Consumers wield this power through their desktops or laptops, but more likely, through a small, powerful device that sits nicely in the palm of their hand. When consumers have a question, a complaint, or a compliment, they turn to their smartphone and share it with hundreds, thousands, and maybe even millions of other consumers on social media. If a company cannot give them what they want, they discount them with a swipe of their finger or the click of a button. The balance of power has shifted.

For a company to succeed today, they need to embrace the power of social media, to make it part of who they are and what they do. Companies need to evolve into a social business. Those who fail to make this transition may, in time, find themselves left behind. As a wise person once said, companies must innovate or die. Innovation is not just about new product development; it is also about developing new ways of doing business. In this chapter, we will explain what it means to be a social business and why it is important for your company to embrace this change. We will also explain the stages of social business development and how social tools can be integrated to become part of your company's DNA. Interspersed throughout the chapter are examples of companies that have successfully made the transition. Hopefully, they will inspire you to do the same.

The Social Business

Social business is "activities that use social media, social software and social networks to enable efficient, effective and mutually useful connections between people, information, and assets" (Kiron et al. 2012). When a company becomes a social business, they no longer view social media solely as a marketing or public relations communication tool, but as a tool that can be used throughout various strategic, innovative, and functional areas of a company. A study of 3,478 managers from 24 industries in 115 countries revealed a growing interest in and need for companies to make the transition to becoming social businesses (Kiron et al. 2012). Making the transition is not easy; it requires leadership, resources, and time.

Social Business Maturity Model

The social business maturity model presented in Table 3.1 was developed based on a combination of academic frameworks and industry models

Table 3.1 Social business maturity model

	Trial	Transition	Maturity
Current status	• No clear goals • No formal policy • No plan • No control • Ad hoc and experimental social initiatives • Using social as a broadcasting channel	• More focused activities • Allocation of some resources • Movement from listening to engaging with consumers • Social primarily used for marketing and PR purposes • Some, but inconsistent interaction with consumers	• Social media monitoring • Communicating feedback • Employee, consumer, and influencer engagement • More focused use of social in a number of functional areas
Next steps	• Learn how your consumers use social media • Listen to what they are saying • Conduct a competitive audit • Develop, implement, and learn from pilot projects • Prioritize initiatives	• Creation of a Social Media Advisory Board or Center of Excellence • Policy formation and rules for engagement • Goal alignment with strategic business goals • Encourage employee engagement • Providing employee support and training • Identifying social influencers • Exploration of how social can be used in other functional areas—HR, Sales, Finance, and so on • Measuring and communicating results • Ongoing monitoring	• Obtaining C-level support and engagement • Social media moves into all areas of the business—HR, Sales, Finance, and so on • Social media is now part of the business planning process • Policies and procedures updated to allow for companywide participation • Review Advisory Board or Center of Excellence role and composition
Resources required	• Obtaining support from senior management • Human resources • Identify social media evangelists • Listening or monitoring platform	• Allocation of additional human resources • Social media management system	• Ongoing education and support

Source: Adapted from (van Luxemburg 2011; Li and Solis 2013; Effing and Spil 2016).

(van Luxemburg 2011; Li and Solis 2013; Effing and Spil 2016). The model describes three phases of social business. It identifies activities that typically take place during each phase, the steps and the resources required to move your company to the next phase.

Trial Phase

The trial phase of social business is not unlike Hollywood's portrayal of the Wild West, chaotic and lawless. In this phase, social media is not a formal part of the business. Company social media accounts are often created in silos, functioning independently from other company social media accounts. Those that do exist were created by individual departments or social-savvy, and (in some cases) not-so-socially savvy, employees. These accounts were more than likely created without undergoing a formal approval process. There may even be duplicate accounts, inconsistent posting and engagement practices, and unauthorized or inappropriate use of company intellectual property (e.g., logos, trademarks). During this phase, there is no strategy or goals in place. There is little synergy between accounts. Your company may be using social media as a broadcasting channel—posting the same information on each platform, instead of customizing information for each platform and using specific platforms to engage consumers in conversation and build relationships. Your company may not have a social media policy that outlines what employees can and cannot post. Your employees are often unaware of laws and regulations that they are required to be followed. Sometimes, the intern(s) is solely charged with crafting your company's social media presence (Tip: Don't do this). In this phase, the mindset is "let's give it a shot and see what happens."

Chaos aside, there is value in experimentation. However, this value will go unrealized if no one is paying careful attention. Social businesses need to listen and learn. So, let's get a little more focused. There are at least four valuable sources of information you can draw upon to learn about how to use social media for business purposes: (1) publically available information, (2) information about your social media connections, (3) information about your current consumers base, and (4) information about your competition.

Public Information

The beauty (and curse) of social media is that it is constantly growing and evolving. Platforms that were once popular (e.g., MySpace) lose their appeal and are replaced with other platforms (e.g., Facebook). New platforms are launched and become hugely successful (e.g., Instagram and Snapchat), others transform by adding new features (e.g., Pinterest), and some simply fail to catch on (e.g., Gowalla). The ways in which consumers use and engage with social media also change overtime. A decade ago, social media was used primarily for connecting or reconnecting with family and friends. Today, as we learned in Chapter 2 consumers use it for a variety of additional purposes, such as to meet new people, be inspired, research products, catch up on the latest news, find employment, and be entertained. Social media has certainly come a long way. Strategies that worked well on social media five years ago may not work well today. Companies need to keep up-to-date on the growth and popularity of different platforms and understand who and how consumers are currently using them. Fortunately, there is ample publicly available information on this topic. Pew Internet (pewinternet.org), eMarketer (emarketer.com), Social Media Examiner (socialmediaexaminer.com), Nielsen (nielsen.com), Forrester (forrester.com), and McKinsey (mckinsey.com) are all good places to start. See the Appendix of this book for a list of resources.

Social Connections

The key to marketing success is by understanding your consumers. This truism is no different in the social space. Therefore, you need to learn as much as you can from your existing social connections. To begin, select a sample of 20–30 of your social media followers and review their accounts to see when they use social (day/time), how frequently they use it (frequency of posts), and what type of content they appear to be interested in (evident by status updates, shares, likes, comments, and so on). You are likely to find that there are platform differences in how consumers are using and engaging with your brand. For example, consumers may be more active on Facebook than they are on Twitter. They may like watching the videos you share on Facebook but do not engage with those you post to Twitter. Next, examine your social accounts carefully to see what type of content resonates the strongest with your followers. Look for content that receives the greatest level of engagement from your followers (i.e., likes, shares, comments, retweets). Take note of specific content that fails to ignite a response. A final step is to conduct a sentiment analysis, a process by which you perform a keyword search, typically your company name to see what people are saying about your company across social media. Sentiment analysis also quantifies and categorizes comments as either positive, negative, and neutral. There is a large number of free and fee-based sentiment analysis services available: Social Mention (socialmention.com—free), WhosTalkin (whostalkin.com—free), HowSociable (howsociable.com—fee-based), Mention (mention.com—fee-based), and Keyhole.co (keyhole.co—fee-based). These will allow you not only to see what people are saying about your company, brand, product, competition, or industry in real time, but also help you determine if they like you.

Consumer Base

While social media can provide a valuable window into the lives of your consumers, you may still need a better view. If you need more information on your consumers' social media habits, then it is a good idea to survey them. A formal survey can be drafted and distributed via e-mail or social media. Alternatively, you could add a couple of questions to an existing task (e.g., order form) or interaction (e.g., customer service call). An informal, exploratory survey format using social media is another option. A company could simply ask or post a question on Twitter or Facebook and document consumer feedback.

Competition

There is a lot that you can learn about how to and how not to use social media by simply monitoring the social activities of your competitors. Identify three or more competitors to monitor. Select the industry leader and a couple of your immediate competitors and audit their social media activities. Identify which platforms they use, how active they are on each platform, how they use their brand voice, how they embody their brand story, what they post, and the kind of response these posts generate. Try to identify the combination of content and timing of posts that works for each platform. Similarly, identify what does not appear to work. In other words, what posts did not generate much consumer engagement (i.e., likes, retweets, comments). You can learn just as much from their failures as you can from their successes.

To monitor your consumers and your competitors' social media habits, it may be worthwhile to purchase a subscription to a social media monitoring platform. There are myriad of options available depending on the amount and level of data you wish to capture and the size of your budget. Getting into the nuances of social media monitoring is beyond the scope of this book, but a low-cost and effective option to start with is Hootsuite (hootsuite.com). Other commonly used options include Salesforce, Sysomos, and Viral Heat. See the resource list in the Appendix for more information.

Once you have observed and learned as much as you can from your connections, consumers, and competitors, you will be able to formulate a set of assumptions about the best way to generate a following and successfully engage with your consumers on social media to encourage social word of mouth (sWOM). Now it is time to test some of these assumptions. Pick one or two social media accounts, and over the period of a couple of weeks, pilot these assumptions. Monitor each and every post to determine success. After a couple of weeks of experimenting with different approaches, you will be ready to prioritize future initiatives. Remember the goal is quality, not quantity. It is better to have a small number of well-executed initiatives on a couple of social media platforms that generate positive results than it is to try and be everywhere and do everything. In other words, do not jump into simultaneously creating a Facebook, Twitter, Instagram, YouTube, and Google+ account. Be realistic about what you can achieve, given the resources you have at your disposal. You have to crawl before you walk, before you run. Your holistic social media efforts are a marathon and not a sprint.

There are two primary social media resources you will need: financial resources for a monitoring service subscription as well as any resources required for your initiatives (i.e., content generation and organization) and human resources to develop, implement, and monitor your pilot projects. During this phase, social media responsibilities largely fall to the marketing department. Someone in the marketing department needs to be assigned the responsibility of managing the company's social media initiatives—Director of Social Media or Social Media Manager. To assist this person now and in the future, it is essential that you identify and recruit social media evangelists—employees throughout and at all levels who recognize the importance of social media as a business tool. These evangelists can be very influential at gaining companywide support, beginning at the senior level.

Executive Buy-In

Executive buy-in and support are essential for success (Kiron et al. 2012). C-level executives differ in their perceptions of social media and the importance and value of creating a social business. Greg Verdino—author, speaker, and founder of Verdino & Co—offers six reasons why many executives are often reluctant to adopt social (Hootsuite Universiy 2012).

They Are Not on Social

Many members of senior management are, shall we say, of a mature generation. They were not born into, nor did they come of age in a digital world. Their birth was not announced on Facebook, and they did not immortalize every birthday on Instagram. Pokemon was a video game they or their siblings played on a Game Boy, not an augmented reality game that required players to scour the neighborhood eyes glued to their smartphone. Senior management's use of social media maybe limited to LinkedIn, and if they have an account on another platform (e.g., Facebook), chances are they are lurkers, or intermittent contributors, rarely posting if at all. They may not have the same understanding of or appreciation for social media as others.

They Do Not Think the Investment Is Worth the Time

Even if members of senior management do use social media for personal reasons, they may feel that the amount of time and effort required to generate and maintain a social media presence is not worth the time. We understand—being social is time-consuming! But, they are also concerned that the resulting impact to the bottom line may not be worth the investment. Return on investment (ROI) is admittedly hard to determine on social media. They see other, perhaps, more traditional media as being a better investment, particularly if those initiatives have proven successful in the past.

Too Much Risk, Not Enough Reward

Whether it is a negative consumer story or a company employee posting something inappropriate, there are plenty of business-related social media horror stories to give any company pause. For example, some years ago, an employee of Best Buy created a series of short YouTube videos illustrating some different sales scenarios. In each scenario, the consumer was presented in an unflattering manner. Best Buy was often, but not always, mentioned by name. Some of these videos were viewed over 1.5 million times. Not surprisingly, the company received a lot of negative feedback (Dunn 2010). In Chapter 1, we offered the example of DiGiorno's incorrectly using the domestic violence hashtag #WhyIStayed to sell pizza. A final example is the case of the breakfast cereal brand Cheerios. In 2016, music artist Prince died suddenly. Cheerios, which is owned by General Mills, sent out the tweet "Rest in peace" against a purple backdrop, with a Cheerio to punctuate the i, and #prince. A storm of angry comments followed in rapid succession. Grieving fans felt that the tweet was exploitative (Kottasova 2016). In each of these cases, the company was quick to issue an apology and removed the offending post, but not before it was seen by the masses and screen captured to live forever in the virtual vault of social blunders. It is easy to see why some members of senior management are uncomfortable with social media. Without sufficient procedures and controls in place, mistakes are common, and it is difficult to control the narrative and the brand's reputation.

They Do Not Think the Target Market Uses Social

Ten years ago, this may have been a valid statement. But not today. Social media is no longer just used by teens and twenty-somethings. Today, social media penetration is strong in all age groups (your grandmother is probably checking you out on Facebook right now!). As we learned in Chapter 2, social media adoption rates have changed dramatically over the years. Notably, older adults are increasingly signing up for social media (Perrin 2015).

Another argument is that social media is only appropriate for business-to-consumer (B2C) companies; business-to-business (B2B) companies simply won't reap its rewards. First, it is important to remember that people run companies. Social media can be an effective way of creating awareness of your brand, building and maintaining a relationship with people who are decision makers, buyers, users, influencers, and gatekeepers. Second, and as you will learn later in this chapter, B2B companies can be very successful at using social media. For B2B companies, being on social media is not about having an account on every platform—not every platform is relevant to you and your consumers. Instead, it is about identifying and adopting a small number of platforms and using them to enhance your business through sWOM.

They Do Not Know How to Measure Results

CEOs, CMOs, managing directors, and board members are those members of senior management who are most likely to view social business as somewhat important. CFOs who focus on return on investment (ROI) place less value on social in part because of the difficulty in measuring results (Kiron et al. 2012). Measuring results in general and ROI specifically has been a challenge. But, social media results can be measured. If your company is unable to measure results, it may be because you did not tie social initiatives to company business goals—key performance indicators (KPI) were not defined (e.g., share of conversation, traffic from social media platforms). Aligning social media with business goals or KPIs and developing specific, measurable, realistic, aggressive, and timely objectives is necessary.

You Are Not Making a Compelling Case

The last reason why senior management is often unwilling to adopt social media is that the person advocating for a social media program is not making a compelling case. In other words, the social media advocate needs to work on his or her sales technique. Social media expert Verdino recommends avoiding the use of dramatic case studies that have little or nothing to do with your industry. He also advises against relying too much on statistics from outside of your company and data from consultants whose primary purpose is to gain business. Instead, he suggests tying your social sales pitch to core business objectives, understand who you are selling to, and adapt your sales pitch to cater to senior management's understanding of social media and what is important to them. He also suggests enlisting the support of social media evangelists and other potential influencers. Finally, brush up on your sales skills (Hootsuite University 2012).

Transition Phase

The transition phase is the evolutionary phase. Having completed the steps of listening and learning, conducting a competitive audit and piloting initiatives, it is time to put all of this knowledge to good use. During the transition phase, social media activities become more focused. Instead of trying to do it all and be something for everyone, the company directs its social media efforts toward specific consumer groups and social platforms. There is a movement from listening to consumers to engaging with them. Resource allocation has improved, but likely has room to grow. To gain support for additional resources, it is important for you to keep monitoring, measuring, and reporting results. Senior management needs to see that social media is worth the investment. Now may be an appropriate time to acquire or trade up to a more robust social media monitoring and management system. Hootsuite may continue to be a good long-term option for small to medium-size companies. Larger companies may eventually need to upgrade to a more sophisticated system with additional features. Social monitoring leaders include Salesforce, Sysomos, Visual Technologies, and Viral Heat.

When the focus becomes engagement, it is time to establish a social media advisory board. An advisory board is a group of individuals whose purpose is to craft a company social media policy and provide appropriate guidelines for using social media in the workplace. We cover social media policies and advisory boards in Chapter 5.

Employee Engagement

The primary reason why many companies adopt social media is to connect with and motivate external consumers. This is a legitimate reason, but do not forget your internal consumers, your employees. Social media can be used to build and maintain business relationships between employees, and between employees and senior management. Social media can be an effective communication channel for sharing company news and fostering a sense of company pride.

In their book, *The Social Employee*, authors Cheryl and Mark Burgess stress that the primary drivers of social business are employees (Burgess and Burgess 2014). They are right. Your employees are the face of your company, engaging with consumers and the public every day. It will be difficult to succeed as a social business without employee support. Company employees are "low-hanging fruit" when it comes to increasing your social media following. Employees have expertise that can be shared on social media and maybe very helpful at spreading positive sWOM. Through social media, employees can foster long-term relationships with social consumers. Empowering your employees to share company information on their personal accounts may make your company more accessible to people outside of your company network.

In truth, not all employees are socially savvy, especially about how to use social media for business purposes. Some employees may also be reluctant to take on additional social responsibilities. To build a culture of collaboration and social sharing among your employees, you need to identify your social media evangelists. Seek out those employees throughout all levels of the company, who are early adopters of technology, those who see the value in social, who believe in your mission, who are good communicators, listeners and are consumer-centric (Burgess and Burgess 2014). Provide these employees with the training and guidance to be brand ambassadors and empower them to lead the charge and spread the word.

Integrating Social Throughout the Company

The chances are good that your company is using social media primarily for marketing and public relations purposes. This is great, but the deep integration of social media into multiple areas of the organization is necessary to transform your company into a social business. It is now time to start exploring opportunities for incorporating social throughout the company.

The following section provides a brief overview of some ways in which social media can add value to a company and increase company-related sWOM.

Strategic Insights and Execution

Social media can help business leaders by offering strategic insights and improve strategic execution. In the case of strategic insights, a company can analyze consumer comments and perform brand sentiment analysis to identify problems with existing products and anticipate shifts in consumer preferences. Personal care brand, Nivea, provides one example of a company that uses social media for social insights. The company assumed that when it came to purchasing deodorant that consumers were most concerned about skin irritations and length of protection. However, when they analyzed social media comments about the brand, they learned that consumers were most concerned about the stains on their clothes caused by the deodorant's residue (Roberts and Piller 2016). Nivea used these insights to create a new product—Nivea Invisible for Black and White.

Comments can live online forever. Positive comments help consumers evaluate products, make purchase decisions, and also reaffirm their selection. This helps with product sales and brand reputation. However, when a complaint or criticism is shared on social media, it has the potential to do harm. After a comment is posted, it moves from being a private matter to a public one. The source of the complaint will determine the impact that it will have on the brand's reputation and sales. When the complaint comes from a consumer, who has a high number of social connections, and if these social connection are not closely connected to each other, there is the potential for a firestorm (Stich, Golla, and Nanopoulos 2014). A firestorm is a "sudden discharge of large quantities of messages containing negative WOM and complaint behavior against a person, company, or group in social media networks" (Pfeffer, Zorbach, and Carley 2014, 118). In other words, negativity may breed negativity. Recipients or readers of the complaint may contribute to the conversation by voicing their complaint or sharing the initial complaint with their social networks. For this reason, companies need to have a strategy for handling the negative sWOM. We will talk more about negative sWOM in Chapter 6.

Social media can also be used as a tool for executing strategies. Cara Operations is a Canadian restaurant chain with 11 brands, 840 franchisees, and over 26,000 associates. The CEO of the company wanted to engage the company's associates in improving service delivery. The challenge was that many of the company's associates are young part-time workers with a high employee turnover rate, which made it difficult for the company to implement an effective training program. To help engage associates, the company decided against using traditional communication methods of training and instead turned to social media. The company selected a platform that their associates were already familiar with and used on a regular basis, Facebook. Associates were encouraged to connect with the company on Facebook. On the page, the company shared tips on customer service and encouraged associates to post their success stories. Psychological research reveals that consumers share "up to 90 percent of their emotional experiences with others" (Berger 2014, 593). When good things happen, we want to share this news with others. In this case, employees were sharing their good news with their social networks. Fellow associates were able to learn about, recognize, and celebrate their accomplishments. Family and friends who were on Facebook were also able to acknowledge their personal success (Kiron et al. 2012). Just as a rolling snowball increases in size and importance, so too can sWOM as friends, and friends of friends are exposed to and share the good news.

Innovation

Social media can be a great tool for solving problems with existing products and sourcing ideas for new ones. In the case of Nivea, the company was able to use social insights on their deodorant products to solve a problem and create a new product. Nivea Black for White turned out the be company's most successful product launch (Roberts and Piller 2016). Another company who uses social insights for a product developed is the toy manufacturer, Lego. Lego boasts a team of 120 designers and an active online social community of over 120,000 Lego enthusiasts. The company states that 99 percent of the brand talent does not come from the company, it comes from the community (Highfield 2014). Minecraft Micro World is a Lego product based on the popular video game Minecraft. The idea for Micro World came from a Lego fan who submitted his idea through Lego Cuusoo, a website hosted by Lego for fans to submit ideas for new products. Once an idea is posted, other Lego enthusiasts are invited to voice their support for the idea. Within 24 hours of being posted, the idea for Minecraft Micro World received over 10,000 votes. This is a significant amount of exposure, attention, and positive feedback in a short period. Lego management interpreted this high level of support as social proof that this idea would result in a successful product. Within one month, the idea was approved for production (Kiron et al. 2012). The product was such a success that Lego added two additional models to its Minecraft play theme (Terdiman 2013).

Social can also help extend or enhance your current product offerings. The Tate is an institution that houses the British art from 1500 to current day and comprises four physical galleries (Tate Britain, Tate Modern, Tate Liverpool, Tate St Ives). The Tate's fifth gallery is virtual, consisting of a website and social media accounts (Twitter, Facebook, YouTube, Google+, Instagram, Pinterest, and Tumblr). On each of these platforms, art lovers around the world can learn about art, enjoy exhibits, and create personal experiences at a time and place convenient to them. In addition to moving art from the physical to the digital world, Tate successfully blends the digital back into the physical world by integrating social media into their art galleries. Visitors to Tate's physical art galleries are encouraged to share their opinion of live performances on social media. Comments that visitors post on Facebook, Twitter, and LinkedIn are immediately projected on the walls of the art gallery contributing to the live performances. During the *Art in Action* festival, more than 122,000 consumers shared their opinions on social media, each of which was projected on the walls of the art gallery. In the Tate Modern gallery, there are 75 interactive screens installed in the staircases. Comments and photographs shared by consumers on social media are projected onto the screen. A drawing bar allows visitors to create art, which is immediately uploaded to the social web for all to see and share (Avery 2014). The fusion of the real and digital worlds becomes a catalyst for sWOM.

In addition to sharing their experiences with their network, social media can enhance the consumer's experience. Sporting venues around the world are turning to social media to enhance the live fan experience and heighten team spirit. Many venues now encourage fans to tweet about the game. Tweets are then shared on stadium screens (Miller 2014). Social media can also improve bricks and mortar retailing experiences.

Women are notorious for using their smartphones to take photographs of themselves in change rooms trying on new outfits. They frequently share these images with their social network. Italian fashion brand Diesel identified a way to embrace this activity that would both benefit the shopper and the brand. The brand installed Facebook mirrors in changing rooms of their physical stores. Dubbed "Diesel Cam," the interactive mirror allows in-store shoppers to take a photograph of themselves wearing Diesel clothing and share it with their friends by posting it directly to Facebook and Instagram. The photos are stamped with the Diesel logo in the corner. This is a clever and effective way of enhancing the in-store shopping experience while also encouraging social sharing and building brand awareness (Marsden 2010).

Human Resources

If you have been employed in the same position for a while, you may not realize just how the recruitment process has changed. Help wanted ads and paper resumes are artifacts of yester year—say "hello" to social recruiting. Social recruiting is the use of popular social media platforms to advertise, source, and recruit potential candidates for a job. At least 84 percent of the organizations use social media for recruiting purposes (publicly owned for-profit—88 percent, privately owned for profit—89 percent, government—68 percent). The top three reasons for using social are to recruit passive job candidates—identify potential candidates who may not be currently looking for a job (82 percent)—increase employer brand recognition (77 percent), and to target candidates with a specific skill set (71 percent). The most popular networks for recruiting are LinkedIn (96 percent), Facebook (60 percent), Twitter (53 percent), and other professional social networking sites (35 percent) (Society for Human Resource Management 2016).

A 2014 survey found that 65 percent of the respondents would consider a job opportunity if they heard about it from a personal connection (Budzienski 2015). Internal recommendations can be a successful way of finding the right people. Therefore, it is wise to enlist the help of your employees to share and talk about the current openings with their social networks. For many companies, including Google, this is the primary method of finding potential candidates (Sannelli 2014).

In addition to identifying potential candidates, social is also used to screen applicants (43 percent). Recruiters report that social media allows them to obtain more information about a candidate than is contained in his resume or cover letter (61 percent). It also allows recruiters to verify the accuracy of the information recorded in an applicant's resume (50 percent) (Society for Human Resource Management 2016). Despite the popularity and benefits of social recruiting, care should be taken when using social media or other Internet search tools to vet job applicants. Information obtained through social media may be outdated, inaccurate, unreliable, or protected by Title VII of the Civil Rights Act of 1964. Title VII prohibits employment discrimination based on race, color, religion, sex, and national origin. This information is typically omitted from a resume and job application form, but maybe inadvertently obtained while viewing the applicant's social media account (Global HR Research 2015).

Marketing Communications

Social media is first and foremost a communication channel. It is a channel that provides a two-way dialog between consumers, between a company and its consumers, and between companies. Social media is a conversation tool. It allows you to communicate with consumers by either broadcasting a general message or to deliver a personalized, individual message. Broadcasting is akin to a megaphone—a company reaches a large number of people with a single message (mass communication). The company crafts a message and talks to the consumer, not unlike the traditional mass media (TV, radio, and print). The difference, however, between traditional and social media is the timeliness of the communication. Social media allows immediate access and real-time communication with your consumers at a fraction of the cost of traditional media.

Broadcasting general messages to your entire network may be appropriate some of the time, but certainly not all of time. On social media, you have a direct line to your consumers, much like a telephone. You should use this opportunity to engage specific segments of your network and individual consumers in conversations. Thus, your social media efforts should consist of a combination of mass and targeted and personalized communications.

> The best way to sell a product is not to sell it at all.

Companies should not view social media as purely a sales channel, but as an as an important contributor to the consumer decision-making process. In truth, the best way to sell a product is not to sell it at all. Instead, a good sales representative will have a conversation with you, she or he asks questions, listens, and provides guidance. Social media allows companies to have one-on-one conversations with individual consumers. It is like chatting with someone on a telephone. As a company engages in a conversation with a specific consumer, other social media users can eavesdrop and may even chime in on the conversation. The conversation may eventually lead to a sale. In Chapters 6 and 7, we will talk more about how to have conversations with consumers by crafting persuasive social media messages.

Humanizing the Brand

Consumers respond positively to brands that represent who they are or who they want to be. Have you ever heard yourself say something to the effect of "Yes, it (brand) is nice, but it's just not me?" If the answer is yes, then you may be saying that the personality of the brand is not consistent with your identity. When consumers choose to follow and engage with a brand on social media, they do so because they identify with the brand. As we discussed in Chapter 2, this is a motivating factor in why we share. Consumers see their real or aspirational sense of self (i.e., who they want to be) reflected in the brand. Once they follow the brand on social media, the brand becomes part of their online social identity. This brand association becomes one of the many important data points connected to a consumer's profile(s). Collectively, this information paints a picture of a consumer's social identity that is broadcasted across the social media network(s). You are who you like. The brand and consumer social identity association, provides numerous benefits, such as, increasing brand awareness, extending your communication reach, and increasing the consumer's brand involvement. It may also increase consumer engagement, stimulate sWOM, improve the reputation of your company, drive traffic to your website, and improve your search engine ranking. To encourage consumers to make this connection, a company needs to humanize their brand.

To humanize your brand is to imagine your brand as it were a person, to give your brand a personality—a set of traits that people attribute to your product as if were a real person (Aaker, Vohs, and Mogilner 2010). A brand personality makes your brand more relatable and helps to distinguish it from the competition. The greater the congruence between a brand's personality and the real or aspirational personality of the consumer, the stronger the preference for the brand (Aaker 1997). If your brand were a person, how would you describe his or her personality? Is he (or she) formal or relaxed? Feisty or timid? Conservative or progressive? Innovative or conventional? Energetic or easy-going? If you are uncertain, look to your brand values for guidance.

Brand Voice

Once you have determined your brand personality, you then need to develop your brand voice. That is, you need to decide not only the types of content that you will share, but also *how* you will communicate with consumers on social media. For example, fast casual restaurant, Smashburger is unlikely to post content related to the virtues of a vegetarian diet or low-fat food. Instead, they celebrate "holidays" such as National Bacon Lovers Day (FYI: It's August 20). If your company is very formal then when replying to consumer posts, you may decide to address the consumer by his last name (e.g., Mr. Jones). On the other hand, if your company is very informal and spontaneous, you may choose to share witty content and use the consumer's first names (e.g., Hi Bob!).

Some examples of companies with strong and distinct brand voices include Taco Bell, Intel, and Adidas (Figures 3.1–3.6).

Taco Bell's personality and brand voice could be described as humorous and somewhat wacky.

Taco Bell @tacobell · Jul 24

In the mood for endless Taco Bell.

⬆ ⬆ 2.9K   ♥ 3.4K   ···

Figure 3.1 Taco Bell Twitter example 1

Taco Bell @tacobell · Jul 19

Happy Birthday, @ShaneDawson, you dreamy human. 🎤

Figure 3.2 Taco Bell Twitter example 2

Source: Images courtesy of Taco Bell's public Twitter account.

Intel's voice is smart and enlightening.

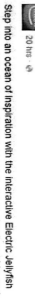

Intel
20 hrs ·

Step into an ocean of inspiration with the interactive Electric Jellyfish installation. With the help of Intel tech, visitors can shoot, wobble, and bounce light with the touch of a finger. http://intel.ly/29VGvXf

Figure 3.3 Intel's Facebook example 1

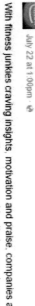

Intel
July 22 at 1:00pm ·

With fitness junkies craving insights, motivation and praise, companies are eager to oblige. Check out these 7 wacky wearables that go way beyond the typical fitness tracker: http://intel.ly/29QBkl3

Figure 3.4 Intel's Facebook example 2

Source: Images courtesy of Intel's public Facebook page.

Adidas is inspirational.

adidas @adidas · Jul 17
When you run out of obstacles, create new ones. Create Chaos = Football + Motorbikes. @S3Society, #heretocreate

Figure 3.5 Adidas Twitter example 1

adidas @adidas · Jun 8
Today we start a journey to save the oceans.
Support @Parleyxxx's Ocean Plastic Program.
Create a movement.

Figure 3.6 Adidas Twitter example 2

Source: Images courtesy of Adidas public Twitter account.

Once you have developed your voice, you will need to provide guidelines for employees to follow, guidelines on acceptable content and manner of speech. Employees and third parties who are authorized to post on behalf of the company will need direction to ensure a consistent brand voice, which is essential for presenting an accurate and consistent brand identity. You do not want Jim in accounting being super serious, Jenny in human resources being feisty, and your social media influencers or paid endorsers being totally irreverent.

It is also important to meet periodically with your social media team to review whether or not your social media posts are consistent with your brand voice. Find emblematic social media posts and examples of consumer engagement that embody the essence of your brand. It is also helpful to pinpoint posts that are not consistent with your brand and identify the reasons why (i.e., word choice, tone, subject matter). And it goes without saying, learn from your social media mistakes (there will be many!). Archive and revisit these positive and negative examples.

Up to this point, we have focused primarily on business to consumers (B2C) use of social media, but there are many B2B companies that are effectively employing social media. As we mentioned earlier in this chapter, social media can be an effective way of creating awareness of your brand, building and maintaining relationships with key influencers, and decisions makers. Take, for instance, Maersk Line, a member of the Maersk Group, the world's largest shipping container company. Headquartered in Copenhagen, Denmark, Maersk Line has 324 offices in 115 countries. The company operates 605 container vessels and employs 7,600 seafarers and 22,400 land-based employees (Maersk Line 2016). Maersk turned to social media to share news about the company, as a way to get closer to their consumers and to potentially influence the industry. The company has accounts on nine different social platforms, Facebook, Twitter, LinkedIn, Flickr, YouTube, Instagram, Tumblr, Google+, and Weibo. Each platform has a different target market and purpose. For example, Instagram and Flickr are used to inspire people and to keep the name Maersk top of mind. Google+ allows consumers and experts to engage, and LinkedIn is their corporate platform. Maersk's strategy for building a social presence began with their employees. The company recognized that social was a great way for them to connect with their employees around the global. Social media helped Maersk build a sense of company pride among employees, which in turn helped to spread positive sWOM. When employees contributed to company posts, these messages were shared with the employee's extended network of family and friends which were instrumental in increasing Maersk's reach.

Sharing their extensive digital archive of 14,000+ photographs of ships on social media helped to humanize the brand. Each photograph the company shared on social media was accompanied by a short story. Collectively, these stories help to tell the history of Maersk. Shipping enthusiasts were drawn to these posts and even began posting their photos of Maersk ships (Figure 3.7). By contributing their materials, these followers help to craft and share the story of Maersk throughout the social web. Maersk's Facebook posts frequently attract thousands of likes and hundreds of shares. To determine the effectiveness of their social media efforts, Maersk conducted a survey. Sixty-seven percentage of the respondents stated that Maersk's social media efforts had enhanced their perception of the company. Maersk's success can in part be attributed to senior managements' understanding that social media is not just a marketing tool, but a communication tool (Katona and Sarvary 2014).

Maersk Line
May 2 ·

#Spotted at #Terneuzen Port, Netherlands. #MaerskLine #OnTheMove #GlobalNetwork #Monday (image by Louis van der Hooft)

Figure 3.7 Maersk Facebook example

Source: Image courtesy of Maersk's public Facebook page.

Customer Services

If you had a question about a recent purchase, how would you contact the company? Would you call them on the 1–800 number? Jump in your car and head to the store? Try the live chat feature on their website? Perhaps, you would send them a tweet? Or, post a question on the company Facebook page? Maybe you would not contact the company. Perhaps, you would post a message on social media and let members of your social network respond. Social customer service or s-Care is the delivery of customer service via social networks rather than call centers, retail stores, service centers, and company websites. A recent study of U.S. consumers revealed that while the preference and use of s-Care currently skew toward the younger generation, it is and will continue to be an important service channel for all customers. Over four in five (81 percent) millennials reported that they would use social media to engage with a brand's customer service, versus 63 percent of Gen Xers and 44 percent of Baby Boomers. Even 40 percent of those who do not currently use social media indicated that they would be willing to engage with customer service through social channels. The most popular platform for s-Care is Facebook (82 percent). Millennials are more willing to use a selection of s-Care channels (Facebook 78 percent, Twitter 45 percent, Instagram 25 percent) than are Gen X (Facebook 84 percent, Twitter 33 percent, Instagram 11 percent) and Baby Boomers (Facebook 86 percent, Twitter 16 percent, Instagram 4 percent). That is not to say that traditional customer service channels are no longer important, rather consumers today expect multiple options and one of them should be social (Dalla Pozza, Wood, and Burkhalter 2015).

s-Care access also appears to be an important factor in deciding which brand to purchase. One-third (35 percent) of the Baby Boomers and nearly one-quarter (20 percent) of Gen Xers and millennials surveyed reported that not having access to their preferred method of customer service interaction would prevent them from making a purchase (Bianchi, Schiavotto, and Svoboda 2014).

In addition to meeting consumers expectations for customer service and potentially impacting future sales, s-Care may significantly lower the cost of customer service operations and increase customer satisfaction (Bianchi, Schiavotto, and Svoboda 2014). That is, assuming a company can live up to service response times. Expectations of the speed of response vary based on age with 27 percent of Gen Xers and Boomers believing that it would take at least two days to receive a response via social media. Millennials (22 percent), on the other hand, expect a ten minute response time (Salesforce 2015). They are not exactly the most patient bunch!

Social media is not only important and effective for dealing with consumers directly, but it is also important for sharing information internally to help solve consumer problems. Take for example, Nationwide Mutual Insurance Company. A Nationwide customer was stranded on vacation—his RV had broken down. He called the Nationwide call center for assistance—did his policy cover this situation? The call center agent was uncertain and decided to post the case on the company's internal social collaboration platform. People from all across the company chimed in to help solve the problem. Within 30 minutes, the call center representative had an answer and a detailed approach to help the customer. Without this internal social collaboration system, the problem may have taken hours or even days to resolve, and Nationwide could have lost a customer (Kiron et al. 2012). Furthermore, unanswered questions, unresolved issues, and unreturned calls can often lead to negative word of mouth (WOM). It is not uncommon for dissatisfied consumers to turn to social media to publically air their grievances. This has the potential to create a firestorm. Even if it does not motivate others to complain, it can still discourage consumers from doing business with your company.

Maturity Phase

During the maturity phase, the company's social media moves beyond marketing to include other functional areas. Policies and procedures may need to be updated, and the role and composition of the social media advisory board modified to accommodate the enhanced use of social media and to include representation from additional areas. Hopefully, all of the C-level executives now see the value of social. If some members of senior management are still wavering, it may be worthwhile to involve them with a specific social initiative that will help achieve one of their goals (Li and Solis 2013).

The key to determining if you have successfully made the transition to a social business is when social is an integral part of the business planning process and when there is companywide support and usage of social. Social is now part of the fabric of your business; it is part of the company's DNA.

An example of an organization that has successfully transitioned to a social business is the American Red Cross. The American Red Cross was founded in 1881 with the mission to "prevent and alleviate human suffering in the face of emergencies by mobilizing the power of volunteers and the generosity of donors" (American Red Cross 2016). To help them achieve their mission, the Red Cross made the commitment to infuse social media into every aspect of the organization. First and foremost, they have the commitment of senior management. Senior management recognizes the unique capabilities of social media to mobilize the masses to prepare for and respond to disasters.

The Red Cross operates accounts on a variety of social platforms, each with a specific purpose. To share the history of the company and to help build an emotional connection with the public, they use Instagram, Flickr, and Pinterest. Instagram is used primarily to share pictures of aid workers around the world and pictures of aid recipients. Flickr is used to host photographs of disaster relief responders in the field. The Red Cross Pinterest page contains a selection of boards. For example, there is a board of photos that show the history of the Red Cross, a board that contains promotional posters dating back to the early 1900s, and a board that contains a series of images communicating the importance of giving blood. The Red Cross YouTube account informs the public about disaster response and helps to educate the public on topics such as CPR. Job opportunities are posted on LinkedIn. The Red Cross Google+ account is a place for supporters to engage with each other. Blogs are also to share

American Red Cross @RedCross · Apr 19

#RedCross has opened 13 shelters to help communities devastated by #houstonflood

rdcrss.org/1XH7GU0

Figure 3.8 Red Cross Twitter example

Source: Image Courtesy of Red Cross public Twitter account.

more detailed information and allow supporters to connect. Facebook is used to share current information with supporters, volunteers, blood donors, and the general public. Twitter is used for real-time updates on disasters and Red Cross services (Figure 3.8).

In addition to using social media to educate, communicate, and build relationships with supporters, the Red Cross also uses social to make business decisions. By monitoring social chatter and public sentiment, they can identify how to respond to public needs. For example, by tracking keywords like "tornado" on Twitter, the Red Cross can spot exactly when and where disasters are happening and use this information to help manage and track resources and supplies.

Social is also an important tool for fundraising. Supporters can make a donation through one of their blogs or on Facebook. They use Twitter to post messages encouraging followers to donate to specific disasters (Kane 2014).

If a 135-year-old charitable organization, with over 600 chapters, 35,000 employees and 500,000 volunteers in the United States alone can make the commitment and transition to becoming a social business what is stopping your company?

Social B2B Companies

For companies that operate in the B2B market, social media use is often limited to a LinkedIn profile and perhaps a blog. Some B2B companies do not see the value in operating a Facebook page or an Instagram account. After all, who on earth would be interested in a photograph of your frontend loaders, sea containers, or industrial equipment? But, as we saw in the case of B2B company Maersk Lines, social media can be very important for internal and external communications, customer service, and sales (Wichmann 2013). Therefore, we feel it is important to revisit some important facts for those readers who work for a B2B company:

- **Decision makers are on social media:** Although the buying process in the B2B market is fundamentally different to the B2C market, purchase decision makers are more than likely on social media, and this is a great way to reach and influence them.

- **Social media can help create brand awareness:** Brand awareness is still very much a goal for B2B businesses. Other B2B companies are active on social media. Like traditional consumers, they will hear about your company through social media posts and your company's social media profiles.

- **Social media can build connections:** Social media provides unique opportunities to not only research other companies, but also to make connections with decision makers and industry influencers.

- **Social media can humanize your brand:** B2B companies have a personality that also needs to be shared.

- **Social media can be used to help educate the public:** You should take the opportunity to use social media to educate other companies (and consumers) on the importance of your product. While you may not be directly selling to consumers, if they perceive actual or real problems with your product, they can voice their concerns to others, which could create public relation problems.

- **Social media is not just for marketing:** As we have seen in this chapter, social can be infused throughout the entire company to connect people, information, and assets with the goal of making your company more efficient and competitive.

We conclude this chapter with one more example, the case of SAP (Systems Applications and Products). SAP is a B2B company who has successfully made the transition to becoming a social business.

SAP

SAP makes enterprise software to manage the business operation and customer relations. Headquartered in Walldorf, Baden-Württemberg, Germany, SAP employs almost 80,000 people in 130 countries. SAP's vision is to "help the world run better and improve people's lives" (SAP 2016). To achieve this vision, SAP harnessed the power of social media to become a social business. They embedded social media into their organization for strategic insight and execution, innovation, human resources, marketing communications, and customer services. Like many other businesses, they have a wide selection of accounts on multiple platforms including, Facebook, Twitter, YouTube, LinkedIn, Google+, and Instagram.

The most powerful illustration that SAP is a social business is the SAP Community Network, a global online community of almost 2 million IT people, technologists, partners, business experts, students, professors, consultants, and influencers from more than 200 countries (SAP 2015). The community that is hosted by SAP includes blogs, wikis, and discussion forums. It is a place where members can discuss SAP products, programming languages, industries, and technology. How-to guides, white papers, and free downloads are all available on the site. Community members can post questions that are answered by either a company representative or other members of the community. The SAP Community Network also has Twitter, Facebook, Google+, and YouTube accounts.

A valuable feature of SAP's community is Idea Place, an online forum where community members offer suggestions for new features and enhanced functionality to existing products. When a community member submits an idea or enhancement, it is visible to all community members. Community members have the opportunity contribute their ideas to the proposed improvement. Members then vote the idea up or down. From here, product managers identify the most popular requests for further investigation.

Crowdsourcing product development and enhancements in this manner benefit both the customer and the business. Allowing a customer to suggest improvements and to vote on each suggestion makes him or her feel part of the development process, that his or her contribution is important and that his or her needs will be met. In return, the company benefits from the collective wisdom of community members, which enables the company to solve existing problems promptly, produce better products, prioritize development initiatives, and continue to meet the needs of their customer base. Over the course of one to two years, SAP community members will submit as many as 15,000 ideas (Kiron 2012).

For a company to be successful in today's hyper-connected world, the company needs to embrace social media. sWOM begins internally; it begins with engaging with and empowering your employees to use social media for business purposes. Social media needs to be integrated into your company, much in the same way the telephone and the computer did decades ago. Social media is the telephone of this generation—ringing loudly and constantly. The question is, are you going to answer it?

References

Aaker, J.L. 1997. "Dimensions of Brand Personality 1997." *Journal of Marketing Research* XXXIV, no. 3, pp. 347–56. doi:10.2307/3151897

Aaker, J., K.D. Vohs, and C. Mogilner. 2010. "Nonprofits Are Seen as Warm and For-Profits as Competent: Firm Stereotypes Matter." *Journal of Consumer Research* 37, no. 2, pp. 224–37. doi:10.1086/651566

American Red Cross. 2016. "Mission & Values." Retrieved from www.redcross.org/about-us/who-we-are/mission-and-values

Avery, J. 2014. "The Tate's Digital Transformation." *Harvard Business School Publishing*, No. 314122.

Berger, J. 2014. "Word of Mouth and Interpersonal Communication: A Review and Directions for Future Research." *Journal of Consumer Psychology* 24, no. 4, pp. 586–607.

Bianchi, R., D. Schiavotto, and D. Svoboda. 2014. "Why Companies Should Care About E-Care." *McKinsey.* Retrieved from www.mckinsey.com/business-functions/marketing-and-sales/our-insights/why-companies-should-care-about-ecare

Budzienski, J. 2015. "3 Ways to Be Constantly Recruiting Star Talent Through Social Media." *Entrepreneur.* Retrieved from www.entrepreneur.com/article/245295

Burgess, C., and M. Burgess. 2014. *The Social Employee*. New York, NY: Mc-Graw Hill.

Dalla Pozza, I., N.T. Wood, and J.N. Burkhalter. 2015. "Tweeting for Service: Twitter as a Communication Channel for Customer Service." In *Maximizing Commerce and Marketing Strategies through Micro-Blogging*, eds. J.N. Burkhalter and N.T. Wood, 111–29. IGI Global. doi:10.4018/978-1-4666-8408-9

Dillerm, C. 2015. "CodeCrush 2015: IT Innovation." Retrieved from http://slideplayer.com/slide/5788528/

Dunn, B.J. 2010. "Best Buy's CEO on Learning to Love Social Media." *Harvard Business Review* 88, no. 12, pp. 43–8.

Effing, R., and T.A.M. Spil. 2016. "The Social Strategy Cone: Towards a Framework for Evaluating Social Media Strategies." *International Journal of Information Management* 36, no. 1, pp. 1–8. doi:10.1016/j.ijinfomgt.2015.07.009

Global HR Research. 2015. "The Pros and Cons of Social Media Screening." Retrieved from www.ghrr.com/blog/2015/11/13/the-pros-and-cons-of-social-media-screening/

Highfield, V. 2014. "Lego's Community Does All the Marketing It Needs." *Total Customer*. Retrieved from www.totalcustomer.org/2014/07/07/legos-community-marketing-needs/

Hootsuite University. 2012. *Social Selling to the CEO with Greg Verdino*. Hootsuite. Retrieved from https://learn.hootsuite.com

Kane, G.C. 2014. "Why Social Media Will Fundamentally Change Business." *MIT Sloan Management Review*. Retrieved from http://sloanreview.mit.edu/article/why-social-media-will-fundamentally-change-business/

Katona, Z., and M. Sarvary. 2014. "Maersk Line: B2B Social Media—'It's Communication, Not Marketing.'" *California Management Review* 56, no. 3, pp. 142–56. doi:10.1525/cmr.2014.56.3.142

Kiron, D. 2012. "SAP: Using Social Media for Building, Selling and Supporting." *MIT Sloan Management Review* 54, no. 1, pp. 1–4. Retrieved from http://sloanreview.mit.edu/feature/sap-using-social-media-for-building-selling-and-supporting/

Kiron, D., D. Palmer, A.N. Phillips, and N. Kruschwitz. 2012. "Social Business: What Are Companies Really Doing?" *MIT Sloan Management Review* 53, no. 4, p. 1.

Kottasova, I. 2016. "Cheerios Angers Grieving Fans with Prince 'Tribute' Tweet—Apr. 22, 2016." *CNN Money*. Retrieved from http://money.cnn.com/2016/04/22/media/prince-death-cheerios-tweet/

Li, C., and B. Solis. 2013. *The Evolution of Social Business: Six Stages of Social Media Transformation*. Retrieved from www.altimetergroup.com/2013/03/new-research-the-evolution-of-social-business-six-stages-of-social-business-transformation/

Maersk Line. 2016. "Maersk Line Facts." Retrieved from www.maerskline.com/en-us/about/facts-figures

Marsden, P. 2010. "Brands @ Social Commerce/Diesel: Facebook in the Fitting Room." *Digital Intelligence Today*. Retrieved from http://digitalintelligencetoday.com/brands-social-commerce-diesel-facebook-in-the-fitting-room/

Miller, K. 2014. "Smart Stadiums Are Redefining the Fan Experience." *Digitaria*. Retrieved from www.digitaria.com/news/blogs/smart-stadiums-are-redefining-fan-experience

Novell. 2013. "Enterprise Technology Through the Years." Retrieved from http://b-i.forbesimg.com/drewhendricks/files/2013/09/technology_through_years2.png

Perrin, A. 2015. *Social Media Usage: 2005–2015.* Retrieved from www.pewinternet.org/2015/10/08/social-networking-usage-2005-2015/

Pfeffer, J., T. Zorbach, and K.M. Carley. 2014. "Understanding Online Firestorms: Negative Word-of-Mouth Dynamics in Social Media Networks." *Journal of Marketing Communications* 20, no. 1–2, pp. 117–28. doi:10.1080/13527266.2013.797778

Polt, R. 1995. "A Brief History of Typewriters." *The Classic Typewriter Page.* Retrieved from http://site.xavier.edu/polt/typewriters/tw-history.html

Roberts, D.L., and F.T. Piller. 2016. "Finding the Right Role for Social Media in Innovation." *MIT Sloan Management Review* 57, no. 3, pp. 41–7. Retrieved from http://search.ebscohost.com/login.aspx?direct=true&db=bth&AN=114181472&site=ehost-live&scope=site

Salesforce. 2015. "Crossing The Generational Divide: Providing Customer Service for Today's Consumers," 16. Retrieved from http://webassets.desk.com/static/ebooks/desk-customer-service-across-generational-divide-report.pdf

Sannelli, R. 2014. "6 Strategic Tips for Employers to Recruit on Social Media." *Fox Business.* Retrieved from www.foxbusiness.com/features/2014/07/11/7-strategic-tips-to-recruit-on-social-media.html

SAP. 2015. *2015 Annual Report.* Retrieved from http://go.sap.com/docs/download/investors/2015/sap-2015-annual-report.pdf

SAP. 2016. "Company Information." Retrieved from http://go.sap.com/corporate/en/company.fast-facts.html

Society for Human Resource Management. 2016. *Using Social Media for Talent Acquisition—Recruitment and Screening.* Retrieved from www.shrm.org/hr-today/trends-and-forecasting/research-and-surveys/Documents/SHRM-Social-Media-Recruiting-Screening-2015.pdf

Stich, L., G. Golla, and A. Nanopoulos. 2014. "Modelling the Spread of Negative Word-of-Mouth in Online Social Networks." *Journal of Decision Systems 23*, no. 2. pp. 203–21. doi:10.1080/12460125.2014.886494

Terdiman, D. 2013. "Lego Doubles down on Minecraft." *CNET*. Retrieved from www.cnet.com/news/lego-doubles-down-on-minecraft/

van Luxemburg, A. 2011. "Social Media Maturity Model." Retrieved from www.socialmediamodels.net/social-media-adoption-models-category/social-media-maturity-model/

Wichmann, J. 2013. "Being B2B Social: A Conversation with Maersk Line's Head of Social Media." *McKinsey & Company*. Retrieved from www.mckinsey.com/business-functions/marketing-and-sales/our-insights/being-b2b-social-a-conversation-with-maersk-lines-head-of-social-media

Williams, T. 2012. "The Evolution of Technology & Its Impact on the Development of Social Businesses." *Forbes*. Retrieved from www.forbes.com/sites/sap/2012/01/10/infographic-the-evolution-of-technology-its-impact-on-the-development-of-social-businesses/#2c03a2612c9b

CHAPTER 4

Legal and Regulatory Issues: Clear and Conspicuous Disclosures

Singer and songwriter Rihanna tweeted "Listening to ANTI" to her more than 55 million fans. Included with the tweet was a photo of Rihanna wearing Dolce and Gabanna gold jewel-encrusted headphones. The image was retweeted over 175,000 times and received over 284,000 likes. The headphones, which retailed for $9,000, sold out within 24 hours (Wouk 2016).

Engaging celebrities in sharing positive word of mouth (WOM) with their legions of fans is a popular strategy offline and now online. Marketers are knocking on the virtual doors of A, B, C, and even D-list celebrities to solicit their help with spreading positive WOM with their legions of fans on social media. One can only imagine the jubilation in Dolce and Gabanna's marketing department after the success of Rihanna's tweet.

Celebrity support for a brand can be priceless. It can not only increase brand exposure, but it may also increase sales. However, their support is not always free. In fact, celebrity endorsement often comes with a hefty price tag. Celebrities understand the potential influence they have over fans and they expect to *be handsomely compensated*. The cost of employing a celebrity to share positive social WOM (sWOM) varies based on their social status and their number of followers. Some celebrities charge as little as $1,000 a tweet, but big names demand and receive more. A tweet from NBA player LeBron James costs $140,000 (Rovell 2015). If you can afford that, then you may want to consider model and pseudo-Kardashian, Kendall Jenner, who commands $125,000—$300,000 for a single social post (Avila 2015). But what are small to medium-size businesses with limited marketing budgets to do? How can they spread positive sWOM?

The answer lies, at least in part, in their ability to harness the influence of everyday social media users.

Unfortunately, companies face a fine line between encouraging consumers to share positive sWOM and incentivizing them to do so. And, if that line is crossed, you may find yourself in some legal hot water. In this chapter, we will examine the Federal Trade Commission's (FTC's) Endorsement Guidelines and what they mean for marketers who want to embrace and encourage sWOM.

Social Influencer Examples

The best way to begin our discussion on legal and regulatory issues is to offer some examples, each of which highlights a different way in which everyday consumers and social influencers can help spread positive information about brands:

Cole Haan: Global lifestyle brand Cole Haan hosted a contest on Pinterest. The "Wandering Sole" contest asked fans of the brand to pin (or repin) images of their favorite shoes for a chance to win a $1,000 shopping spree. To be eligible to enter the contest, users had to repin five images from the Cole Haan Pinterest page and pin another five images of their favorite places to wander. Each image was to be accompanied by the hashtag #WanderingSole (Sterling 2014).

Lord & Taylor: U.S. department store Lord & Taylor hired 50 fashion bloggers to take pictures of themselves wearing a paisley print dress and post them to Instagram. Each photo was captioned with positive statements (e.g., so excited to be dressing for spring in this dress from @lordandtaylor's new #DesignLab collection!).

Sour Patch Kids: Mondelez International, a leading manufacturer of candy, enlisted the help of teenage social media influencer, Logan Paul, to help promote Sour Patch Kids. The goal of the campaign was to increase awareness of the candy brand among the core market—teens. Once a day for one week, Paul posted a Snapchat story that incorporated the popular candy.

Despite the appeal of these sWOM strategies, each of them suffers from a similar legal problem. To the average social media user, these social media messages (tweets, pins, posts) may appear organic—independent evaluations or support for a product or brand. However, these messages were not created and posted independently. Each of these was a planned marketing promotion, in which the brand or appointed agency incentivized social influencers to engage in sWOM. In other words, a material connection existed between the consumer and the company, and this relationship was not disclosed to the public. In orchestrating and sharing these posts on social media, the brand and the participating social media users failed to adhere to FTC's Endorsement Guidelines. Under Act 5 of FTC's Endorsement Guidelines, these social messages are misleading and potentially deceptive. Such practices can lead to enforcement action by the FTC and substantial fines. So, how does the FTC determine whether an act is deceptive?

Deception on Social Media

An analysis of deception first begins with determining whether a representation, omission, or practice is *likely to mislead* the consumer. Most deception involves written or oral misrepresentations, or omissions of material information, such as failure to disclose a material connection between an endorser and a brand. The FTC need not determine that consumers are misled to conclude that an act or practice is deceptive (Burkhalter, Wood, and Tryce 2014). The key is "likely to mislead". The second element is that the representation, omission, or practice must be likely to mislead *reasonable consumers under the circumstances*. The FTC will evaluate the entire advertisement or transaction, to decide how a reasonable consumer is likely to respond (Dingle 1983). The FTC holds that "reasonable consumers may be less skeptical of personal opinion (i.e., endorsements) than of advertising claims" (Petty and Andrews 2008, 12). Nonetheless, "reasonable consumer" is difficult to define and often leads to protracted litigation (Burkhalter, Wood, and Tryce 2014). The third element is materiality. A representation, omission, or practice must be a *material* one for deception to occur (*F.T.C v. Transnet Wireless Corp* 2007). A material representation, omission, or practice is the one that is likely to impact a consumer's decision making related to a product (Burkhalter, Wood, and Tryce 2014).

If you have never heard of FTC's Endorsement Guidelines and were unaware that such requirements exist, do not panic (yet), you are not alone. In 2014, it was reported that 40 percent of all marketers and nearly 60 percent of the content creators surveyed had little or no awareness of FTC Endorsement Guidelines (Quittner 2014). B2B marketers appear to be even more in the dark. In 2015, more than half of the B2B marketers surveyed in North America reported having used sponsored social, yet as little as 8 percent of them were aware of and understood the FTC's Endorsement Guidelines (eMarketer 2015). So, who is the FTC, what is the extent of their power, and what are the guidelines that you need to follow?

The FTC

The FTC is a bipartisan federal agency with the broad responsibility of promoting competition while protecting consumers from acts and practices that may cause them harm. One practice that the FTC monitors is deceptive advertising (Federal Trade Commission 2016a). Here, the FTC's duty is to enforce truth-in-advertising laws—federal laws that say advertising "must be truthful, not misleading, and when appropriate, backed by scientific research" (Federal Trade Commission 2016b). In addition to enforcing these laws, the FTC also educates businesses on how to comply with the law. Educational resources are typically in the form of published guides. One of the guides published by the FTC specifically addresses the use of testimonials and endorsements in advertising. Before we go any further, we should note that the FTC uses the terms "endorsement" and "testimonials" interchangeably for the purpose of enforcing the FTC Act (Federal Trade Commission 2008). The FTC literature that references social media also utilizes the term "advocate" when referring to individuals who deliver endorsements through social media. To keep things simple from this point forward, we will use the term "endorsement" when referring to the act of voicing approval for a brand and "endorser" when referring to those social media users (consumers, social influencers, and celebrities) who are responsible for these social media posts.

The FTC's Guide to Testimonial and Endorsements was first published in 1975. The purpose of this guide was to ensure that advertising messages were clear and truthful. The growing use of social media for endorsements forced the FTC to revisit these guidelines, and in 2009, a substantially revised version of the guides was published. The need for revision was based on the fact that, on social media, it is difficult to determine whether a relationship exists between the individual posting the message and the brand they have mentioned. In traditional advertising (i.e., television, radio, print), the consumer can readily identify an endorsement message and the endorser's association with a particular brand. For example, when British actress Keira Knightley appears in a TV commercial or magazine advertisement for Chanel perfume, we understand that she is being paid to appear in these advertising messages. However, when this endorsement appears on social media, it is difficult for consumers to determine if the posting is consumer-generated earned media. In other words, it is difficult to tell if the message was posted by the endorser, independent of the brand, or if the endorser posted it in consideration for some form of payment. The endorsement confusion on social media can be attributed to an individual's personal account being used to send the message. When an endorsement is shared from a personal account, the typical consumer may not be aware that a relationship, referred to by the FTC as a "material connection," exists between the marketer and the person who posted the online message—the endorser.

When to Disclose—Material Connection

The key to determining if and when disclosure is required is the presence or absence of a material connection.

"Material connections may be defined as any connection between an advocate [endorser] and a marketer that could affect the credibility consumers give to that advocate's statements. Important examples of 'material connections' may include; (i) consideration (benefits or incentives such as monetary compensation, loaner products, free products or services, in-kind gifts, special access privileges, affiliate commissions, discounts, gift cards, sweepstakes entries or non-monetary incentives) provided by a marketer to an advocate, or (ii) a relationship between a marketer and an advocate (such as an employment relationship) (WOMMA 2012)."

The following may help improve your understanding of what constitutes a material connection:

Imagine that you follow a non-celebrity fashion blogger. In one blog post (e.g., tweet, status update, or blog entry), your favorite blogger writes a positive review of a particular item of clothing. You, the reader, may feel inclined to take this blogger's opinion into consideration when deciding to purchase the item. What if you were told that she was paid to discuss and endorse the item, would this alter how you view her recommendation? This incidence occurred with the Lord & Taylor example presented early in this chapter. The department store paid 50 bloggers between $1,000 and $4,000 to promote a particular paisley print dress. Bloggers posted a photograph of themselves wearing the dress on Instagram and other social media sites. These posts reached 11.4 million individual Instagram users over two days and amassed 328,000 brand engagements (Federal Trade Commission 2016c). The dress quickly sold out. A material connection existed between the marketer and the endorser in the form of monetary compensation (Beck 2015a).

In the Cole Hahn example, Pinterest users were asked to repin Cole Hahn images for a chance to win a $1,000 shopping spree. The material connection was in the form of consideration—entry to a sweepstake.

In both of these examples, the social media users who were responsible for sharing sWOM failed to disclose their connection with the band they were endorsing. The FTC asserts that consumers have the right to know who is behind these sponsored messages, particularly if they could influence their purchase decisions (WOMMA 2014). According to the FTC, regardless of the type of message (e.g., visual or text), each of these sWOM messages was misleading and potentially deceptive.

When a Disclosure Is Not Required

There are a few scenarios when a material connection does not exist, and therefore, disclosure is not required. The first is when a consumer mentions a product that he or she paid for himself or herself. If the consumer posts about an item he or she purchased and is not being compensated for that post, then a material connection, as defined by the FTC does not exist (Federal Trade Commission 2013a). In our Chewbacca example (Chapter 2), Star Wars fan Candace Payne independently posted the video. There was no relationship between Payne and the marketer. Nor was there was any consideration offered to post the video. Therefore, there was no material connection and no need for disclosure (Federal Trade Commission 2013a). However, (and there is always a however) after posting the original video Payne received, free of charge from Kohl's department store, a large selection of Star Wars merchandise, and $2,500 in Kohl's gift cards (Griner 2016). If Kohl's gave Payne these items with the understanding that she would share, discuss, or promote them on social media, a material connection would, at that point, exist between Payne and Kohls. She would then need to disclose her connection with the store in any future posts.

Another instance when it is not necessary to disclose is when the posting is made from the brand's official account, as was the case with the Sour Patch Kids promotion. Logan Paul, the teenager, recruited for the campaign was a well-known social media influencer among teenagers. A material connection exists because Paul was financially compensated for his participation in the promotion. But, because Paul posted some of his Snapchat videos from the official Sour Patch Kids account, it is not necessary for him to disclose his material connection. Paul did, however, also post from his personal account. It is necessary to disclose the connection on the posts from his personal account. The FTC contends that one cannot assume that consumers would have seen his posts on the official account and would have been aware of the fact that he was a paid endorser (Federal Trade Commission 2015).

Another common scenario is when a company gives out free samples of a product to consumers one of whom decides to write a favorable review or comment on social media. Once again a material connection does not exist because the company gave these samples free of charge to many consumers, without any expectation of a favorable endorsement. The focus of the FTC's Guides is when the company pays or gives something of value to a consumer *in return for* a favorable mention on social media (Federal Trade Commission 2013a).

Who Is Responsible?

The FTC Guidelines themselves do not have the force of law. However, any practice that is deemed to be inconsistent with or in violation of the guides may result in law enforcement actions. The FTC can and does conduct investigations and has the power to bring cases involving such endorsements under Section 5 of the FTC Act (Unfair or Deceptive Acts or Practices) (Federal Trade Commission 2015). This raises the question, "In the instance of a violation of the FTC Act, who exactly is responsible, the company or the endorser?" If law enforcement is required, the primary focus will be on advertisers, their ad agencies, and public relations company involved. However, the account holder or endorser could also be held accountable (Federal Trade Commission 2013a). For that reason, both brand marketers and endorsers need to be aware of these guidelines. Brand marketers should monitor all posts made by endorsers to ensure that each contains a clear and conspicuous disclosure. To date, the cases investigated by the FTC have not resulted in fines. Instead, a series of conditions were imposed on each company. Common conditions include the development of an internal compliance system, submission of regular reports to the FTC to demonstrate compliance—a process to educate social influencers on the guidelines—and a requirement to cut off payments to those social influencers who fail to comply. These conditions can and have been imposed on some companies for as much as 20 years (Coffee 2016; Roberts 2016).

The FTC's Endorsement Guidelines for Clear and Conspicuous Disclosures

The FTC's 2009 Guide to Endorsements and Testimonials focuses primarily on *when* to make disclosures (material connections). In 2013, the FTC released the *.Com Disclosures* report with updated guidance that now included *how* to make effective disclosures (WOMMA 2014). Both documents help businesses and endorsers avoid deceptive acts and advocate for clear and conspicuous disclosures. Whereas there is no set formula for creating a clear and conspicuous disclosure, the *.Com Disclosures* report

Guidelines for clear and conspicuous disclosures

 Placement and Proximity
- Place disclosure close to the claim
- Avoid pop-up disclosures
- Restrict hyperlinked disclosures to space constrained platforms

 Prominence
- Make disclosure prominent
- Font size at least as large as the message
- Where possible use contrasting colors for the disclosure and message
- Do not bury the disclosure in text

 Distracting factors
- Avoid all distracting factors such as graphics, sound, and additional text

 Repetition
- Repeat disclosure if there are multiple entry points to the blog or video endorsements
- Consumers must be exposed to the entire disclosure
- Repeated endorsements require repeated disclosures

 Multimedia
- Match audio endorsements with audio disclosures
- Video and text disclaimers to be displayed for a sufficient duration for consumers to notice, read, and understand them

 Language
- Language should be understandable - simple, straightforward, with clarity and syntax
- Avoid legalese
- Avoid technical jargon

Figure 4.1 Guidelines for clear and conspicuous disclosures

does provide some guiding principles for marketers to ensure that disclosures are communicated effectively (see Figure 4.1). In evaluating whether a particular disclosure is clear and conspicuous, the FTC offers the following considerations:

Placement and proximity: A disclosure is deemed to be more effective if it is placed as close as possible to the claim it qualifies. For example, if the endorsement is in the form of a tweet or status update on Facebook, the disclosure can be placed at the beginning or the end of the message. Pop-ups, which are blocked on many, but not all (e.g., blogs), social platforms should be avoided. If the endorsement appears on a blog or personal website, it should be placed on the same page and as close as possible to the claim. If the disclosure is lengthy or the consumer has to scroll down to read it, then the consumer should be alerted via text or through visual cues (e.g., "see below for important information about this post/message"). Hyperlinks disclosures should be avoided for two **reasons**. First, a hyperlink is likely to take a consumer away from the claim, and therefore, disregards the requirement for proximity. Second, the consumer is often not informed why it is important for him or her to click on the link. Hyperlinking a single word (e.g., "disclaimer" or "details") or phrase (e.g., "terms and conditions" or "more information") within the text may not be effective. These approaches may not alert the consumer to the nature of the information and its significance. As a result, motivation to and the likelihood of clicking on the link and being exposed to the disclosure is reduced. However, on space-constrained platforms, where it is necessary but impossible to include a lengthy disclosure, a hyperlinked disclosure may be used. The hyperlinked disclosure needs to be clearly labeled, using an easy-to-understand language and be sufficiently prominent, so that that it is obvious, unavoidable, and conveys the importance of the information to which it leads (e.g., "Brand Relationship Statement") (Federal Trade Commission 2013b). Asterisks (*) or other symbols by themselves may not be effective.

Prominence: Each disclosure should be prominently displayed. That is, it should be noticeable to the consumer. The disclosure should be in a font size at least as large as the message. If the platform permits it, the disclosure can be presented in a contrasting color to make the disclosure more noticeable. The disclosure should not be buried in any lengthy text where it may go unnoticed. See Figure 4.2 for an example of disclosures buried in text.

Snickers. You're not you when you are hungry.
At least I know I'm not. #snickers. ad.
snickers.com/Product/Snicke…

2:12 PM · 28 May 2016

Figure 4.2 Twitter disclosure 1

Distracting factors: If the message contains distracting factors such as graphics, sound, text, and so on the consumer may not notice the disclosure. Therefore, extreme care should be used when adding these features to the message. Avoid all distracting factors.

Repetition: Repetition makes it more likely that a consumer will notice and understand a disclosure. Repetition is particularly important if there are multiple entry points to a website, blog, or video. Consumers must be exposed to the entire disclosure not just a portion of it. It is insufficient to endorse a product multiple times, but only be exposed to a disclosure once. If a consumer is going to be exposed to repeated claims or endorsements, then the disclosure too should be repeated.

Multimedia: In the case where the endorser uses audio claims (e.g., in a video, or podcast), then the disclosure should also be offered in an audio format. Video and text disclaimers should be displayed for a sufficient duration for consumers to notice, read, and understand them.

Language: The disclaimer should be simple, straightforward, presented in a clear language and syntax. Endorsers need to avoid the use of legalese or technical jargon.

Commonly Used Method of Disclosure

The requirement for understandable language seems relatively simple and straightforward—you need to communicate your material connection in layman's terms. This may be as simple as stating verbally or in text *"I received XXXXX for this post,"* *"This post was paid for by XYZ,"* or *"Paid for by XYZ."* This language may be appropriate for platforms that do not have message length constraints (e.g., blogs, YouTube), but they are problematic on sites that limit the length or duration of each message. For example, a Vine video is six seconds (6.5 seconds to be exact) in length. A tweet has a 140-character restriction—including punctuation and spacing. If an endorser was to include a disclosure such as, *"Paid for by XYZ,"* this consumes 15 to 18 characters depending on punctuation, leaving 122–125 characters for the endorsement. This may or may not be enough room. Therefore, marketers need to be creative in crafting succinct endorsed messages.

The FTC offers some strategies to overcome this problem. The FTC suggests that in space-constrained messages disclosing a material connect may be achieved by using abbreviations such as "Ad" for advertisement, and "Paid" for a paid message or post. This is a common strategy on Twitter. See Figure 4.2 for an example of a tweet created to promote the Snickers candy bar. Notice that the inclusion of the "ad," but also consider the placement of the disclosure. Is there a possibility that this could go unnoticed?

The FTC acknowledges that short-form disclosures may not be adequate for all readers, as some may not understand the meaning of these abbreviations (Federal Trade Commission 2013b). An academic study of 167 Twitter users confirmed that consumers do, in fact, have difficulty understanding the intended meaning of popular disclosures. In this study, researchers examined three commonly used short-form disclosures: Ad (short for advertisement), Spon (short for sponsorship), and Samp (short for sample), and two long-form disclosures—Paid and Endorser. The findings of the study revealed that of the three short-form disclosures "Ad" was the easiest for consumers to understand. For the long-form disclosures, "Endorser" was the most effective at communicating a material connection between the individual posting the tweet and the brand mentioned in the message. The researchers concluded that full words (e.g., "sponsored") are preferable to abbreviations (e.g., "spon"). In the case of long-form disclosures, such as "Paid," the researchers recommend changing this to "Paid Ad" (Burkhalter, Wood, and Tryce 2014). "Contest" and "Sweepstakes" are other commonly used disclosures when an endorser posts a message in return for entry into a draw. One of these would have been an appropriate method of disclosure for the Cole Haan Wandering Sole Pinterest posts.

In addition to using abbreviations, the inclusion of hashtags to attempt to draw the consumers' attention to the fact that the word (e.g., Ad) is not part of the actual message is another common strategy. For example, it is not uncommon to see #Ad or #Sponsored included in a social post. See Figure 4.3 for an example. In this instance, the endorser has used #ad. But once again, do you think that this may go unnoticed?

Whereas this may be effective on some social media platforms, there are other platforms where hashtags are used in abundance, making it easy for the disclosure to get lost in the post. In such instances, the disclosure may not meet the FTC's guideline of being prominent. A good

Summertime sippin' with some delicious @sparklingice. Show me how you #FlavorUp #ad bit.ly/1VkhEfC

2:59 PM · 28 May 2016

Figure 4.3 Twitter disclosure 2

I have fallen in love with this new energy drink!!!! Can't believe how good it tastes. 🖤🖤🖤 #thebest #givememore fav flavor is cherry lots of #energy #mojo #toogoodtobetrue gotta try #ad #cool #hot #nextbestthing #somuchenergy #bam #ilovecherry #musthave #wherehaveyoubeenallmylife #canihavesome #tasty

Figure 4.4 Instagram disclosure

example of this is Instagram, where due to the liberal 2,200 character limit hashtags are used extensively. How quickly can you spot the disclosure in Figure 4.4?

Even in the Twitter example offered in Figures 4.2 and 4.3, it could be argued that the disclosure is not prominent and may be overlooked. For platforms where there is a strong likelihood that consumers will miss the disclosure, and may not be able to understand, it may be appropriate to create a disclosure using full words, place the disclosure at the beginning of the message, and to use an additional strategy to draw attention to it (e.g., all capital letters or asterisks). See Figures 4.5 and 4.6 for examples. In Figure 4.5, the endorser has posted the disclosure in all caps surrounded in parenthesis. The disclosure is longer, making it easier to understand. Its placement at the beginning of the message helps to draw attention to it. In Figure 4.6, we see a similar approach, except for this time, instead of parentheses, attention is drawn to by the addition of asterisks.

(PAID AD)Sharing my newest @Walgreens Hawaiian Tropic favs just in time for Memorial Day! #alohatherapy

3:12 PM - 28 May 2016

Figure 4.5 Twitter disclosure in caps with parentheses

"PAID AD" Shop this Plaid dress from here >> http://bit.ly/1WWRcXn #Dress #Bag #Fashion#Shopping

Just now

Figure 4.6 Facebook disclosure in caps with asterisks

I'm now partnered with @snickers, b/c we all know "you're not you when you are hungry. At least I'm not #snickers snickers.com/Product/Snicke...

12:29 PM - 12 Jun 2016

Figure 4.7 Disclosure as part of the message

Another strategy is to rewrite the message, so that the disclosure is included as part of the endorsement copy (Figure 4.7).

Industry Regulations

In addition to the FTC Guidelines for Clear and Conspicuous Disclosures, businesses need to follow guidelines that apply to their industry and profession. There are many highly regulated industries and professions for which there are specific guidelines regarding the use of social media in general and the online endorsements specifically. These include, but are not limited to, the banking and finance, medical, pharmaceutical, and health-care industries (Lagu et al. 2008). In one study, researchers analyzed the content of blogs written by health care professionals. Their findings revealed that 11 percent contained endorsements of specific health care products. Not one of these postings contained a disclosure (Lagu et al. 2008). See the Appendix of this book for a links to various industry regulations.

Employees on Social Media

So far, we have offered examples of celebrities, everyday consumers, and social influencers to endorse brands on social media. You may be wondering, what about employees? If a business encourages employees to talk about the company or individual brands on social media, do they need to include a disclosure? The answer to this depends on if they are using the official brand account or their personal account. If employees are discussing the company on the company's official account, they do not need to disclose. However, if they are discussing the company on their personal account, they do need to disclose their connection. There is a material connection between the employee and the company, and not all of the people who see the post from the personal account may be aware of that connection. Even if an employee is answering a question on social media, he or she must disclose his or her connection with the brand (Federal Trade Commission 2013a).

In 2012, advertising agency Deutsch LA created a marketing campaign on behalf of their client, Sony. The campaign was to promote Sony's new handheld gaming device, the PlayStation Vita. One campaign strategy was to encourage users to tweet positive statements about the Sony device using the hashtag #GameChanger (Beck 2014). In this case, consumers were not offered any consideration for sharing their positive feedback via Twitter. Thus, a material connection did not exist between the brand and their consumers. However, not all of the positive tweets originated from consumers; some originated from employees of Deutsch LA (the advertising agency behind the campaign). See the problem? A material connection did exist—an employment relationship between the employee and Deutsch, who in turn had a contractual relationship with Sony. The Deutsch LA employees failed to disclose their material connection. After the FTC had conducted an investigation, Deutsch settled. Needless to say, the agency no longer represents Sony (Beck 2015b). There is an important lesson here—do not assume that your advertising agency is aware of and adhering to the FTC Endorsement Guidelines.

Another commonly asked question is, "What if my employee has his or her place of occupation listed in the bio of his or her Twitter or the About section of Facebook. Is it still necessary to disclose?" To answer this, simply ask yourself, "Do I know the names of the employers for all of my Facebook friends and Twitter followers?" (Answer: You don't). Therefore, disclosing a material connection in the biographical section of any social media account is an insufficient method of disclosure. Think about what it would take to read an employment disclosure found in a bio. A consumer would have to click on the endorser's name, which, through a hyperlink, will take him or her to the endorser's home page where the bio or about sections are located. Most consumers will not take this extra step. As such, the employee endorser should disclose his or her material connection in each post (Federal Trade Commission 2013a). An alternative strategy is to have the employee create a separate account for work purposes with the name of the brand incorporated in the account name or handle. For example, "@DaveFromDell." In the case of LinkedIn, the name of the employer appears alongside the endorser's name. However, this does not guarantee that the consumer will read this information, as it may not meet the guidelines for prominence, placement, and proximity. Also, many employees list the parent company name on LinkedIn. The reader may not be familiar with the parent company, and therefore may not realize that a relationship exists between the endorser and the brand (Federal Trade Commission 2013a). For example, not many people know Sun Capital Partners, Inc is the owner of Boston Markets (restaurant), Hannah Anderson (apparel), and Flamingo Horticulture (consumer goods). The method of the disclosure can vary depending on the social media platform on which it appears (e.g., "Disclosure: I work for XYZ," XYZ employee), but it needs to meet the requirements for clear and conspicuous disclosures (Castillo 2014).

Meeting the FTC Guidelines

All businesses should have a social media policy that includes a section on sWOM activities and that mandates a disclosure policy for employees and endorsers that comply with the FTC guidelines. However, having a policy is one thing, understanding and being able to apply it is something completely different. To help ensure FTC compliance, training should be provided to both employees and endorsers. It is a brand's responsibility to educate and train employees and endorsers. Refresher training may be required periodically to keep abreast with any changes to the FTC Guides.

As part of the endorser recruitment process, you should inform all potential endorsers that they are required to disclose their connection with the company in each and every post. You may even want to go as far as specifying the methods of the disclosure that you would like them to use. To ensure compliance, you can inform endorsers that the incentive is contingent upon the disclosure being included. You also need to systematically monitor posts to ensure compliance. There should be scheduled review times and consequences for noncompliance.

When outsourcing this activity to an advertising agency, public relations company, or any third party, you should confirm that they will be following and enforcing the FTC Guidelines. Ask for regular reports to verify compliance. Outsourcing your promotional activity to an outside agency will not absolve you of your responsibility to abide by the FTC Act. More on this in Chapter 5.

Commonly Asked Questions

Admittedly, understanding and adhering to the FTC Guidelines is easier said than done. Also, social media continually presents new problems and situations that test our understanding of these important rules. To help ease you into FTC compliance, following are the answers to some additional commonly asked questions.

Material Connection and Compensation

Q: "Is there a monetary threshold for disclosing a relationship? What if we (the business, e.g., a coffee shop) are only offering a 'token of appreciation' for an online recommendation or endorsement, such as a free cup of coffee?"

A: When it comes to material connections, there is no monetary threshold. The key is whether the likelihood that the "token of appreciation" will affect the weight and credibility of the endorsement. One might argue that a cup of coffee is not such a sufficient weight to influence a consumer, but a month's supply of free coffee may be viewed differently (Beck 2015c). It is both easier and in everyone's best interest to adopt a consistent practice and habit of disclosing on each platform, regardless of the actual or perceived value of the incentive.

Q: "For a material connection to exist, does there have to a monetary value attached to the incentive? For example, what if I move a customer to the top of a waiting list, invite him or her to a product launch event, seat him or her at a better table in my restaurant?"

A: There does not need to be a financial arrangement for a material connection to exist. In this case, the incentive is a special access privilege. The FTC states that if the customer is offered privileges in return for social media mentions, then yes, there is a material connection, and it should be disclosed (Federal Trade Commission 2013a).

Q: "If I offer my customers a discount on a future purchase, or offer to enter them into a draw to win a prize, do they need to disclose?"

A: The customer is still being incentivized to post, and therefore a material connection exists, and a disclosure should be included. Similar to "tokens of appreciation," the value of this incentive will determine the importance of the disclosure. The greater the incentive, the greater the importance of the disclosure, and the more likely a business and endorser will come under scrutiny for failing to disclose. For instance, a significant discount or entry into a draw to win a substantial item is more likely to be questioned than one where the discount or prize is very small (Federal Trade Commission 2013a). The challenge here lies the interpretation of "significant" and "substantial."

Endorsers

Q: "I have a well-known spokesperson (noncelebrity) who endorses my product in print ads. Does he or she now need to start disclosing when he or she endorses us through his or her Twitter and Facebook accounts?"

A: The answer to this depends on whether his or her social media followers are aware that he or she already endorses your product. If there is a chance that his or her followers are unaware, then yes, he or she would need to disclose his or her connection in each of his or her posts (Beck 2015c).

Q: "What if the person who endorses my product is a well-known celebrity and has appeared in some traditional advertisements (TV, print, and so on)? If he or she starts mentioning us on social media, does he or she need to disclose?"

A: If the celebrity is a known endorser of your product, then it may not be necessary to disclose the connection when posting on social media. However, if a significant number of the people who follow his or her social media accounts do not know that he or she is an endorser, then he or she will need to disclose (Federal Trade Commission 2013a). Take for example, a celebrity who is a spokesperson for a regional business appearing only in regional TV and print advertisements. Knowledge of his or her affiliation with the business may be geographically confined to areas where these advertisements air. His or her social media followers may be more geographically disbursed.

Remember, just because some consumers may be aware of the connection between the endorser and the brand does not mean that all consumers are (Federal Trade Commission 2015). An act is considered deceptive if it leads "a significant minority" (Federal Trade Commission 2015).

Disclosure Format

Q: "I cannot fit a message and disclosure in a Tweet, what do I do?"

A: If there is not enough room, then you should rewrite your message, so that you can include a disclosure. Character limits are not a valid excuse for excluding a disclosure (Beck 2015c). Furthermore, disclosures must be present on all messages, regardless of the device (e.g., computer, tablet, cell phone) used by the intended audience (WOMMA 2014).

Q: "What if the social media posts are posted in another language. What language should the disclosure be in?"

A: The disclosure is to be presented in the same language as the endorsement (Federal Trade Commission 2013a).

Q: "What are some of the phrases we can use to disclose a material connection?"

A: The type and length of the phrase will vary depending on the platform. In Figure 4.8, we suggest some methods of disclosure. This list is by no means exhaustive. Disclosures can be presented in all capital letters, contrasting colors, or accompanied by symbols (e.g., #, ***) to draw attention to them.

Q: "What is the best way to disclose in a video?"

A: It is advisable to have the disclosure at the beginning of the video. The disclosure can be communicated verbally and appear on the screen in text. It is important that the text disclosure is visible long enough for the viewer to read it in its entirety. When posting videos to platforms such as YouTube, care should be taken to ensure that the disclosure is

Sample Methods of Disclosure

- PAID AD
- ADVERTISEMENT
- PROMOTION
- CONTEST
- SWEEPSTAKE
- COMPETITION
- BRAND ADVOCATE
- SPONSORED POST
- PAID POST
- PAID PROMOTION
- (WORK@(company name)
- (company name)EMPLOYEE
- EMPLOYEE
- "I work at (company name)"
- "I am a brand advocate for (brand name)"
- "I was compensated for this post."
- "I was paid by (company name)"

Figure 4.8 Sample methods of disclosure

not obstructed by advertisements. For long videos or even live streams, where viewers can enter and exit a video at any time, it is necessary to include multiple disclosures throughout the video or stream (Federal Trade Commission 2013a).

Q: "Do product reviews that appear on my company website or websites such as Yelp need to include disclosures?"

A: That depends on whether or not there is a material connection between the consumer posting the review and the brand he or she is referencing. If the reviewer received a benefit or incentive for writing the review, then yes, a disclosure is necessary. If no benefit or incentive was offered then, no material connection exists and the reviewer does not need to disclose (Federal Trade Commission 2013a).

Q: "When an endorser posts on the brand's official account, does he or she need to disclose?"

A: If the post only appears on the official brand account, then the answer is no. However, if he or she is also posting from his or her personal account, then yes, he or she needs to disclose. Alternatively, he or she can create a separate social media account for these posts where the brand name is incorporated in the account name or handle. For example "@ JoeFromPepsi."

Q: "Does an endorser need to disclose details of his or her compensation?"

A: No, endorsers do not need to confirm the specifics of their compensation. They just need to disclose that they have a connection with the brand. They can simply say that they were paid or received a gift for their posting.

Q: "Do all types of social media posts promoting a brand need include a disclosure? What if the post is a photo or a video without any text, do these need a disclosure?"

A: Positive sentiment and endorsement for a product can be communicated in many ways, including through a simple photograph. Take, for example, the case of Jason Peterson. Peterson, an advertising executive, was reportedly given a first-class ticket to Iceland and $15,000 in cash in return for sharing four images of Dom Perignon with his 300,000+

Instagram followers. In another example, freelance photographer Alina Tsvor shared a photograph of her flight with Chicago Helicopter Experience with her 55,000+ Instagram followers in return for free helicopter rides for her and her friends. In both of these cases, the advocates relied on images to communicate their endorsement. Disclosures should have been included (Mann 2014).

Q: "Do I need to hire a lawyer to write these disclosures?"

A: If your disclosure is written in clear, easy-to-understand language and avoids legalese and technical jargon, then you do not need a lawyer (Federal Trade Commission 2013a).

The importance of complying with the FTC and industry guidelines for sWOM cannot be understated. Your company needs to ensure that all employees and endorsers understand the importance of and appropriate method of disclosure. This information is often documented in your company's social media policy. Our next chapter delves into how to create a social media policy.

References

Avila, T. 2015. "Here's How Much Kendall Jenner Makes on a Single Instagram Photo." *Mic Network Inc.* Retrieved from http://news.yahoo.com/heres-much-kendall-jenner-makes-151205729.html

Beck, M. 2014. "FTC's First Twitter Disclosure Crackdown Is a Wake-Up Call." *Marketing Land.* Retrieved from http://marketingland.com/ftc-social-media-disclosure-110310

Beck, M. 2015a. "Did Lord & Taylor's Instagram Influencer Campaign Cross The Line?" *Marketing Land.* Retrieved from http://marketingland.com/did-lord-taylors-instagram-influencer-campaign-cross-the-line-123961

Beck, M. 2015b. "FTC's First Twitter Disclosure Crackdown Is a Wake-Up Call." *Marketing Land.* Retrieved from http://marketingland.com/ftc-puts-social-media-marketers-on-notice-with-updated-disclosure-guidelines-132017

Beck, M. 2015c. "FTC Puts Social Media Marketers on Notice with Updated Disclosure Guidelines." *Marketing Land.* Retrieved from http://marketingland.com/ftc-puts-social-media-marketers-on-notice-with-updated-disclosure-guidelines-132017

Burkhalter, J.N., N.T. Wood, and S. Tryce. 2014. "Clear, Conspicuous, and Concise: Disclosures and Twitter Word-of-Mouth." *Business Horizons* 57, no. 3, pp. 319–28. doi:10.1016/j.bushor.2014.02.001

Castillo, M. 2014. "FTC after Deutsch L.A. Case: No, Agencies Can't Ask Staffers to Casually Tweet About Clients | Adweek." *AdWeek*. Retrieved from www.adweek.com/news/technology/ftc-no-agencies-cant-ask-staffers-casually-tweet-nice-things-about-clients-161755

Coffee, P. 2016. "FTC Slams Lord & Taylor for Not Disclosing Paid Social Posts and Native Ads." *AdWeek*. Retrieved from www.adweek.com/news/advertising-branding/ftc-slams-lord-taylor-deceiving-customers-not-disclosing-its-native-ads-170229

Dingle, J.D. 1983. *FTC Policy Statement on Deception*. Retrieved from www.ftc.gov/sites/default/files/attachments/training-materials/policy_deception.pdf

EMarketer. 2015. "Many B2B Marketers Not Aware of FTC Sponsored-Content Guidelines." Retrieved from www.emarketer.com/Article/Many-B2B-Marketers-Not-Aware-of-FTC-Sponsored-Content-Guidelines/1013239

Federal Trade Commission. 2008. "Guides Concerning the Use of Endorsements and Testimonials in Advertising—16 CFR Part 255." Retrieved from www.ecfr.gov/cgi-bin/text-idx?SID=745dabff622dbafa30e1ee08f7b4ad2a&mc=true&node=pt16.1.255&rgn=div5

Federal Trade Commission. 2013a. "The FTC's Endorsement Guides: What People Are Asking." *The FTC's Endorsement Guides*. Retrieved from www.ftc.gov/tips-advice/business-center/guidance/ftcs-endorsement-guides-what-people-are-asking

Federal Trade Commission. 2013b. "Dot Com Disclosures." Retrieved from www.ftc.gov/system/files/documents/plain-language/bus41-dot-com-disclosures-information-about-online-advertising.pdf

Federal Trade Commission. 2015. *The FTC's Endorsement Guides: What People Are Asking*. Retrieved from www.ftc.gov/tips-advice/business-center/guidance/ftcs-endorsement-guides-what-people-are-asking#when

Federal Trade Commission. 2016a. "What We Do | Federal Trade Commission." Retrieved from www.ftc.gov/about-ftc/what-we-do

Federal Trade Commission. 2016b. "Truth in Advertising | Federal Trade Commission." Retrieved from www.ftc.gov/news-events/media-resources/truth-advertising

Federal Trade Commission. 2016c. "Lord & Taylor Settles FTC Charges It Deceived Consumers Through Paid Article in an Online Fashion Magazine and Paid Instagram Posts by 50 'Fashion Influencers' | Federal Trade Commission." *FTC*. Retrieved from www.ftc.gov/news-events/press-releases/2016/03/lord-taylor-settles-ftc-charges-it-deceived-consumers-through

"F.T.C. v. Transnet Wireless Corp", 506 F. Supp. 2d 1247, 1266. (S.D. Fla. 2007). Retrieved from www.leagle.com/decision/20071753506FSupp 2d1247_11664/F.T.C.%20v.%20TRANSNET%20WIRELESS%20CORP.

Griner, D. 2016. "Kohl's Sent a Star Wars Treasure Trove to the Woman Behind the Megaviral Chewbacca Video | Adweek." *AdWeek*. Retrieved from www.adweek.com/news/advertising-branding/kohls-sent-star-wars-treasure-trove-woman-behind-megaviral-chewbacca-video-171628

Lagu, T., E.J. Kaufman, D.A. Asch, and K. Armstrong. 2008. "Content of Weblogs Written by Health Professionals." *Journal of General Internal Medicine* 23, no. 10, pp. 1642–46. doi:10.1007/s11606-008-0726-6

Mann, R. 2014. "Influential Instagrammers Part of New Underground Luxury Barter Economy." *AdWeek*, October. Retrieved from www.adweek.com/news/advertising-branding/inside-instagram-s-secret-barter-economy-160905

Petry, R.D., and J. Andrews. 2008. "Cover Marketing Unmasked: A Legal and Regulatory Guide for Practices That Mask Marketing Messages." *Journal of Public Policy & Marketing* 27, no. 1, pp. 7–18. doi:10.1509/jppm.27.1.7

Quitner, J. 2014. "How to Avoid the FTC's Ire When Advertising on Social Media." *Inc*. Retrieved from www.inc.com/jeremy-quitner/social-media-advertising-rules-all-about-transparency.html

Roberts, J. 2016. "FTC Blasts Warner Bros Over Stealth Social Media Campaign." *Fortune*. Retrieved from http://fortune.com/2016/07/11/warner-bros-social-media/

Rovell, D. 2015. "LeBron James Sponsored Tweets to 23.2 Million Followers Can Cost $140K." *ESPN*. Retrieved from http://espn.go.com/nba/story/_/id/13470682/lebron-james-sponsored-tweets-232-million-followers-cost-140k

Sterling, G. 2014. "FTC: Brand-Incentivized Pins on Pinterest Potentially 'Deceptive,' Require Disclosure." *Marketing Land*. Retrieved from http://marketingland.com/ftc-brand-incentivized-pins-pinterest-potentially-deceptive-require-disclosure-78297

WOMMA. 2012. "Social Marketing Disclosure Guide." Retrieved from www.smartbrief.com/hosted/womma_1783/SMDisclosureGuide-Final.pdf

WOMMA. 2014. *Ethical Word of Mouth Marketing Disclosure Best Practices in Today's Regulatory Environment*. Retrieved from https://womma.org/free-womm-resources/

Wouk, K. 2016. "Rihanna Sells Our $9000 Dolce & Gabanna Headphones | Digital Trends." *Digital Trends*. Retrieved from www.digitaltrends.com/music/rihanna-sells-our-9000-dollar-dolce-gabanna-headphones/

CHAPTER 5

Social Media Policy and Guidelines: The Rules of Engagement

At this point, you should see social media as a business tool, not just a marketing channel. Social media will have a big impact on the way in which your business operates for the foreseeable future. Over 2 billion social media consumers cannot be wrong (Smith 2016)! So, your company has a decision to make—is it on or off the social media bus? We hope, given that you have made it all the way to Chapter 5, that you have jumped on board. But proceed with caution. For all the benefits of social word of mouth (sWOM), there can be negative consequences of embracing social.

In Chapter 4, we examined the Federal Trade Commission's (FTC) Guidelines for Endorsements and Testimonials. We considered the growing practice of influencers, social consumers, and employees to endorse brands through social media and the potential legal issues that can arise from failing to adequately disclose when a material connection exists between the brand and the endorser. Unfortunately, this is not the only regulation that your company needs to have on its radar. As social media continues to be further integrated into our daily lives, in some cases, even replacing traditional methods of communication (e.g., telephone), the line between business and personal interactions continues to blur. Social media can increase a business's liability exposure (Hamer 2013). For example, the National Labor Relations Act, Trade Secret Law, the Security Exchange Commission's (SEC) Regulation on Fair Disclosure (Regulation RD), the Electronic Communications Privacy Act, The Copyright Act, and the Communications Decency Act, and much more apply to social media. Failure to comply with these Acts can result in legal action.

The first step to mitigating risk is to develop and implement a social media policy. In this chapter, we will examine the importance of having a well-developed social media policy, the process of creating a policy, and defining appropriate content. We will suggest some social media policies developed by other companies that may offer some guidance and inspiration. The goal of this chapter is to provide you with a framework for developing your policy. In the interest of full disclosure, we are not lawyers, and therefore, we recommend that when preparing your policy you consult your legal department. The framework presented here is offered as a general guide and may need to be modified to fit your company.

What Is a Social Media Policy and Why Do We Need One?

A social media policy is a code of conduct developed and approved by senior management. The purpose of a social media policy is to communicate how the company views social media, and how they will use it in a business context. Guidelines contained within the policy provide direction on how to use social media. These guidelines are often created based on a set of best practices. They protect the company, company employees, and their clients from public relations and legal crises and help the company present and maintain a positive and consistent brand identity. A well-written set of guidelines should also empower employees, providing them with the confidence they need to utilize social media effectively.

A typical policy will, at a minimum, include information on the social platforms the company has approved for business use, who is authorized to speak on behalf of the company, what content may or may not be posted, how to share content, and general rules of engagement.

For the most part, a social media policy is about educating employees to simply use common sense when using social media. But, as a wise person once said, common sense is not so common. A social media fiasco, where a company or an employee posts a cringe-worthy or litigious message on social media, is not that uncommon. As the following examples illustrate, many of these litigious actions were completed by employees who, in many instances, were not aware that what they were doing was wrong.

- The Content Factory, a digital PR, social media, and content-marketing company, wrote a blog post for a client. Included in the blog entry was a photograph they obtained from the Web (without permission). Three months after the blog was posted, the client received a formal complaint letter, revealing they were being sued for $8,000 for using the photo. The Content Factory settled for $3,000 (DePhillips 2014).

- Shereen Way posted a photo on Instagram of her four-year-old daughter wearing a pair of pink Crocs sandals. Crocs took the photo from Instagram and featured it in a website gallery of user-generated photographs before asking for Ms. Way's permission. Eventually, the company did seek her permission—which she did not give. Fortunately for the Crocs company, Ms. Way did not pursue legal action (Murabayashi 2015).

- On the 2013 anniversary of the September 11 attacks, Fox News personality Jeanie Pirro posted a status update on her Facebook page. The post was Thomas Franklin's famous photograph of New York City firefighters raising the American flag over the rubble of the World Trade Center on September 11, 2001. Included with the post was the hashtag #NeverForget. The owners of the photo, North Jersey Media Group, filed a lawsuit against Pirro (Zara 2015). Fox News Network LLC was later added to the suit. In 2016, Fox News and North Jersey Media Group reached a settlement ("Fox News, North Jersey Media Group End Lawsuits Through Settlement" 2016).

- An Applebee's waitress posted a photograph of a customer's receipt (including a legible signature) on Reddit. The post went viral. The waitress lost her job (Weisbaum 2013).

- Reed Hastings, the CEO of Netflix, Inc. posted on his Facebook page that Netflix users were viewing nearly a billion hours of video on Netflix each month. As a result of this post, there was an upward movement in the stock price of Netflix. Netflix is a publically traded company. The Securities and Exchange Commission (SEC) initiated an investigation for a potential violation of the Regulation RD (Required Disclosure). To make a long story short, the SEC decided not to bring an enforcement action, but Netflix still incurred legal expenses in addition to public image problems associated with the investigation (Jennings, Blount, and Weatherly 2014).

The probability of a company becoming embroiled in litigation or being on the receiving end of some bad publicity may in part be attributed to the manner in which the company manages their social media efforts. A company can either outsource their social media efforts to an agency with social media expertise or handle some, if not all, of their social media accounts in-house. A 2016 study of 511 businesses from a variety of industries revealed that approximately 57 percent of those surveyed managed all of their social advertising in-house (Keath 2016). Companies who outsource their social media believing their hired agency will be responsible for compliance may be mistaken and in for a rude awakening. The case of Sony and their advertising agency, Deutsch LA, which was covered in Chapter 4, is a living proof that even big agencies representing even bigger companies do not have it under control. Outsourcing the management of your official social media accounts does not absolve you of legal responsibility of company-related social media posts. Nor does it remove the need to educate all of your employees (even those outside of Marketing and Legal departments) on industry regulations and legal ramifications of using social media. The reality is that even if your official accounts are managed elsewhere, your employees are still using some form of social media (albeit personal), and may inadvertently post something inappropriate that can be associated with your company. They may not even be aware of how to appropriately engage with others on social media. A common misconception is that millennials, who were born into a digital world, have social media expertise. They do not. Millennials are technology-dependent, but not necessarily technology-savvy. They may be competent in using social media for personal use, but not for professional purposes. Therefore, a social media policy is necessary.

Millennials are technology-dependent, but not necessarily technology-savvy.

Having a social media policy is one thing, but understanding and applying it is something completely different. We are sure (or hope) that some of the companies mentioned in the previous examples had a social media policy in place. If they did, it is clear that one or more of the following happened: the policy was incomplete, the employees did not understand the policy, employees did not follow the policy, or social media postings were not monitored. If a detailed policy had been in place, if employees received training on the policy, and if someone had been monitoring online postings, there is a good chance that many of these transgressions could have been avoided. So let us discuss how to develop a social media policy.

Developing a Social Media Policy and Guidelines

Step 1: What Is Your Purpose?

The first step is to determine your purpose for using social media. Is social media to be used purely as a marketing communications tool—a tool to inform, persuade, and build relationships with existing and potential consumers—or does it serve a larger purpose? Do you want it be integrated into multiple functional areas (e.g., HR, purchasing, sales)? Are you striving to be a social business (see Chapter 3)? Clearly articulating your purpose for using social media is like planning a road trip. First, you decide where it is you want to go—why are you using social media? Then, you plan the best way of getting there and what resources and tools you will need (e.g., what platforms you will need, who will use them, what they need to know)? Without a clear purpose, you are likely to develop an ineffective policy. Common reasons for using social media in a business setting include, but are not limited to:

- Increasing brand awareness
- Strengthening the brand's reputation
- Sharing and amplifying stories of success with external audiences
- Building and strengthening relationships with existing and prospective consumers
- Listening to and learning from consumers (i.e., marketing research)

- Engaging with vendors
- Improving customer service
- Increasing conversions (i.e., sales, lead generation)
- Recruiting and retaining high-quality employees
- Fostering pride among employees

It is likely that your company will have more than one purpose. Articulating your purpose and putting it down on paper will help you to identify appropriate social media platforms and content for your policy.

Step 2: Examine Your Company Culture

The next step, examining your company culture, begins by revisiting your company mission and values. Let these guide your policy-development process. Take, for instance, The Coca-Cola Company's mission: "To refresh the world; To inspire moments of optimism and happiness; To create value and make a difference." The Coca-Cola Company's values include leadership, collaboration, integrity, accountability, passion, diversity, and quality (The Coca-Cola Company 2016a). Their social media policy, which is available on company's website, embraces the corporate mission and values, encouraging employees to "Have fun, but be smart." To "use sound judgment and common sense," to "adhere to the Company's values" (The Coca-Cola Company 2016b).

Next, consider the beliefs about social media that exist within your company. Do you have executive buy-in (see Chapter 3)? How do your employees feel about social media? What social media platforms do they use? The answers to these questions will help you to determine how detailed your policy will need to be, the amount of employee education and training required, and who you should invite to be a member of your social media advisory board.

Step 3: Create a Social Media Advisory Board—A Center of Excellence

A Social Media Advisory Board, or if you are looking for a name with little more pizzazz, a Social Media Center of Excellence, is a group of individuals whose purpose is to craft the social media policy and appropriate guidelines. Charlene Li, CEO and Principal Analyst at Altimeter Group, a research and strategic consulting company, contends that the Center of Excellence is a company's moral compass. The Center collectively decides which platforms the company will use, creates policies on how to use these platforms, identifies best practices, and provides training for employees and any third party who may be posting on behalf of the company (e.g., social influencers), and ensures that the brand voice is appropriate and consistent (see Chapter 3) (Hootsuite University 2013). The Center should also sample social media posts within and across each of the company's social media accounts to ensure that the content, language, and tone is consistent with the company's brand personality and brand voice.

The size and composition of your company's Center should be based on your purpose for using social media (Step 1). For instance, if you are only using social media for marketing purposes, the large majority of your Center will comprise of marketing employees. If you are a social business, then your Center should include representatives from all areas of your business (i.e., HR, Finance, Marketing, and so on). Even if your purpose is restricted to a particular business function, such as marketing, it is wise to have additional representation. An outsider may offer a different perspective, play "devil's advocate," and reduce the occurrence of groupthink. A Center may also include experts (industry and social media) as well as consumers. You may decide to include a member of your legal team to navigate potential legal landmines. However, it is important to remember that legal team is a participant in the process, not the sole driver. If you choose not to add a member of your legal team to your Center, you will still need them review your policy prior to implementation. Above all, when forming your Center, it is important to recruit "social-media-friendly" people. Seek out the "social media evangelists," those individuals who see the value in social media and who will become internal advocates for the policy (Black 2010).

During the early stages of policy development, the Center may need to meet on a regular basis. Once the policy has been developed and employees trained, meetings may be less frequent. The work undertaken by the Center will also evolve over time. When the policy is first introduced, the Center may work as a centralized body, vetting planned social media activities and monitoring online activities. As the workforce becomes more skilled, the approval and monitoring process may become decentralized. The Center may only need to meet a few times a year to review and update policies. We recommend meeting at least twice a year.

Step 4: Research

Once the Center of Excellence has been formed, the next step is to conduct research. The research phase involves reviewing existing business policies, researching best practices, identifying potential laws and regulations, and benchmarking against other companies. It is advisable to create a centralized system for posting and sharing information collected. An internal website, Google Documents, or Dropbox folder are all suitable options.

Review Existing Policies

The first step is to determine if there are existing policies in place that address the use of social media in the workplace for business or personal purposes (e.g., HR policies). If policies exist, the Center needs to decide whether the existing policies can be amended or whether new policies are required. As social media is integrated into multiple functional areas; it is likely that existing policies will need to be updated. For example, if a business decides to use social media as a recruiting tool, current human resources policies are likely to be impacted and will need to be updated. The new social media policy crafted by the Center may reference the use of social media for recruiting; however, the recruiting policies that reside in HR may be silent on social media or offer conflicting guidelines. For this reason, it is advisable to review all existing policies to determine those that need to be updated so as to avoid conflicting policies.

Best Practices

Social media platforms are constantly in a state of flux. Platforms such as Facebook frequently update their interface and newsfeed algorithms to enhance user experience (and maximize revenue). The manner and purpose behind consumers' use of social media also changes over time. Two years ago would you have considered ordering pizza via Twitter? Probably not. However, today Domino's Pizza offers a "Tweet to Order" system for their consumers. This illustrative example highlights a social media truth: social media is a moving target. As such, some best practices will change over time.

Best practices can be categorized into two areas: rules of engagement and platform approach. Rules of engagement are appropriate behaviors for social posting and engaging with consumers on social media. The mission and values of the business will guide the creation of these approved behaviors, as will the rules of professional communication etiquette. To illustrate, some of Best Buy's values are respect, humility, and integrity (Best Buy 2016). Best Buy's social media policy and guidelines call on employees to be smart, respectful, and human. Employees are required to disclose their affiliation with Best Buy, act responsibility and ethically, and to honor differences (Best Buy 2014). Rules of engagement can also be formulated from a variety of external sources including industry and consumer expectations, published research, social media experts, professional and industry organizations (e.g., WOMMA.org), and societal expectations. See the Appendix of this book for some valuable resources.

Platform approach refers to appropriate methods of communicating and engagement on specific social media platforms. Approaches to using specific platforms can be general (what type of content can be posted on which platform) or specific (the best days of the week and times of the day to post). Similar to rules of engagement, these approaches are formulated from a variety of sources, including an analysis of those activities that generate the greatest level of engagement of the company's account (views, positive comments, likes, shares, downloads, and so on) and published research reports (academic, industry, and organizational). Please note, companies often publish an abridged version of their social policy and guidelines on the company website. It is unlikely that this public version of the policy will include how the company will approach each platform. A more detailed document containing guidelines for how employees should use specific platforms may exist offline.

Laws and Regulations

Federal and state laws, as well as industry regulations, may apply to social media. The majority of these fall into three categories: intellectual property, employment-related issues, and marketing activities. A policy will, at a minimum, provide a statement requiring that employees comply with government laws and industry regulations. A list of these laws and regulations is often included. A more robust policy will include details of or links to a detailed description of each law and regulation, with instructions and guidelines to ensure compliance. The closer a company moves toward being a social business, the greater the number of laws and regulations to which the company, their employees, and third parties must comply. The Social Media Center of Excellence should seek legal advice on laws and regulations that apply to their industry and social media activities. See the Appendix of this book for a link to some industry resources.

Your company is also bound to the terms of service for each social media platform (Facebook, Twitter, and so on) that you use. As such, platform-specific terms of service and policies should be reviewed in advance to identify any potential obstacles (Smith, Gambrell, and Russell 2016).

Benchmarking

The task of developing a social media policy and guidelines can, at first, appear overwhelming. But there is no need to reinvent the wheel. There are many examples of comprehensive, well-written social media policies available online. Begin by contacting industry associations for sample policies and guidelines. Next, research competitors to identify the breadth and depth of their social policies and guidelines. Finally, it may be helpful to review the policies of leading corporations, such as IBM, Microsoft, The Coca-Cola Company, Intel, and Adidas, which are available on each company's website. Keep in mind, the policies and guidelines available online may be an abridged version. If you are still looking for more examples, the Social Media Governance Website (http://socialmediagov-ernance.com/policies/) maintains a database of over 100 social media pol-icies (Black 2010).

Step 5: Draft a Document and Distribute for Feedback

Drafting a policy is like writing a book. It takes time and multiple drafts to get it right. The first draft may be quite lengthy. Do not worry, remem-ber, it is easier to reduce the size of a document than it is to add to it later. Keep the document simple. Use simple, easy-to-understand language. To reduce the need for frequent updates, try to avoid including information that may outdate quickly. Keep lengthy paragraphs to a minimum and use bullet points to emphasize key points. A draft of the policy should be submitted to your company's attorney and senior management for feed-back and final approval. If the final document is large, consider develop-ing an abridged version for easy daily reference.

The Social Media Policy: What to Include

The following is a brief overview of each section in a typical social media policy.

Policy Statement

Begin by stating the policy. In your policy statement, you should include whom the policy applies to (scope) and the reason for the policy (purpose). If appropriate, you can link the policy to the company's mission and values.

Approved Platforms

This section will list the social media platforms that the company has approved for official business purposes. These terms of services and policies of each platform should be vetted by the legal department before adoption.

Account Status

There are two categories of accounts, official accounts and unofficial accounts. Official accounts are those accounts approved, created, and managed by the company. A list of and links to all official accounts should be included in the policy document.

Unofficial accounts are created by employees, individual departments, and consumers. These accounts may include your company name or logo, but were not vetted by the company, and the content that is being posted to these accounts is not being monitored. To the average consumer, these unofficial accounts may look like authorized accounts. For that reason, your company needs to decide the manner in which they handle these accounts. The policy document should clearly state how the company will address unofficial accounts.

There are three options for managing unofficial accounts.

- Independence: Allow the account to exist and independently operate. You should carefully consider this option. By allowing these accounts to operate independently, your company has little to no control over the content. This could have negative implications for your company.

- Compliance: Contact the account holder and encourage him or her to apply for official account status. In this case, the company will allow the account to remain as long as the account administrator abides by the company's social media guidelines. In return, the company may offer to list the page on the company website and will grant the account administrator permission to use company images and logos. Transitioning an unofficial account to become an official account may be a viable option if the account has a large following and has achieved positive results. Someone within the company will need to be responsible for monitoring the account to ensure continued compliance with company guidelines. If the account holder declines your offer to make their account official or does not respond to your request, you may decide to move to option three—termination.

- Termination: Contact the account administrator and request that he or she remove all company intellectual property (logos, trademarks, and so on). Also, request that they must clearly indicate on the account (in the bio or account description) that this is an unofficial account, and that all posts are made by a specific individual (and include his name). If the account holder fails to comply, you may want to issue a cease and desist letter. You should also file an unauthorized trademark use report with the specific platform.

Legal Issues

The policy document should, at a minimum, include a statement requiring that employees comply with federal and state laws and industry regulations. A list of these laws and regulations should be included. An additional step is to include details of or links to detailed descriptions of each law and regulation along with instructions and guidelines to ensure compliance.

Account Access

The policy document should indicate who is permitted to post on behalf of the company. If employees are required to complete training before being granted permission to post, then this should also be stated.

Account Ownership

There may be instances in which an employee creates a social media account that is granted "official account" status, yet the account was created with the employee's work e-mail address (e.g., janedoe@socialgurus. com), rather than using an administrative e-mail address (e.g., social@ socialgurus.com). Common sense would dictate that once the account receives an official status that the e-mail address associated with the account would be updated. If this slips through the cracks, it may be worthwhile to include a statement that states that all accounts that have been granted official status are the property of the company. That way, if an employee leaves the company, the account ownership (login) will transfer to the company.

Brand Voice

In Chapter 3, we discussed the importance of humanizing your brand. To convey this personality, you need to develop a brand voice. Brand voice is how that personality is portrayed through communications. Creating a brand voice begins by reviewing the mission of your company to help you identify the appropriate language and tone to use in your social communications. Regarding language choice, you need to decide whether you want your posts to be written using simple or complex words, should the message be serious or fun, and should you include or avoid the use of technical jargon. Another factor related to language choice is the need to establish a consistent message tone. What is the appropriate tone that reflects your brand personality? Is it direct, personal, scientific, fun, sassy, humble, and so on? Communication is certainly not just about word choices. You must also consider the appropriate type of photographs and video. Visual components of the message must be aligned with the brand voice and accurately reflect the brand's personality. In Chapter 3, we offered the example of Taco Bell. Taco Bell's brand voice is humorous and wacky. The Taco Bell Facebook page recently contained a post titled "This just happened: I got engaged to a Doritos Locos Tacos." Accompanying the announcement was a picture of high school student dressed in a suit proposing to a taco. On Twitter, the company posts visuals, which include funny taco gifs, and pictures of taco t-shirts, all of which support the company's brand voice. In the same chapter, we described Adidas's brand as inspirational. During the 2016 Summer Olympics, the Adidas Facebook page included a number of posts that included photographs of inspiring paralympians. Developing guidelines that include appropriate language, tone, and content is important to ensure that all employees and third parties posting on behalf of the company are all using the same voice.

Best Practices: Rules of Engagement

When educating employees on how to engage with followers on social media, it helps if you include both specific directions and examples. Following are some suggested, although generic, guidelines that companies may adopt. Please note that depending on the expectations of your industry, your company and the laws and regulations that apply a company may decide to elaborate on each item.

Know the rules

Before posting content to a company account, make sure that you have read and that you understand the company's social media policy. Ensure that you are familiar with federal, state, and industry laws and regulations.

Be yourself

Social media is a great communication and community-building tool—a place where you and your audience can share information, engage with one another, and build and maintain relationships. Write in the first person and allow your personality to show.

Be respectful

At all times, post meaningful and respectful comments. Do not post negative comments or engage in negative conversations about competing companies. Resist the urge to respond to negative posts. Your engagement needs to be focused and professional, and should aim to add value.

Be transparent

Be transparent about your affiliation with the company and avoid misrepresentation. If you are endorsing the company or one of their products, ensure that you include a disclosure that meets the FTC Guidelines. If you make a mistake (e.g., share inaccurate information), you need to admit it. Be upfront and quick with your correction.

Maintain confidentiality

Do not discuss confidential or proprietary information on social media. Do not discuss or disclose business partnerships or employee information on social media.

Respect proprietary content

Be respectful of proprietary information and content. Do not use copyrighted materials (print, media, or any other digital files) and intellectual property without first gaining permission from the owner. Also, give credit to the source of this content in your postings.

Best Practices: *Platform Approach*

People are motivated to use different social media outlets for different purposes. For example, Facebook is popular for communicating with family and friends, whereas LinkedIn is more appropriate for communicating with company and industry associates. Furthermore, each platform has its nuances that will impact how information is shared. If your company decides to restrict specific communications to particular platforms or has a preference for how that information is presented, then this should be outlined for employees. Platform approach guidelines may be appropriate when a large percentage of the workforce is permitted to post to and engage with consumers on social media. Walmart is an example of a company that offers separate guidelines for Facebook and for Twitter (Wal-Mart Stores 2016).

Policy Enforcement

In addition to providing rules of engagement, it is also important to explain to employees the consequences of failing to adhere to the policy or follow the guidelines. The severity of the punishment will largely depend on the infraction, ranging from a warning to termination. It is up to your company to decide on the appropriate punishment for a specific infraction. Your human resources and legal department can assist in crafting a statement for inclusion in the document.

Introducing the Policy

Once the policy has been approved by the legal department and senior management, it is ready to be presented to employees and relevant third parties. The manner in which the policy is introduced to the workforce is a function of the size and culture of the company, geographic disbursement of employees, and how social-media-savvy your employees are. The obvious place to introduce the policy and guidelines is during new employee orientation. For existing employees, an alternative strategy will be required. For a small business, a short in-person information and training session may be sufficient. For larger organizations with a more disbursed workforce, a more creative approach may be required. One suggestion is to create a short educational video. The global auditing company KPMG created a four-minute video to explain their social media policies and guidelines (Tung 2014). Another alternative is to offer training through a series of webinars.

Whereas a four-minute video or a brief in-person information session may be sufficient for providing a general overview of the policy and guidelines, a lengthier, more detailed training session may be required for those employees authorized to post on behalf of the company. As an example, the computer and technology company Dell requires employees to undergo a certification process before being granted permission to post on behalf of the company. Dell created their own Social Media and Communications University (SMaC U—pronounced "smack you") to train Dell employees on the best way to use social media. The certification process includes the completion of three mandatory classes and one class on a specific social media platform. The mandatory classes include, SMaC Principles—a class that covers Dell's five core principles for proper engagement; Getting Started SMaCing—a class where employees learn how to engage in social media and the social media tactics and tools that are at their disposal—Building Brand on SMaC class where employees learn how to support the Dell brand through content, voice, and actions. Platform-specific classes are offered for Facebook, Twitter, Community, LinkedIn, and Google+. Upon successful completion of the certification program, employees are permitted to speak on social media on behalf of the company. The certification program, which takes approximately eight hours to complete, has reduced the company's need to monitor social media communications (Deshpande and Norris 2014). As of July 2015, over 15,000 Dell employees were SMaC U-certified (Petrone 2015).

Regardless of the method of delivery—in-person, webinar, or video—the best way to develop an informed and skilled social media workforce is not just to tell them what to do, but to show them how to do it. Employees should, in a controlled environment, be given the opportunity to put it into practice what they have learned. A sound training session will use stories and examples to help employees understand the rules. It will also present them with some common scenarios to which they are asked to apply the guidelines they have learned.

Periodic Review

The final step of the process is to periodically review both the policy and guidelines to ensure that they are current. It is also important to revisit the legal aspects of social media. As updates are made, refresher training for all employees will be required. Even if there have been no changes to the policy or guidelines, it is advisable to offer a brief refresher training, perhaps once a year. A short video may be an effective approach.

Social Media Policy Examples

As stated earlier, there are many great examples of social media policies available online (simply search using the company name and the words "social media policy"). You may want to consider reviewing some of these for inspiration. Keep in mind that some of these policies may be the abridged version of a larger policy that is accessible only to company employees. The following discussion summarizes a few examples of policies that are worth reviewing. Links to access these social media policies and others are located in the next section and in the Appendix.

Intel

Intel has created a clear and straightforward policy. The policy begins with an overview of how Intel views social media and reminds readers that "social computing on behalf of Intel is not a right but an opportunity, so please treat it seriously and with respect." It informs readers how to obtain approval to post on behalf of Intel, how to participate in training, and references the role of Intel's Social Media

Center of Excellence. Guidelines for engagement are presented as three fundamental rules: disclose, protect, and use common sense. A brief explanation and instructions for each of these rules are provided. The document also devotes an entire section to contractors and endorsements, explaining the importance of material connections when a post is sponsored or incentivized (Intel 2016). If your goal is to craft something that is simple and easy to understand, this would be an appropriate policy to model. See http://www.intel.com/content/www/us/en/legal/intel-social-media-guidelines.html.

Coca-Cola

The Coca-Cola Company provides a slightly more detailed policy and a set of guidelines. The document begins by explaining what social media means to the company and then outlines how the company and their employees are expected to engage with the public on social media. There is a section devoted to employees' personal use of social media, and similar to Intel, expectations for spokespersons. A nice feature of this policy is that it can be downloaded as a pdf document in 29 languages (The Coca-Cola Company 2016). For those companies with an international workforce, this may be worth reviewing. See http://www.coca-colacompany.com/stories/online-social-media-principles.

Target

The Target Corporation has developed a very structured policy. The document begins by describing the purpose of the policy and offers a definition of social media. From here, the document explains who the policy applies to and what the policy does not cover or when it does not apply. The company's guidelines on how to use social media are listed in easy-to-read bullet format. Responsibilities of team members and line managers are listed separately. A particularly noteworthy feature of this document is the examples of online actions that are in breach of the policy and subsequent consequences for the employee (Target Corporation 2013). If your workforce is diverse in their understanding and experience with using social media, this may be an appropriate policy to model. See https://www.target.com.au/medias/marketing/corporate/aboutus/Careers/Social+Media+Policy.pdf.

Environmental Protection Agency (EPA)

The EPA has divided their policy and procedures into five separate documents. The main document entitled "Social Media Policy" explains the purpose, scope, and audience. Roles and responsibilities and definitions are provided. Not surprisingly, because this is a highly regulated agency, there are links to other procedures, standards, and guidelines. The remaining documents include policies and procedures for (1) using social media to communicate internally, (2) using social media to communicate with the public, and (3) representing the EPA online using social media. Each of these documents follows a similar format. The fourth and final document is a flowchart that helps employees determine if, when, and how an employee should respond to social media postings. For those who work in a highly regulated industry, this policy may be appropriate to benchmark against (U.S. EPA 2011). See https://www.epa.gov/irmpoli8/policy-and-procedures-using-social-media-epa.

Now that we have provided the framework for establishing a social business, outlined the legal issues surrounding social word of mouth (sWOM), and offered suggestions on how to create a policy, the remainder of the book will guide you on how to create a shareworthy persuasive message for a variety of popular platforms.

References

Best Buy. 2014. "Best Buy Social Media Policy." Retrieved from http://forums.bestbuy.com/t5/Welcome-News/Best-Buy-Social-Media-Policy/td-p/20492

Best Buy. 2016. "Culture." Retrieved from www.bestbuy-jobs.com/culture/ (accessed July 1, 2016).

Black, T. 2010. "How to Write a Social Media Policy." *Inc.* Retrieved from www.inc.com/guides/2010/05/writing-a-social-media-policy.html

DePhillips, K. 2014. "The $8,000 Mistake That All Bloggers Should Beware." *The Content Factory*. Retrieved from www.contentfac.com/copyright-infringement-penalties-are-scary/

Deshpande, R., and M. Norris. 2014. "Building a Social Media Culture at Dell." HBS No. 514096 Boston: Harvard Business School Publishing, Retrieved from http://hbsp.harvard.edu

"Fox News, North Jersey Media Group End Lawsuits Through Settlement." 2016.

Hamer, S. 2013. "Creating an Effective Workplace Social Media Policy." *HRFocus* 90, no. 10, pp. 17–20.

Hootsuite University. *Securing Your Organization in the Social Era with Charlene Li*. Hootsuite. Retrieved from https://learn.hootsuite.com

Intel. 2016. "Intel Social Media Guidelines." Retrieved from www.intel.com/content/www/us/en/legal/intel-social-media-guidelines.html

Jennings, S.E., J.R. Blount, and M.G. Weatherly. 2014. "Social Media—A Virtual Pandora's Box: Prevalence, Possible Legal Liabilities, and Policies." *Business and Professional Communication Quarterly* 77, no. 1, pp. 96–113. doi:10.1177/2329490613517132

Keath, J. 2016. "5 Unpublished Stats on the Future of Social Media Marketing." *Socialfresh*. Retrieved from www.socialfresh.com/the-future-of-social-media-marketing-stats/

Murabayashi, A. 2015. "Did I Just Give My #Permission? Hashtag Consent for Photo Usage Is Trending." *PetaPixel*. Retrieved from http://petapixel.com/2015/09/22/did-i-just-give-my-permission-hashtag-consent-for-photo-usage/

Petrone, P. 2015. "How Dell Turned Its Workforce Into an Army of Recruiters." *LinkedIn*. Retrieved from https://business.linkedin.com/talent-solutions/blog/2015/06/how-dell-turned-its-workforce-into-an-army-of-recruiters

Smith, G., and LLP. Russell. 2016. "Social Media Marketing; The 411 on Legal Risk and Liability." Retrieved from www.sgrlaw.com/resources/trust_the_leaders/leaders_issues/ttl28/1597/ (accessed July 2, 2016).

Smith, K. 2016. "Marketing; 96 Amazing Social Media Statistics and Facts for 2016." *Brandwatch Blog*. Retrieved from www.brandwatch.com/2016/03/96-amazing-social-media-statistics-and-facts-for-2016/

Target Corporation. 2013. *Social Media Policy*. Retrieved from www.target.com.au/medias/marketing/corporate/aboutus/Careers/Social+Media+Policy.pdf

The Coca-Cola Company. 2016a. "Mission, Vision & Values." Retrieved from www.coca-colacompany.com/our-company/mission-vision-values (accessed July 1, 2016).

The Coca-Cola Company. 2016b. "Social Media Principles." Retrieved from www.coca-colacompany.com/stories/online-social-media-principles

Tung, E. 2014. "How to Write a Social Media Policy to Empower Employees." *SocialMedia Examiner*. Retrieved from www.socialmediaexaminer.com/write-a-social-media-policy/

US EPA. 2011. "Policy and Procedures for Using Social Media at EPA." Retrieved from www.epa.gov/irmpoli8/policy-and-procedures-using-social-media-epa

Wal-Mart Stores, Inc. 2016. "Walmart Policies and Guidelines." Retrieved from http://corporate.walmart.com/policies

Weisbaum, H. 2013. "Applebee's Waitress Canned after Posting Pastor's Tip." *NBCNews*. Retrieved from www.nbcnews.com/business/applebees-waitress-canned-after-posting-pastors-tip-1B8198406

Zara, C. 2015. "Fox News, Jeanie Pirro Facebook Lawsuit Could Change Copyright Landscape on Social Media." *International Business Times*. Retrieved from www.ibtimes.com/fox-news-jeanie-pirro-facebook-lawsuit-could-change-copyright-landscape-social-media-1865246

CHAPTER 6

Storytelling: What Do You Say and How Do You Say It

No one is going to share your message if it is not worth sharing. Not a novel idea—yet, marketers are spending a considerable amount of time thinking about the types of information or content they should post online. There is now recognition that the old outbound model of marketing—where marketers seek out consumers via cold calls and unsolicited advertisements—is not working. Consumers need to come to you (i.e., inbound marketing). However, you need something of substance to lure them in; good content embedded in a larger brand story. You also need to be a darn good storyteller.

This focus on delivering valuable content underlines the growing area of content marketing. Content marketing is defined by the Content Marketing Institute as "a strategic marketing approach focused on creating and distributing valuable, relevant, and consistent content to attract and retain a clearly-defined audience—and, ultimately, to drive profitable customer action" (Content Marketing Institute n.d.). Since 2011, interest in content marketing has steadily grown (Snow 2015). A cottage industry has been developed resulting in numerous dedicated software platforms designed to help you create, curate, optimize, analyze, and distribute digital assets (Lieb, Groopman, and Li 2014). In addition, there are also content marketing conferences and the Content Marketing Institute dedicated to the topic. Content marketing is essential because it is not only the backbone of social media marketing, but also Search Engine Optimization (SEO) practices, inbound marketing, and e-mail marketing. Success is measured by web traffic, search engine rankings, brand awareness, lead generations, sale revenue, downloads, and engagement such as social media.

The Content Marketing Institute definition provides a procedural overview of content marketing, yet it misses the mark somewhat, in that, it neglects the heart and soul of content marketing—storytelling. For this, we turn to the content marketing tech agency Contently who defines content marketing as "the use of storytelling to build relationships with consumers by providing them something entertaining or useful" (Contently 2016). In truth, storytelling is only a part of the message communication process. In an analysis of blogs, researchers Kozinets et al. (2010) found that word of mouth marketing (WOMM) was influenced by "character narratives" (i.e., personal stories), the specific forum or message context, communal norms found within the forum (i.e., norms impacting communication message "expression, transmission, and reception"), and the marketing message and meaning (i.e., marketing promotional elements) (Kozinets et al. 2010). This chapter will explore each of these WOMM influences within the context of brand story development, message development, textual storytelling, and visual storytelling process. The chapter concludes with how to write a more persuasive story that will ultimately drive consumer action.

What Is Your Brand Story?

Storytelling is central to this chapter because WOMM is about *sharing* stories—stories that engage and excite consumers; stories that consumers consider valuable. Understanding the social consumer, their interests and passions, and preferences when it comes to media consumption is at the core of spinning a good, authentic tale. Social media brings with it a whole set of storytelling tools—the written word, pictures, video, and even virtual reality are all at our disposal. Social media also provides brands with easy ways to retell stories by allowing retweeting, sharing, and embedding to be so accessible.

Marketers who want to excel in social word of mouth (sWOM) marketing must think of themselves as storytellers and consumers not just as their audience, but also as their coauthors. And, like any good storyteller, they need to tailor their story and manner of delivery for their audience. Marketers need to be able to both identify and cultivate storytellers from the consumer rank and acknowledge that they are "co-producers" of marketing communications (Kozinets et al. 2010). Consumers should be encouraged to share their experiences, and marketers should routinely select and profile key stories that are consistent with the overall brand narrative. In the end, the focus needs to be on *telling before selling*. So, how do you capture a consumer's attention for them to not only view but share your content? What story will you share? How is your story going to be different than their competitors?

There are numerous examples of companies and individuals who have successfully embraced storytelling in their marketing efforts. Arguably, one of the best-known examples of applying storytelling in their marketing efforts is Red Bull. In fact, Red Bull's marketing is so interwoven with content development that it can be thought of as a "publishing empire that also happens to sell a beverage" (O'Brien 2012). Red Bull's content covers a variety of extreme sports and documents their sponsored events, individual athletes, and teams through a variety of social media platforms. All of these efforts are consistent with their lifestyle brand narrative of extreme action and sports. Red Bull has also involved consumers in the cocreation of their brand story content through hashtag campaigns, such as #summeriscoming. Consumers who received the most likes on their extreme photos got a paid trip to the X Games (Edmondson 2014).

Another example of a company putting brand stories at the center of their marketing efforts is the Coca-Cola Company. In 2011, Coca-Cola began to focus on "content excellence." The underlying theme of which was to create "contagious ideas" communicated through dynamic brand stories that would drive conversation online. Coca-Cola even changed its company website from a corporate presence to one more along the lines of a digital magazine—called "Coca-Cola Journey" (Elliot 2012). Coca-Cola's overriding brand story is helping the world live positively. Coca-Cola's "online magazine" (aka website) delivers a variety of entertainment, health, environmental, and sports articles consistent with "living positively." In Fall 2016, Coca-Cola launched a mobile road trip from Atlanta to Los Angeles to "discover, capture and amplify stories about the 130-year-old company's deep ties to American culture." Uniquely, content was not only created by Coca-Cola millennial staffers, but also fans (Moye 2016). Lastly, TOMS shoes present a story about improving lives. For every pair of shoes purchased, TOMS gives a pair away to someone less fortunate. The company's philanthropic efforts also include helping to improve access to water, restoring vision, providing safe births, and preventing bullying. This desire to help is illustrated through a variety of social media posts highlighting how they are helping impoverished communities.

So, Red Bull's story is about extreme action infused with energy, Coca-Cola wants the world to live positively, TOMS is improving lives—but what is your big brand story? The rules of writing and communicating your brand story are very similar to those contained in your local public library. You need good, relatable characters, an interesting and compelling story reinforced by supporting content, and a descriptive and effective way to execute it (Content Marketing Institute n.d.; Gunelius 2013). Social media, thankfully, has provided us with numerous platforms that make this process easier.

Keys to Successful Storytelling

There are six keys to successful storytelling: character, brand voice, "big" story brand idea, story arc, story execution, and coauthorship.

- **Character:** Whether it is an influencer, employee, or a pro-filed consumer, characters that convey your brand's content should be someone that your buyer persona can relate to and finds credible. They can pay a leading or supporting role in your story, but your consumer needs to develop an emotional connection with your character(s). Therefore, ensuring the message is ripe with information for charac-ter development (i.e., video or images) will increase the likelihood that the consumer will not only be engaged, but also share the message.

- **Brand voice:** The voice of your brand—conveyed through text and visually oriented posts must be consistent; con-sistent between posts and consistent with the brand image and story. Is the brand voice and subsequent language used informal or formal? Is the personality conveyed—fun, sarcastic, witty, stoic, and so on? Can consumers quickly pick up on personality characteristics (i.e., Intel's voice is smart and enlightening, Taco Bell is a little wacky). As we discussed in Chapter 5, it takes a lot of work to establish, achieve, and maintain a consistent brand voice.

- **"Big" brand story idea:** The story should be simple and get at the core of your brand's identity. It may seek to explain why your company exists or delve into a problem that your product seeks to resolve. Ultimately, the big brand story must be appealing to your consumers—it must emotionally connect with them. It is hard to think of a more compelling brand story than TOMS shoes. Look to your company's mission to help develop your brand story.

- **Story arc:** Brand stories are a collection of information or posts—not told in one sitting. However, posts must be consistent with the larger brand story. Also, like any good story, there should be hurdles and ways to overcome them delivered in regularly scheduled increments. The presented conflict should be something that relates to your consumer's needs and stage in the purchasing cycle. A great example of a compelling story can be found with TOMS shoes chronicling a staff trip to Nepal on Facebook. The series of images highlights the recent earthquake there, the number of children in need, and how TOMS has a partnership with a sight-giving agency.

- **Story execution:** Social media is the instrument of story delivering and also provides a framework for the types and methodology of how the stories are told. Stories can be short (e.g., Vine) or complex (e.g., YouTube channel). They also can be told across multiple social media platforms. The key to selecting where to execute your story is both understanding which social media platforms your consumers are using and knowing the type of content or story they want and expect told within a specific network. For example, content on Pinterest tends to be more "home-orientated" (i.e., food, and so on) (Moon 2014; Libert 2014).

- **Coauthorship (with consumers):** Lastly, it is essential to remember that brand stories are not just the product of orchestrated marketing campaigns born out of corporate boardrooms—they are cocreated with consumers. Consumers are routinely sharing their brand stories, experiences with the product. Messages on social media related to products are stories—tales of consumers' experiences and connection with the product that are positive, negative, and neutral. Brands must nurture and encourage their consumers to tell their stories. In Chapter 7, we offer the example of Tourism Australia who successfully included their consumers to tell their brand story.

Later in this chapter, we will discuss many strategies to help your message's virality—but at a minimum, it is about good storytelling.

Story Content and Making It Contagious

When you visit TOMS' Instagram account, you are immediately drawn into their story of improving lives and the emotional connection that their brand has cultivated. Pictures of young children getting shoes, beautiful foreign landscapes as the backdrop of profiled TOMS shoes, and numerous heart-infused pictures all seek to reinforce TOMS' story of improving lives around the world. In general, the pictures depict happiness, interpersonal connections, and a sense of giving back. They are aesthetically rich. Each of TOMS' philanthropic causes provides unique content that contributes to the larger brand story and is consistent with TOMS' brand image and voice. They are also engaging and interesting to TOMS' consumers.

So, how will you tell your story within social media? As mentioned, your individual posts must reinforce your brand story, but above all, they must be interesting and valuable to consumers. This is especially true if you want consumers to share your story. However, simply getting a consumer to view or read your post does not guarantee its virality. Let's face it, the vast majority of posted content within social media is simply not shared with others. In fact, most fans of branded pages do not even see the Facebook posts in their newsfeed, let alone "like" or "share" them. So, what should you do? The answer to not only getting exposure on platforms like Facebook but also getting users to share, retweet, and repin comes down to one simple truth: you must provide content that *your* consumers value.

Value, much like beauty, is in the eye of the beholder. And, it will also vary from consumer group to consumer group. Fortunately, research examining virality and word of mouth (WOM) communication provides us with some tools to increase the likelihood of creating shareable content. Jonah Berger, Wharton Professor and author of *Contagious*, identified six principles (STEPPS) that drive WOM: Social Currency, Triggers, Emotion, Public, Practical Value, and Stories (Berger 2013). We will briefly explore each of these principles as they relate to social media content. We have chosen to vary the order provided in his STEPPS acronym and discuss emotion last—given its importance in the academic literature.

- **Social currency**: We care deeply concerned how we appear to other people. And, social media affords us the ability to craft, in some cases, a new and improved digital identity. Consumers, therefore, seek out and share interesting information that is consistent with their desired self. They want to stand out and look good in the eyes of their peers. This can also explain the sharing success of social media posts that include "quotes" (Zarrella 2013c). As a marketer, you need to think about the types of information that consumers will want to share to look "good" and also how to put a spotlight on consumers. This may mean rewarding or simply acknowledging consumers who actively post their product reviews or get the most views on social media. You can also give certain consumers the "inside track" on new product-related information. At a minimum, you should highlight what makes your product or rather your product benefits interesting to consumers.

- **Triggers:** The secret behind triggers is getting your content to be "top-of-mind." In other words, people will readily be prompted to think about the content (and then share it). Use specific events (i.e., holidays or big news events), activities (i.e., vacation time), or obstacles (i.e., the morning rush out the door with your children) that your target consumer encounters and align them with your content. Think—Star Wars "may the force be with you" aligned with May 4 "May the fourth be with you." Also make sure you time messages to when these events and obstacles occur.

- **Public:** Make something stand out, so that people can identify it and imitate it. While this suggestion was made about creating a highly visible product (i.e., silver-colored Apple computers that contain a backlit apple versus the typical black laptops), it is also relevant in the context of social media. To illustrate, make your content more visible by simply creating a post that contains a photo, video, animated GIF, or cinemagraph. Increasing its visibility allows it to be more easily noticed and shared (more on this later). You can also create a branded sound that begins or ends each of your videos. Think about the very beginning of TED talk videos—the distinctive sound of chimes, a water drop, and then drums (can you hear it?). Another idea is to always include identifiers on your branded content to quickly and readily assign its ownership to you. This can be easily accomplished by putting a small logo in the corner of a post or video.

- **Practical value:** Many of us simply enjoy useful information and want to spread its value to others. It should come as no surprise that some of the most valuable content are, in fact, instructive and educational posts. For example, a 2015 Content Marketing Trend Survey found that articles or case studies (54 percent), videos (46 percent), infographics (43 percent), and research or white papers (36 percent) were the top four types of content that respondents considered to be the "most effective" (Ascend2 and Leading Marketing Solution Providers 2015). When analyzing retweets, Quicksprout found that tweets linked to "how-to" and "list-based" articles performed well with retweets (Patel 2014). Another study sponsored by HubSpot found almost 80 percent of retweets were related to news. Retweets, more often than not, also include a link offering readers additional value for the tweet (Zarrella 2009). So, the question is—What does your target consumer consider valuable and how can you simply convey this information? Lists, videos, infographics, how-to guides, and frequently asked questions are a good place to start.

- **Stories:** Up to this point, we have discussed the broad brand story, but within this larger context, there are smaller stories, individual consumer, or employee stories that work to support the bigger story theme. Take, for example, the storied posts on Coca-Cola's Facebook page. Within it, Coca-Cola highlighted, in the summer of 2016, specific athletes' Olympic gold moments #Rio2016 #THATSGOLD. This focus on a "gold feeling" is about "accomplishing something great, however, simple, in an everyday moment" (Coca-Cola 2016). The emphasis on this joyful, special feeling is consistent with their larger "live positively" brand story.

- **Emotions:** Content that conveys emotion readily goes viral. Yet, all emotions are not created equal. Emotions that are high in arousal (e.g., anger and awe) tend to have higher rates of sharing. Whereas, low-arousal emotions (e.g., sadness) do not inspire as much sharing—no one wants to feel or responsible for making others feel miserable. Research suggests that just having a more emotional headline for your content can lead to higher rate of share (Moon 2014). There is a free analyzer tool, the Emotional Marketing Value Headline Analyzer, that will rate the emotional impact of your headline (Advanced Marketing Institute 2009). A message's overall associated emotion and the general valence of a message—positive, negative, and neutral—have garnered a lot of research in the academic literature. As such, we provide a further elaboration of both message valence and emotional arousal in the next section.

Message Valence and Emotional Arousal

Academics and industry frequently look at WOM messages from a valence or sentiment perspective. In other words, is the information or comment positive, negative, or neutral? While marketers can certainly communicate positive, negative or neutral information, most often discussions about sentiment relate more to product related consumer comments and reactions and their consequences. Traditional WOM research has found negative WOM to be more influential on both brand evaluations and on purchase intentions (Bone 1995; Richins 1983; Brown and Reingen 1987). The same has been found for eWOM communications—negative eWOM significantly impacts experiential, more sensory dependent type goods (Park and Lee 2009). For better or worse, social media allows for the rapid diffusion of negative sWOM information. As we talked about in Chapter 3, a "firestorm" may prove to be detrimental to the credibility of a company or brand (Pfeffer, Zorbach, and Carley 2014). This dissemination of negative information within social media differs from other WOM and eWOM in its speed and volume, ability to weigh into the conversation in simplistic terms ("like" or retweet), the "echo chamber" of social media (i.e., when consumers are not exposed to new ideas within your network, instead existing ideas are amplified through repetitive postings), the amount of information, and cross-media dynamics (i.e., blurring of online and offline media) (Pfeffer, Zorbach, and Carley 2014). Negative sWOM can be particularly detrimental if it originates with key social influencers such as "hubs" and "bridges" (Stich, Golla, and Nanopoulos 2014). This can be incredibly harmful to a business ("Pink Slime Case Study").

Texas mom Bettina Elias Siegel ignited a social media firestorm that destroyed a business. Siegel was on a mission to improve the quality of school lunches. She was concerned with the widespread use of a product known as Lean Finely Textured Beef (LFTB)—lean beef that has been extracted from the fat trimmings, a staple of the fast-food industry commonly found in burgers, tacos, and school lunches. Whereas the name LFTB sounds harmless enough, the product because of its color and texture acquired the unappetizing moniker, "Pink Slim."

Siegel turned to her blog, The Lunch Tray, to express her disgust and outrage, calling on lawmakers to ban the product from the federal school lunch program. Within eight days of her posting, more than 200,000 concerned parents had signed an online petition. Siegel's beef (pun intended) spread like wildfire and was picked up by ABC news. In response, supermarkets abandoned the product and fast-food chains, such as Wendy's, felt the need to reassure consumers—Wendy's took out a series of newspaper advertisements to assure consumers that they have never used the product. Beef Products Inc. (BPI), the producer of "Pink Slime" suffered irreversible financial losses and was forced to suspend operations in three of its four plants. AFA Foods, a meat processing company, declared bankruptcy and U.S. sales of ground beef hit a ten-year low (ElBoghdady 2012).

Industry and academic research reveal that there are differences in how users of various social media platforms respond to a positive, negative, or neutral sentiment. In a study using simulated Pinterest boards, consumers paid more attention to negative sWOM than positive or neutral (Daugherty and Hoffman 2014). An analysis of Facebook posts revealed that neutral posts received fewer likes than positive or negative posts, whereas very negative posts received more comments (Murphy 2012). Finally, Buzzsumo and Fractl conducted an industry study that examined the sharing of 1 million articles across five different social media platforms and found that some users on platforms had sentiment preferences. Specifically, users on LinkedIn and Pinterest tended to share more positive stories, whereas Facebook shared the most negative among the five platforms reviewed. Twitter and Google+ had the "most balanced range of sentiments" (Libert 2014).

Should we simply view social media posts as positive, negative, or neutral? What about specific emotions and their strength? What role do they play in virality? The strength of the emotion—or emotional arousal—is what leads people to take action or share the message. To be more specific, high emotional arousal content that generates awe, excitement, or humor performs well. In addition, even negative high-arousal emotions such as anger or anxiety are very shareable (Berger 2013). However, emotions that do not elicit high arousal, such as general sadness and contentment, are not viral. An examination of the most frequently e-mailed *New York Times* articles found that articles that instilled a sense of awe defined as "emotion of self-transcendence, a feeling of admiration and elevation in the face of something greater than the self" performed the best (Tierney 2010). Positive content was shared more often than negative content (Berger and Milkman 2011). These findings were reinforced in a separate study that looked at viral videos—high-arousal, positive valence specifically those that inspired the emotion of exhilaration were shared the most frequently (Karen Nelson-Field, Riebe, and Sharp 2013). In contrast, a study that addressed emoticons use within the Chinese social media platform Weibo found that rage was more viral than joy, sadness, or disgust (Shaer 2014). While the studies contained different conclusions, the importance of high-arousal emotions in sharing remained the same. Furthermore, it may be wise to stay away from negative high-arousal emotions as we do not yet understand the long-term effects it would have on a brand (Karen Nelson-Field, Riebe, and Sharp 2013).

The problem for companies is, of course, how do you create content that arouses our sense of awe, humor, anger, excitement, or anxiety enough to get shared? The answer lies at least, in part, in selecting an appropriate creative strategy.

Creative Strategies

Creative strategies can be thought of as "executional factors and message strategies used to bridge the gap between what the marketer wants to say and what the consumer needs to hear" (Ashley and Tuten 2015, 18). Some different typologies on traditional media have been developed (Laskey, Day, and Crask 1989; Aaker and Norris 1982). But, how do they relate to social media? In a review of the social media content posted on 28 popular consumer brands across multiple social media platforms, researchers Ashley and Tuten (2015) identified the most popular message strategies (see Figure 6.1 for an overview). They found a variety of creative strategies were being used; the most popular of which was a functional appeal. A functional appeal demonstrates the utility of a product. Despite its popular use, functional appeal approaches were not related to the

◈ Message Strategies

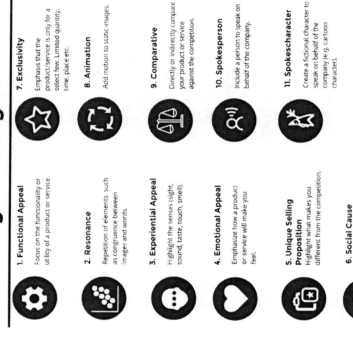

1. Functional Appeal
Focus on the functionality or utility of a product or service.

2. Resonance
Repetition of elements such as congruence between images and words.

3. Experiential Appeal
Highlight the senses (sight, sound, taste, touch, smell).

4. Emotional Appeal
Emphasize how a product or service will make you feel.

5. Unique Selling Proposition
Highlight what makes you different from the competition.

6. Social Cause
Associate your company with a social cause.

7. Exclusivity
Emphasis that the product/service is only for a select few. Limited quantity, time, place etc.

8. Animation
Add motion to static images.

9. Comparative
Directly or indirectly compare your product or service against the competition.

10. Spokesperson
Include a person to speak on behalf of the company.

11. Spokescharacter
Create a fictional character to speak on behalf of the company (e.g. cartoon character).

Figure 6.1 Creative message strategies

levels of engagement, social influence, or the number of Facebook fans or Twitter followers.

Ashley and Tuten (2015) also found that brands attempted to engage with consumers by inviting them to share some content, and half of the brands studied encouraged sharing by providing incentives. The results found that there was a significant relationship between the incentive to share content and the number of people following a brand, Facebook fans, social influence score (i.e., Klout), and engagement scores. Contests that offered consumers the chance to win a prize were twice as popular as discounts (Ashley and Tuten 2015). Outside of identifying a variety of appeals and illustrating which appeals are more successful in driving consumer action, these findings highlight an important truth: Do not focus on selling within social media. As the poor performance on the functional appeal illustrates, content posted on social media cannot be solely about your product. Instead, engage with your consumers, provide value, and focus on appeals that include text and images, emotion, which engages the senses and associates your company with a cause.

Textual Storytelling

Now that you have figured out your brand story and general content of your story, you need to decide how to execute it. For better or worse, you need to adjust your writing style to conform to the ever-evolving social media lexicon and technology platforms. There are also some other considerations that you need to make if you want to increase the likelihood of your posts being shared.

Length: If you want to increase shareability, in most cases, shorter is better. For example, if retweeting is your goal, then a tweet should comprise of 71–115 characters (Lee 2014; Zarrella 2013b). So, what is wrong with the full 140 characters? After 115 characters, an individual cannot add a comment in the retweet without editing it. And, who wants to edit a retweet? In the case of Pinterest, the optimal length is 200–300 characters, as this allows for more detailed information about the item (Dougherty 2015). Chapter 8 provides additional recommendations on the length of posts for various platforms.

Acronyms: Acronyms—immigrants from texting language—have become an integral part of the social space. Marketers have a vast number of acronyms at their disposal, and they can be an effective and fun way to communicate with your consumers (Figure 6.2). While most of the acronyms are familiar and self-explanatory (e.g., OMG, LOL), some are a little more complicated. Take, for instance, BAE (Before Anyone Else), which can mean a close friend or a person's spouse, girlfriend, partner, or FBO (Facebook Official), which marks a life event change that you are making public.

Before you jump on the acronym bandwagon, you need to understand whether using particular acronyms is consistent with your brand voice, and are these acronyms used by your target market? Chances are your target market actively uses only a small number of the acronyms, or they have developed new terms unique to their cohort. According to

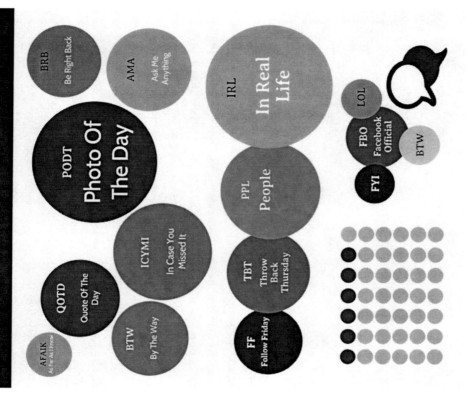

Common Acroynms

Figure 6.2 Common acronyms

Source: Washenko (2015).

Askfm (a popular youth-driven social networking site), teens readily use a host of novel acronyms to capture their zeitgeist (TBR = to be rude; SMH = shaking my head; IDEK = I don't even know) (Mullins 2016). There is some evidence that using an acronym can make your social media post less sharable. This has been found to be true with "LOL" (Zarrella 2009). And, when comparing the use of RT versus actually spelling out "retweet" or "please retweet," the full-length version comes out on top.

Word choice: It is not just what you say, but how you say it! Word choice and phrases can dramatically impact whether a post is shared. Some industry studies have examined word choice and sharing behavior. Although most of these have focused on Twitter, many of these observations can also be applied to other platforms. One finding that may seem somewhat counterintuitive is that longer words are more frequently retweeted (Zarrella 2009). However, somewhat conflicting results can be found on studies that have examined sharing behavior on Facebook—short, simple words are more likely to be shared (Solis 2010). The lesson here is that word selection (simple vs. sophisticated) and word length (short vs. long) should be based on your intended audience.

There is also data that provides insight into specific words that can increase or decrease the likelihood of sharing on specific social media platforms. Figure 6.3 summarizes the most popular words used in shared, retweeted, and repinned social posts as analyzed and discussed by social

The most shareable words by social media platform

Facebook	Twitter	Pinterest
1. Facebook	1. You	1. Recipe
2. Why	2. Twitter	2. Chicken
3. Most	3. Please	3. Minutes
4. World	4. Retweet	4. Bake
5. How	5. Post	5. Cake
6. Health	6. Blog	6. Cheese
7. Bill	7. Social	7. Cut
8. Big	8. Free	8. Bottle
9. Says	9. Media	9. Step
10. Best	10. Help	10. Mix

Media Bottle Post Please
Big Chicken You Cut Step
Bill Most Recipe Why
Social Facebook How
Blog Cheese Free Says

Figure 6.3 *The most shardable words by a social media platform*

Source: Facebook (Zarrella 2010), Twitter (Zarrella 2009), Pinterest (Zarrella 2012a).

media scientist, Dan Zarrella (Zarrella 2012a; Zarrella 2010; Zarrella 2009). It should be noted that these findings are considerably dated, yet these do provide useful insights.

Instead of looking at the content of tweets, another approach is to look at article headlines to determine common word choices in shared posts. A study cosponsored by Buzzsumo and Fractl analyzing 1 million most shared articles across multiple social media platforms found that found that verbs that were more knowledge-based, such as "know," "understand," and "prove," were commonplace in article headlines. Positive adjectives (i.e., greatest and hilarious) in headlines were also frequently used (Libert 2014). Analyzing more than 1 million WordPress blog headlines shared across social media, Buffer and Coschedule also identified the top shared word and phrases in shared headlines (Moon 2014). The top words and phrases included: List, Post, You and Your, Free and Giveaway; How To, DIY, I, Me, My, Easy, Win, and New.

While these three studies differed on their units of analysis shared across social media, some common themes arose. Each points to the importance of disseminating knowledge "how-to," "list post," "blog post," and so on. Subject pronouns (e.g., I, you, he, she), object pronouns (e.g., me, you, him) also do well (Kwon and Sung 2011). This can perhaps be attributed to the humanizing, more informal, conversational tone they give to the post (Moon 2014). Each of these studies highlights the uniqueness of each social platform, underscoring the nuanced and differing approach you should take when posting across platforms.

Call-to-action (CTA): Marketers must also ask for what they want. If you want a retweet, ask for a retweet. If you want a like, ask, share, then ask, follow, ask, reply, ask, download, ask (you get the idea). The adage—ask, and you will receive is alive and well on social media. However, that is not to say that every social post should include a CTA—you do not want to come across as needy or pushy. CTAs should be incentivized by posting good content or creating a contest (Romanek 2013). That said, some CTAs work better than others. Following is a list from highest to lowest of the top seven words or phrases that when included in a tweet garnered more retweets than did similar tweets that did not contain these words—(Zarrella 2013a). As you can see, having good manners pays off.

- Please Help
- Please Retweet
- Please RT
- Please
- Retweet
- Spread
- Visit

While the preceding list pertains to Twitter, Facebook posts containing CTA words, such as "like," "comment," and "share" also result in higher levels of compliance than posts that did not integrate these words (Zarrella 2012b). Similar results with CTA words were also found on Instagram and Pinterest (Ripen Ecommerce 2014; Zarrella 2014). Specifically, Instagram captions that included CTA words asking to "like" and "comment" had higher levels of engagement (Zarrella 2014). On Pinterest, "Please Repin" and "Please Like" should also drive action. The lesson here is that when you include a CTA, remember to say please.

Links: One of the big benefits of social media for marketers is that social can drive traffic outside of the platform through the use of URL links and linked images. Not only do links offer the potential to drive up advertising revenue and conversion rates, but they also provide increased value to consumers by supplementing the information that can be contained in a short post. This increased value is apparent in that consumers are much more likely to retweet and share information from posts that include a link. To illustrate, one study found that retweeting was 86 percent higher with texts that included links (Patel 2014).

Hashtags: The history of hashtags began in the late 1990s as a way to group items together on Internet Relay Chat. Designer and now-Uber employee Chris Messina co-opted their use to organize group conversation on Twitter in a tweet on August 23, 2007. Three years later, in 2010, Twitter reinforced their usage by emphasizing hashtags through "trending" topics on their front page (Bennett 2014a)—today they are ubiquitous. Users of Facebook, Twitter, Google+, Instagram, Pinterest, and more use hashtags to organize subjects and photos as well as express their opinion or support on a topic. Hashtags have even entered in every-day face-to-face conversational vernacular.

Not surprisingly, hashtags impact sharing. Industry research has found that using hashtags matters when it comes to retweets. Twitter's analysis of over 2 million tweets reported that hashtag use resulted in a 16 percent increase in retweets (Rogers 2014). Dan Zarrella's research found an even higher retweet rate—tweets that contained a hashtag were 55 percent more likely to be retweeted than tweets that did not use hashtags—#Amazing (Zarrella 2013c). However (and as we discussed in Chapter 4), too many hashtags can be problematic and may present legal problems if they engulf disclosures. On Twitter, hashtags should be limited to two or less particularly if you want to leave room for retweeting comments and substance. Two also seems to be the magic number on Facebook. A study completed by Social Bakers found that engagement on Facebook also significantly decreased after two hashtags (Ayres 2015).

One of the reasons that hashtags successfully impact sharing is that consumers can quickly find relevant content by searching within a specific social media platform or via Google. Similar to SEO practices, it is essential to create or identify meaningful hashtags that your consumers can relate to and that are relevant to your product. When creating hashtags, make sure they are unique to your brand, easy to remember, and relatively short. Also, make sure that there is not a secondary meaning or the chance that consumers could misread, and therefore misinterpret your intended hashtag meaning (e.g., The 2009 Britain's Got Talent Susan's Boyle PR team use #susanalbumparty to announce the album release party—do you see the problem?). When you participate in an ongoing hashtag conversation, make sure you know what you are jumping into (remember our earlier DiGornio Pizza example). Many marketers have not fully understood the meaning behind the hashtag conversation or were ignorant of the larger cultural context a trending topic was meant to illustrate and have quickly regretted their participation. Take, for instance, the dessert company Entenmann's who tweeted about not feeling bad or #NotGuilty about eating some of their lower-calorie options. Unfortunately, #NotGuilty was currently being used to discuss the Casey Anthony trial verdict (Guido 2016). To assist you in finding the perfect hashtag, check out Hashtagify located in the Appendix.

Quotes: Quotes do well across social platforms. To illustrate, Twitter's analysis of over 2 million tweets found tweets that contained a quote received a retweet rate 19 percent higher, whereas social media scientist, Dan Zarrella, found that tweeted quotes were more likely to be retweeted by 30 percent (Zarrella 2013c; Rogers 2014). While you have the option of including the quote with attribution in a tweet or on a Facebook post, a better approach is to overlay a quote over an awe-inspiring photo for maximum effect. The power of visuals in social media cannot be over-stated. Visual storytelling is an essential part of social media—as the next section will reveal.

Visual Storytelling: A Picture (or Video) Says a Thousand Words

Social media is increasingly becoming a visual medium. A 2014 report covering global Citrix customers revealed that 63 percent of mobile social networking site's data volume consists of images, whereas thirty-two percent was videos. Only 5 percent was text (Citrix 2014). In the first quarter of 2016, Snapchat video attracted a staggering 10 billion views *per day* (Meeker 2016). Smartphone adoption rates, continued advancements in digital camera technology, and a growing number of image- and video-centric social media platforms have led to a perfect storm of consumers wanting to use more images in their communications. This increasing reliance on visuals is consistent with research that has found that our visual IQ (as measured by Raven's Progressive Matrices nonverbal exam) is increasing faster than other aspects of our IQ (Kremer 2015). In 2015, the critical reading scores of high school graduates in the United States were the lowest they have been in 40 years. In the same year, writing scores, which they began testing in 2005, were the lowest on record (Kitroeff and Lorin 2015). The fact that our visual IQ is increasing and our reading and writing skills are decreasing highlights the importance of making your social posts rich with visual content.

Power of Images

The ability to get noticed within social media's ever-changing, information rich environment is crucial. Consumers are experiencing information overload. E-mails, texts, articles flood our screens. Photos, videos, and infographics assist consumers in their ability to digest data quickly. This is happening, in part, because by the time we reach 18 years of age, most of us will be visual learners. Simply put, many of us learn more through visual modalities: symbols, diagrams, pictures, and videos (Felder and Silberman 1988). Our brains also seem predisposed to visuals; approximately 30 percent of our cortex is dedicated to visual processing, whereas hearing only makes up 3 percent and touch is 8 percent (Grady 1993).

Research on traditional advertising and WOM has established that images are superior to text in garnering attention (Pieters and Wedel 2004; Singh et al. 2000). One study found that consumers are 90 percent more likely to look at an advertisement's primary picture before they look at the copy (Werner 1984). This could help explain why engagement is higher with social media posts that include images. There is, however, evidence to suggest that consumers may pay more attention to the text, opposed to images when promoting luxury brands on social media. This maybe attributed to the high level of perceived risk (e.g., monetary, social, and psychological risk) that consumers may associate with purchasing luxury items, resulting in a need for detailed information, which is typically contained in the text. Images were still more attention grabbing for the nonluxury product (Hoffman and Daugherty 2013).

Images are also powerful because, as research suggests, we remember images (recall and recognition) more than we remember text (Childers and Houston 1984). This phenomenon has been called The Picture Superiority Effect (Stenberg 2006; Paivio, Rogers, and Smythe 1968). This effect may not be unique to static images, but also include videos. Research has shown that television commercials, more so than print ads can influence purchase attitudes and intentions (Grass and Wallace 1974). More specifically, videos that evoke high-arousal emotions are remembered the most (Karen Nelson-Field, Taylor, and Hartnett 2013). This relationship between high-arousal emotions and memory also highlights that one of the biggest benefits of images or videos is their ability influence consumers' emotions. Images and video have an ability to quickly influence not only your consumers, but also general public opinion. There have been numerous instances of a single photograph being credited for changing public sentiment (Pensiero 2015).

The Popularity of Visuals

The sheer volume of digital images captured and shared per day is staggering. To illustrate, in 2014, over 1.8 billion photos *per day* were uploaded to WhatsApp, Facebook, Instagram, Snapchat, and Flicker, and in 2016, this number increased to over 3 billion per day (Meeker 2014; Meeker 2016). Snapchat users shared 8,796 photos every second in 2015 (when their user base was 200 million) (Morrison 2015). The quick rise of visual-centric platforms (e.g., Pinterest and Instagram), Facebook's Timeline redesign, which focuses more on images, the visibility of images and video included in tweets, and the integration of the "cover" photo across multiple platforms (i.e., Facebook, Twitter, and LinkedIn) all reinforce that we have entered "the age of visual culture" (Bullas 2012). Indeed, some marketers would argue that social media as a whole is shifting away from text and embracing the visual medium (Gupta 2013). The fact that the highest levels of engagement for millennials, as measured by average monthly minutes, occur on visual platforms (i.e., Facebook, Snapchat, and Instagram), suggests that this is the right strategy. Futurists predict that Generation Z (those born after 1996) will rely even more heavily on images to communication than millennials (Meeker 2016). Smart brands need to make sure they are investing in visually centric social media platforms. In particular, they should be on Instagram, where brand engagement with consumers is considerably higher than Pinterest, Facebook, Google+, LinkedIn, and Twitter (Elliot 2015).

Photos and Consumption Practices

Photos that are shared the most often do not typically contain pastoral images of the countryside, but rather, they capture consumers' daily lives; lives that involve branded clothing, food, and activities and contextualized within cars, stores, and restaurants. The ability to easily and quickly associate and communicate not only your opinion about a product, but also your product aspirations, usage, and ownership are incredibly powerful. In fact, certain types of visual platforms lend themselves to documenting specific points in the consumer decision-making and consumption process, with Pinterest and Instagram representing opposite ends of the consumption spectrum (Gupta 2013). Pinterest images that populate consumer boards are often taken from brand's owned media (e.g., website) (Moore 2012). Pinterest boards become an aspirational, pre-purchase wish list and work to drive sales to e-commerce websites. Ninety-three percent of users are using Pinterest in pre-purchase planning (Shopify 2016), and the average order that originated from Pinterest is almost $59 (Bennett 2014b). In contrast, Instagram documents products that consumers own. It reflects their post-purchase use and conveys their satisfaction.

Photos that are posted on social media are often sanitized, filtered, photoshopped versions. Uploaded photos are cherry-picked from a much larger set (Eveleth n.d.). Teens and adults alike are being careful in which digital artifacts they select to convey their desired digital identity. Part of presenting one's best self online is utilizing filters. Filters are used to correct perceived problems and improve aesthetics, and to create unique fun photos. Highlighting specific objects in the photo, changing the color, and applying vintage effects are other motivations for using filters (Bakhshi et al. 2014). Not surprisingly, filters can impact engagement, although the results are somewhat mixed. A study analyzing 7.6 million Flickr photos found that filtered photos increased viewing by 21 percent and were likely to have attracted 45 percent more comments (Bakhshi et al. 2014). In contrast, an Instagram study found that photos with "no filter" applied generated the highest number of likes per follower (Zarrella 2014). In the Appendix of this book, we have provided a list of websites and applications that you can use to add filters to your photographs.

Videos and Other Digital Assets

Videos are another increasingly important sWOM tool. This is especially true now that Instagram allows the integration of Boomerang's four seconds of stitched together photos, six-second Vine videos, 60-second Instagram videos, and the recent addition, Instagram stories. Each of these platforms serves to capture consumer or brand micro-moments. Consumers seem to appreciate the increased media richness as seen through significant increases in Instagram video viewership (Newton 2016). Snapchat has also evolved from static snaps (images) to an app where the majority of its users are making "Stories"—short, 10-second videos compiled of individual snaps. In 2016, consumers are watching 10 billion "stories" each day (Frier 2016). Instagram, Pinterest, and Snapchat each allow consumers to watch a video within the social media platform.

While our visual storytelling discussion concentrates its efforts on static images and videos, GIFs, cinemagraphs, slides, and infographics are also increasingly popular image choices. In the social media sea of static images, marketers are embracing animated GIFs (i.e., graphics interchange format) and cinemagraphs (i.e., a photo and video combination where one or more image attributes seem alive through their movement) (Piekut 2015). Luxury brands, in particular, are drawn to cinemagraphs because of their ability to bring photos to life and allowing them to articulate both beauty and sophistication in their visual storytelling. Both GIFs and cinemagraphs can be used on websites, e-mail, ads, and embedded within social media posts. Animated GIFs and cinemagraphs boast higher rates of engagement and conversion than static images (King 2016; Johnson 2015; Piekut 2015). However, they are not alone—although waning in popularity, infographics have also demonstrated strong virality (Dugan 2012). Finally, we would be remiss if we did not mention the incredible popularity of Slideshare. Infographics on Slideshare are also liked and shared considerably more than other documents and presentations (Abramovich 2014). Whereas this chapter does not include a detailed discussion on GIFs, cinemagraphs, slides, or infographics, much of the following discussion of the visual storytelling discussion is also applicable to these forms of visuals. In the Appendix of this book, we have provided a list of websites and applications that you can use to locate GIFs, create cinemagraphs, infographics, and lists.

Visual Storytelling Is Not an Option

Visual assets' ability to increase engagement rates and influence purchases has forced companies to acknowledge their worth. A CMO Council and Libris sponsored survey of 177 senior marketers executives, found that 65 percent of those surveyed believed that visual assets, in general, are essential in telling the story of their brand (CMO Council and Libris 2015). Forty-six percent of those surveyed believe that photos were "critical" in marketing and storytelling strategies, followed by video (36 percent), infographics (19 percent), and illustrations (15 percent). They also believe that visual asset use and importance will continue to grow (CMO Council and Libris 2015). Marketers consider their brand editorial images to be the most important in crafting their marketing strategy, followed by consumer-generated images, then brand stock images, influencer images, and finally, partner images (Curalate and Internet Marketing Association 2015). In other words, a combination of company, consumer, and collaborative content is important for telling your brand story.

While some social media platforms are dominated by company-generated images (i.e., Pinterest), most rely heavily on consumer-generated images. Consumers are actively creating and posting their visuals and sharing those created by other consumers on social media. In 2013, Pew Research found that 54 percent of Internet users were posting original visual content online, whereas 47 percent were sharing images and video that others created (Duggan 2013). We can only expect these numbers to be significantly higher today. Both company- and consumer-generated images work to influence consumer decision-making, but consumer-generated content also influences marketers. For example, Pinterest boards were a source of design inspiration for automotive company Buick (Gupta 2013). Engagement with images can be used to predict in-store and onsite product engagement (Curalate n.d.), and consumer photos are now selected for inclusion in branded website's homepages, fan galleries (e.g., Dunkin Donuts, Marshalls from Chapter 1), and even product-landing pages (Curalate n.d.).

A recurring theme in this book is that consumers and marketers must work collaboratively within the social space. Marketers need to not only continue to encourage engagement from consumers, but also actively integrate their content. Visual marketing firm Curalate recommends the 80/20 principle in your visual integration strategy: 80 percent of visuals should be generated by a company, whereas 20 percent should be "outsourced" to consumers and influencers, advocates, and so on (consumer and collaborative). How do we find consumer content to incorporate into our marketing?

Visual Analytics and Commerce

To find and then utilize visually oriented consumer-generated content requires new marketing solutions—enter visual intelligence and analytical tools and visual commerce. Historically, social media analytics have relied solely on textual analysis, ignoring the content of the image itself. As a result, approximately 85 percent of a brand's photos are "lost" because the brand is not mentioned in a post's text (Laughlin 2016). Companies, such as Ditto, Logograb, and Blinkfire Analytics, are using logo recognition software to analyze millions of social images to identify brand logos that are contained anywhere within a photo (e.g., on a cup, shoe, billboard) or even in a video or GIF. The logo may not even be the image's focal point; however, understanding the number of visual mentions within the social realm indicates a brand's popularity and media impact. It also allows marketers to discover affinities with other brands and general types of products relationships that they may not have known existed. In essence, visual analytics contextualizes and shows *how* consumers are using your product. Capturing the organic visual sWOM conversations allows the marketer to find and target consumers that have previously gone unnoticed, develop new products based on discovering new or unknown usage behavior, forge new marketing partnerships with affiliate brands, and understand which promotional materials are working. Some of the visual analytical tools also help you to identify and help connect with frequent brand posters or influencers and their social network. For a list of visual intelligence and analytics companies, check out the Appendix of this book.

Visual commerce is defined as:

The full-funnel approach used in making all of the images both within and outside of a brand's control actionable at every point of the customer journey. This is accomplished by directly linking images to the products or services associated with them, resulting in traffic, conversions and revenue. (Curalate and Internet Marketing Association 2015)

Visual commerce is a growing area. It allows an image to become a point of purchase. Visual marketing company Curalate's "Reveal" technology makes visual purchasing easy. Consumers can click on a specific product in an image and be taken to an e-commerce platform to purchase it. One image can provide multiple purchasing opportunities. Instagram's link to e-commerce can be increased by utilizing the Instagram bio. Instagram users click on the e-commerce link they find in the brand's Instagram bio to purchase products. Consumers can also purchase from Instagram using the "Shop Now" button. There are many platforms (i.e., Like2Buy, Tapshop, and so on) that allow you link Instagram to e-commerce solutions (see the Appendix for more information). Some of these options require a user to first download a third-party app or integrate Instagram accounts between the buyer and seller. Pinterest has also recently included buyable pins—a blue "Buy It" button that appears next to items, allowing consumers to directly purchase within the Pinterest platform. Another feature offered by multiple visual-marketing firms retrieves consumer and influencer pictures from social media platforms, such as Instagram and Twitter, and integrates them within a consumer brand's website or blog gallery.

And, while we now have analytical tools that allow us to analyze photos and visual commerce tools that allow us to make purchases through images, we still do not know the answer to the question…

What Images or Video to Use?

What types of images or videos are consumers more likely to share? If you did not know already, more than likely it is not going to be an image solely of your product (remember: tell, not sell). Do not worry; your product can be part of the image, but there needs to be a positive context and perhaps a friendly face captured in it as well. The type of image or video that is shared is going to depend on the social media platform.

Consumers post a wide variety of images on Instagram. One study identified eight separate categories of Instagram images: friends (i.e., two human faces in the photo), food, gadgets (i.e., electronics, transportation), captioned photos, pets, activity (i.e., concert, landmark), selfies, and fashion (i.e., clothing, shoes, and so on). The most frequent categories of images posted (consisting of almost half of the dataset of photos combined) were friends and selfies. The least frequent were pets and fashion (Hu, Manikonda, and Kambhampati 2014). In contrast, images posted on Pinterest *without* faces received 23 percent more repins than those that included faces (Curalate and Internet Marketing Association 2015). This difference can perhaps be attributed to the varying motives beyond using the social network; Pinterest is more about "things" and Instagram is more about "people."

Video communication provides a much richer communication platform, and arguably, it is harder to pinpoint, let alone create content that can be contagious. However, a content analysis of videos collected from the UK does yield some suggestions. In a study of 800 user-generated and branded social videos, researchers Nelson-Field and Riebe (2013) looked at the average rate of sharing each day, aggregated by the type of creative devices used in the video. The most popular creative device use (by a considerable amount) was personal triumph, followed by weather, science, or nature and baby or young child (remember the popular "Charlie Bit My Finger" video?).

Image Attributes

From the time we opened up our first Crayola box, color has fascinated us. And, we all have our favorite. Color can capture attention, generate emotions, and symbolize ideas. Its effects are both physiological and psychological. And, importantly for marketing, color impacts consumer decision-making. But, does color impact sharing behavior within social media?

Research has readily shown that blue (across cultures) is most often selected as the favorite color, and this preference is also seen online (at least on Instagram). Visual marketing firm Curalate's study of more than

8 million Instagram images found that when blue is the dominant color in an Instagram image, its attracts 24 percent more likes than an image that is predominately red and orange (Dixit 2013). However, this was not found to be the case on Pinterest, where images that contain red, orange, and brown are repinned approximately twice as often than images containing blue images (Lowry 2013). A separate study also found that red and related shades (e.g., pink and purple) increased repinning behavior, whereas black, yellow, yellow–green, green, and blue deterred it (Bakhshi and Gilbert 2015). Instead of focusing on one color within Pinterest, multiple colors might be a better approach. On Pinterest, repinning was 3.25 times higher when an image contained multiple colors opposed to one dominant (Lowry 2013).

Levels of brightness and saturation are other considerations when posting images. On Pinterest, "medium" lightness is best for repinning (Lowry 2013), whereas "high lightness" attracts considerably more likes than dark images on Instagram (Dixit 2013). The background of the image can also make a difference in liking and sharing. On Pinterest, images containing relatively little white space (i.e., less than 30 percent) were repinned at higher rates (Lowry 2013). In contrast, Instagram images with a lot of backgrounds were liked more often (Dixit 2013). Even the texture of an image, determined by the number of edges, makes a difference on Pinterest. Smooth texture images (think rounded surfaces) are repinned at considerably higher rates than images that have many rough edges (Lowry 2013). The opposite was found within Instagram, where a lot of texture led to considerably more likes (Dixit 2013).

Phew! That is a lot of information to digest. So, we helped you out by summarizing this information in Figure 6.4. We added text and images, but unfortunately, we were unable to add color, video, or sound☺.

So, have you figured out your big brand story? Will it be textually and visually rich? Even when you have written your tale, the next hurdle you face is figuring out how you will use it to drive action. In other words, how will you influence others within social media?

STORYTELLING

Keys to Successful Storytelling

Character: The characters in your story should be someone that your consumers can relate to and is perceived to be credible.

"Big" Brand Story Idea: The story should be simple and gets at the core of your brand's identity.

Story Arc: Brand stories are a collection of information/posts - not told in one sitting. Each story presents a hurdle/challenge that must be overcome.

Story Execution: Execute your story on social media platforms your consumers use and know. Makes sure your story fits with the platform.

Brand Voice: Text and visually oriented posts must be consistent; consistent between posts and with the brand image/story.

Co-Author (with Consumers): Nurture and encourage consumers to tell stories.

Story Content

Post content that your consumers value.

Social Currency: Content that helps your consumers improve their digital identity.

Triggers: Content that aligns with current events, activities and obstacles.

Public: Content that stands out and can be easily identified with your company.

Practical Value: Content that is useful.

Stories: Content that tells small stories that work to support the bigger story themes.

Emotions: Content that create high arousal. E.g. Awe, excitement, humor and anger.

Creative Strategies

Choose the right appeal.
Invite consumers to contribute content.
Offer an incentive.
Focus on telling, not selling.

Textual Storytelling

Shorter is often better. However, this varies by platform.
Use Acronyms (simple vs. sophisticated) and length (short vs. long) should be based on the characteristics of your intended audience.
Use verbs, positive adjectives, subject and object pronouns.
When using a Call-to-Action, say 'Please.'
Include a Call-to-Action, say 'Please.'
Limit your use of hashtags. Make them unique.

Visual Storytelling

Visual storytelling is not an option.
Consumers are more likely to remember images than they are text.
Recall is greater for images that evoke high emotional arousals.
Use filters to make photos fun and unique.
Choose colors carefully to evoke emotion.
Gifs, cinemagraphs, slides and infographics are good storytelling tools.
Use videos to create and tell short stories.
Use a combination of company, consumer and collaborative content.
Be conscious of the type of content that consumers expect to see on a given platform. E.g. Pinterest - things, Instagram - people.

Figure 6.4 Storytelling

References

Aaker, D.A., and D. Norris. 1982. "Characteristics of TV Commericals Perceived As Informative." *Journal of Advertising Research* 22, no. 2, pp. 61–70.

Abramovich, G. 2014. "15 Mind-Blowing Stats About Slideshare." *CMO.* Retrieved from www.cmo.com/features/articles/2014/3/10/mind_blowing_stats_slideshare.html#gs.jAcOvsA

Advanced Marketing Institute. 2009. "Emotional Marketing Value Headline Analyzer." Retrieved from www.aminstitute.com/headline/index.htm

Ascend2, and Leading Marketing Solution Providers. 2015. "Content Marketing Trends: Survey Report Summary." Retrieved from http://ascend2.com/home/wp-content/uploads/Content-Marketing-Trends-Summary-Report-150310.pdf

Ashley, C., and T. Tuten. 2015. "Creative Strategies in Social Media Marketing: An Exploratory Study of Branded Social Content and Consumer Engagement." *Psychology and Marketing* 32, no. 1, pp. 15–27.

Ayres, S. 2015. "Tips from 13 Experts on How to Use Hashtags on Facebook." *Post Planner*. Retrieved from www.postplanner.com/how-to-use-hashtags-on-facebook/

Bakhshi, S., and E. Gilbert. 2015. "Red, Purple and Pink: The Colors of Diffusion on Pinterest." *PLoS One* 10, no. 2, p. e011718. Retrieved from http://journals.plos.org/plosone/article?id=10.1371/journal.pone.0117148

Bakhshi, S., D. Shamma, L. Kennedy, and E. Gilbert. 2014. "Why We Filter Our Photos and How It Impacts Engagement." In *International AAAI Conference on Human Factors in Computing Systems*, 12–22. Retrieved from http://comp. social.gatch.edu/papers/icwsm15.why.bakhshi.pdf

Bennett, S. 2014a. "The History of Hashtags in Social Media Marketing." *AdWeek*. Retrieved from www.adweek.com/socialtimes/history-hashtag-social-marketing/501237

Bennett, S. 2014b. "U.S. Social Commerce—Statistics & Trends." *AdWeek*. Retrieved from www.adweek.com/socialtimes/social-commerce-stats-trends/500895?red=at

Berger, J. 2013. *Contagious*. New York, NY: Simon and Schuster.

Berger, J., and K. Milkman. 2011. "What Makes Online Content Viral?" *Journal of Marketing Research* 49, no. 2, pp. 192–205.

Bone, P.F. 1995. "Word-of-Mouth Effects on Short-Term and Long-Term Product Judgments." *Journal of Business Research* 32, no. 3, pp. 213–23.

Brown, J.J., and P.H. Reingen. 1987. "Social Ties and Word-of-Mouth Referral Behavior." *Journal of Consumer Research* 14, no. 3, pp. 350–62.

Bullas, J. 2012. "6 Powerful Reasons Why You Should Include Images in Your Marketing." *Jeffbullas.com*. Retrieved from www.jeffbullas.com/2012/05/28/6-powerful-reasons-why-you-should-include-images-in-your-marketing-infographic/

Childers, T.L., and M.J. Houston. 1984. "Conditions for a Picture-Superiority Effect on Consumer Memory." *Journal of Consumer Research* 11, no. 2, pp. 643–53.

Citrix. 2014. "Citrix Mobile Analytics Report." Retrieved from http://textlab.io/doc/520042/citrix-mobile-analytics-report

CMO Council and Libris. 2015. "From Creativity to Content: The Role of Visual Media in Impactful Brand Storytelling." Retrieved from https://d3kjp0zrek7zit.cloudfront.net/uploads/attachment/file/42928/expirable-direct-uploads_2F09469a4a-87fa-43c8-afe4-a71d013c5bcb_2FCMO-Council_PhotoShelter_Whitepaper_Final.pdf

Coca-Cola. 2016. "Coca-Cola Goes for Gold in Rio 2016 Olympic Games with Global #ThatsGold Campaign." *Press Release*. Retrieved from www.coca-cola

company.com/press-center/press-releases/coca-cola-goes-for-gold-in-rio-2016-olympic-games-with-global-thatsgold-campaign

Content Marketing Institute. 2016a. "Content Marketing Framework: Story." *Content Marketing Institute.* Retrieved from http://contentmarketinginstitute.com/story/ (accessed August 11, 2016).

Content Marketing Institute. 2016b. "What Is Content Marketing." Retrieved from http://contentmarketinginstitute.com/what-is-content-marketing/ (accessed July 31, 2016).

Contently. 2016. "The Content Marketing Encyclopedia." Retrieved from https://contently.com/strategist/2016/06/29/content-marketing-101-arr-storytelling-webinar/ (accessed July 31, 2016).

Curalate. n.d. "The Complete Guide to Visual Commerce: How to Command Attention in a Visual Words." Retrieved from http://pages.curalate.com/the-complete-visual-commerce-guide.html

Curalate, and Internet Marketing Association. 2015. "The State of Visual Commerce." Retrieved from http://pages.curalate.com/rs/496-DAU-231/images/The_State_of_Visual_Commerce.pdf

Daugherty, T., and E. Hoffman. 2014. "eWOM and the Importance of Capturing Consumer Attention within Social Media." *Journal of Marketing Communications* 20, no. 1–2, pp. 82–102. doi:10.1080/13527266.2013.797764

Dixit, P. 2013. "Want Your Instagram Photos to Get Attention? Use the Color Blue." *Fast Company.* Retrieved from www.fastcompany.com/3021407/fast-feed/want-your-instagram-photos-to-get-attention-use-the-color-blue/4

Dougherty, J. 2015. "25 Pinterest Stats, Facts & PR Best Practices | Cision." *Cision.* Retrieved from www.cision.com/us/2015/01/25-pinterest-facts-and-pr-best-practices/

Dugan, L. 2012. "Infographics Shared on Twitter Get 832% More Retweets Than Images and Articles." *Adweek.* Retrieved from www.adweek.com/socialtimes/infographics-on-twitter/468324

Duggan, M. 2013. "Photo and Video Sharing Grow Online." Retrieved from www.pewinternet.org/2013/10/28/photo-and-video-sharing-online/

Edmondson, J. 2014. "3 Brands That Get Storytelling Right—and How You Can Do It Too." *Brandwatch Blog.* Retrieved from www.brandwatch.com/2014/11/3-brands-get-storytelling-right-can/

ElBoghdady, D. 2012. "'Pink Slime' Outrage Goes Viral in Stunning Display of Social Media's Power." *The Washington Post.*

Elliot, N. 2015. "How Does Your Brand Stack Up on Facebook, Twitter and Instagram?" *Forrester: Nate Elliot's Blog.* Retrieved from http://blogs.forrester.com/nate_elliot/15-09-15-how_does_your_brand_stack_up_on_facebook_twitter_and_instagram

Elliot, S. 2012. "Coke Revamps Website to Tell Its Story." *The New York Times*, November 11. Retrieved from www.nytimes.com/2012/11/12/business/media/coke-revamps-web-site-to-tell-its-story.html?_r=0

Eveleth, R. n.d. "How Many Photographs of You Are Out There in the World?" *The Atlantic*. Retrieved from www.theatlantic.com/technology/archive/2015/11/how-many-photographs-of-you-are-out-there-in-the-world/413389/

Felder, R.M., and L.K. Silberman. 1988. "Learning and Teaching Styles." *Engineering Education* 78, no. 7, pp. 674–81.

Frier, S. 2016. "Snapchat User 'Stories' Fuel 10 Billion Daily Video Views." *Bloomberg*. Retrieved from www.bloomberg.com/news/articles/2016-04-28/snapchat-user-content-fuels-jump-to-10-billion-daily-video-views

Grady, D. 1993. "The Vision Thing; Mainly in the Brain." *Discover*. Retrieved from http://discovermagazine.com/1993/jun/thevisionthingma227

Grass, R.C., and U.H. Wallace. 1974. "Advertising Communication: Print vs. TV." *Journal of Advertising Research* 14, no. 5, pp. 19–23.

Guido, M. 2016. "10 Brutal Trend and Campaign Hashtag Fails + Lessons to Learn from Them." *Keyhole*. Retrieved from http://keyhole.co/blog/10-trend-campaign-hashtag-fails-by-big-brands-lessons/

Gunelius, S. 2013. "5 Secrets To Use Storytelling for Brand Marketing Success." *Forbes*. Retrieved from www.forbes.com/sites/work-in-progress/2013/02/05/5-secrets-to-using-storytelling-for-brand-marketing-success/#1e344bfa3dd9

Gupta, A. 2013. "The Shift from Words to Pictures and Implications for Digital Marketers." *Forbes*. Retrieved from www.forbes.com/sites/onmarketing/2013/07/02/the-shift-from-words-to-pictures-and-implications-for-digital-marketers/#586b936c2549

Hoffman, E., and T. Daugherty. 2013. "Is a Picture Always Worth a Thousand Words? Attention to Structural Elements of Ewom for Consumer Brands Within Social Media." In *Advances in Consumer Research*, eds. S. Botti and A. Labroo. Association for Consumer Research. Retrieved from www.acrwebsite.org/volumes/v41/acr_v41_14817-pdf

Hu, Y., L. Manikonda, and S. Kambhampati. 2014. "What We Instagram: A First Analysis of Instagram Photo Content and User Types." In *Proceedings of the 8th International AAAI Conference on Weblogs and Social Media*. Association for Advancement of Artifical Intelligence. Retrieved from www.aaai.org/ocs/index.php/ICWSM/ICWSM14/paper/view/8118/8087

Johnson, L. 2015. "Here's Why GIFs Are Back in Style and Bigger Than Ever for Brands: Creators Race for Marketers' 'Loopy' Business." *Adweek*. Retrieved from www.adweek.com/news/technology/heres-why-gifs-are-back-style-and-bigger-ever-brands-165499

King, C. 2016. "5 Ways to Use Cinemagraphs in Digital Marketing Campaigns." *Flixel Blog*. Retrieved from http://blog.flixel.com/5-ways-to-use-cinema graphs-in-digital-marketing-campaigns/

Kitroeff, N., and J. Lorin. 2015. "Students Bombed the SAT This Year, in Four Charts." *Bloomberg*. Retrieved from www.bloomberg.com/news/ articles/2015-09-03/students-bombed-the-sat-this-year-in-four-charts

Kozinets, R.V., K. De Valck, A.C. Wojnicki, and S.J.S. Wilner. 2010. "Networked Narratives: Understaniidng Word-of-Mouth Marketing in Online Communities." *Journal of Marketing* 74, no. 2, pp. 71–89.

Kremer, W. 2015. "Are Humans Getting Cleverer?" *BBC News*. Retrieved from www.bbc.com/news/magazine-31556802

Kwon, E.S., and Y. Sung. 2011. "Follow Me! Global Marketers' Twitter Use." *Journal of Interactive Advertising* 12, no. 1, pp. 4–16. doi:10.1080/1525201 9.2011.10722187

Laskey, H., E. Day, and M. Crask. 1989. "Typology of Main Message Strategies for Television Commercials." *Journal of Advertising* 18, no. 1, pp. 36–41.

Laughlin, S. 2016. "Q& A: David Rose, CEO, Ditto Labs." *J. Walter Thompson Intelligence*. Retrieved from www.jwtintelligence.com/2016/03/david-rose-ceo-ditto-labs/

Lee, K. 2014. "The Proven Ideal Length of Every Tweet, Facebook Post, and Headline Online." *Fast Company*, April. Retrieved from www.fastcompany. com/3028656/work-smart/the-proven-ideal-length-of-every-tweet-facebook-post-and-headline-online

Libert, K. 2014. "Here's What 2.7 Billion Social Shares Say about Content Marketing." *Marketingland*. Retrieved from http://marketingland.com/heres-2-7-billion-social-shares-say-state-online-publishing-99572

Lieb, R., J. Groopman, and C. Li. 2014. "The Content Marketing Software Landscape: Marketer Needs and Vendor Solutions." Retrieved from www. altimetergroup.com/pdf/reports/Content-Marketing-Software-Landscape. pdf

Lowry, B. 2013. "Beautify Your Content: 8 Image Features That Shine on Pinterest." *Curalate Blog*. Retrieved from www.curalate.com/blog/8-image-features-that-shine-on-pinterest/

Meeker, M. 2014 "Internet Trends 2014—Code Conference." Retrieved from www.kpcb.com/blog/2014-internet-trends

Meeker, M. 2016. "Internet Trends 2016—Code Conference." Retrieved from www.kpcb.com/internet-trends

Moon, G. 2014. "Make Your Content More Sharable with These Simple Tricks, Backed by Research." *Buffer*. Retrieved from https://blog.bufferapp.com/ shareable-content-social-media-research

Moore, R. 2012. "Pinterest Data Analysis: An Inside Look." *The Datapoint.* Retrieved from https://blog.rjmetrics.com/2012/02/15/pinterest-data-analysis-an-inside-look/

Morrison, K. 2015. "How Many Photos Are Uploaded to Snapchat Every Second." *Adweek.* Retrieved from www.adweek.com/socialtimes/how-many-photos-are-uploaded-to-snapchat-every-second/621488

Moye, J. 2016. "JourneyxJourney: The Coca-Cola Company Embarks on Cross-Country Storytelling Road Trip." *Coca-Cola Journey.* Retrieved from www.coca-colacompany.com/stories/journeyxjourney-the-coca-cola-company-embarks-on-cross-country-storytelling-roadtrip

Mullins, J. 2016. "We Attempted to Decode the Most Popular Internet Acronyms Used by Teens and It Didn't Go Great." *E!News.* Retrieved from www.eonline.com/news/732369/we-attempted-to-decode-the-most-popular-internet-acronyms-used-by-teens-and-it-didn-t-go-great

Murphy, S. 2012. "How to Get More Likes, Shares on Facebook." *Mashable.* Retrieved from http://mashable.com/2012/06/19/how-to-get-more-likes-shares-on-facebook-infographic/#SrvzU.0Boiqt

Nelson-Field, K., E. Riebe, and B. Sharp. 2013. "Emotions and Sharing." In *Viral Marketing: The Science of Sharing,* eds. K. Nelson-Field and B. Sharp, First, 13–32. South Melbourne, Australia: Oxford University Press.

Nelson-Field, K., J. Taylor, and N. Hartnett. 2013. "The Pay Off." In *Viral Marketing: The Science of Sharing,* eds. K. Nelson-Field and B. Sharp, First, 69–78. South Melbourne, Australia: Oxford University Press.

Newton, C. 2016. "You Can Now Record 60-Second Videos in Instagram." *The Verge.* Retrieved from www.theverge.com/tech/2016/3/29/11325294/instagram-video-60-seconds

O'Brien, J. 2012. "How Red Bull Takes Content Marketing to the Extreme." *Mashable.* Retrieved from http://mashable.com/2012/12/19/red-bull-content-marketing/#oBPQRljrL5qN

Paivio, A., T.B. Rogers, and P. Smythe. 1968. "Why Are Pictures Easier to Recall Than Words?" *Psychonomic Science* 11, no. 4, pp. 137–38.

Park, C., and T.M. Lee. 2009. "Information Direction, Website Reputation and the eWOM Effect: A Moderating Role of Product Type." *Journal of Business Research* 62, no. 1, pp. 61–67.

Patel, N. 2014. "What Type of Content Gets Shared the Most on Twitter." *Quicksprout Blog.* Retrieved from www.quicksprout.com/2014/03/05/what-type-of-content-gets-shared-the-most-on-twitter/

Pensiero, K. 2015. "Alylan Kurdi and the Photos That Change History." *The Washington Street Journal,* September 11. Retrieved from www.wsj.com/articles/aylan-kurdi-and-the-photos-that-change-history-1442002594

Pfeffer, J., T. Zorbach, and K.M. Carley. 2014. "Understanding Online Firestorms: Negative Word-of-Mouth Dynamics in Social Media Networks." *Journal of Marketing Communications* 20, no. 1–2, pp. 117–28. doi:10.1080 /13527266.2013.797778

Piekut, K. 2015. "How Cinemagraphs Are Helping Brands Break Away from Static Content." *Econsultancy Blog*. Retrieved from https://econsultancy.com/ blog/66568-how-cinemagraphs-are-helping-brands-break-away-from-static-content/

Pieters, R., and M. Wedel. 2004. "Attention Capture and Transfer in Advertising: Brand, Pictorial, and Text-Size Effects." *Journal of Marketing* 68, no. 2, pp. 36–50.

Richins, M.L. 1983. "Negative Word-of-Mouth By Dissatisfied Consumers: A Pilot Study." *Journal of Marketing* 47, no. 1, pp. 68–78.

Ripen Ecommerce. 2014. "Adding Pinterest to Your Ecommerce Strategy." Retrieved from www.ripenecommerce.com/blog/pinterest-for-ecommerce

Rogers, S. 2014. "What Fuels a Tweet's Engagement." *Twitter Blog*. Retrieved from https://blog.twitter.com/2014/what-fuels-a-tweets-engagement

Romanek, J. 2013. "Tweet Tips: Most Effective Calls to Action on Twitter." *Twitter Blog*. Retrieved from https://blog.twitter.com/2013/tweet-tips-most-effective-calls-to-action-on-twitter

Shaer, M. 2014. "What Emotion Goes Viral the Fastest." *Smithsonian*. Retrieved from www.smithsonianmag.com/science-nature/what-emotion-goes-viral-fastest-180950182/?no-ist

Shopify. 2016. "How Pinterest Drives Online Commerce." Retrieved from www. shopify.com/infographics/pinterest (accessed August 15, 2016).

Singh, S.N., P.V. Lessig, D. Kim, R. Gupta, and M.A. Hocutt. 2000. "Does Your Ad Have Too Many Pictures?" *Journal of Advertising Research* 40, no. 1, pp. 11–27.

Snow, S. 2015. "State of Content Marketing 2016: The Tipping Point." *Contently*. Retrieved from https://contently.com/strategist/2015/12/17/state-of-content-marketing-2016/

Solis, B. 2010. "7 Scientific Ways to Promote Sharing on Facebook—Brian Solis." Retrieved from www.briansolis.com/2010/05/facebook-sharing-driven-by-simplicity/

Stenberg, G. 2006. "Conceptual and Perceptual Factors in the Picture Superiority Effect." *European Journal of Cognitive Psychology* 18, no. 6, pp. 813–47.

Stich, L., G. Golla, and A. Nanopoulos. 2014. "Modelling the Spread of Negative Word-of-Mouth in Online Social Networks." *Journal of Decision Systems* 23, no. 2, pp. 230–21. doi:10.1080/12460125.2014.886494

Tierney, J. 2010. "Will You Be E-Mailing This Column? It's Awesome." *The New York Times*, February 8. Retrieved from www.nytimes.com/2010/02/09/ science/09tier.html

Washenko, A. 2015. "The 75 Most Important Social Media Acronyms." *Sproutsocial Blog*. Retrieved from http://sproutsocial.com/insights/social-media-acronyms/

Werner, K.R. 1984. "Effects of Emotional Pictorial Elements in Ads Analyzed by Means of Eye Movement Monitoring." In *Advances in Consumer Research*, ed. T. Kinnear, 591–96. Association for Consumer Research. Retrieved from www.acrwebsite.org/volumes/6313/volumes/v11/NA-11

Zarrella, D. 2009. "The Science of Retweets." Retrieved from www.slideshare.net/danzarrella/the-science-of-re-tweets/24-ReTweets_are_Social_and_Concrete

Zarrella, D. 2010. "The Most Facebook—Sharable Words." *Dan Zarrella*. Retrieved from http://danzarrella.com/the-most-facebook-shareable-words/

Zarrella, D. 2012a. "How to Get More Pins and Repins on Pinterest." *Dan Zarrella*. Retrieved from http://danzarrella.com/infographic-how-to-get-more-pins-and-repins-on-pinterest/

Zarrella, D. 2012b. "New Facebook Data Proves Social CTAs Lead to More Comments, Likes & Shares." *HubSpot*. Retrieved from http://blog.hubspot.com/blog/tabid/6307/bid/33860/New-Facebook-Data-Proves-Social-CTAs-Lead-to-More-Comments-Likes-Shares-INFOGRAPHIC.aspx#sm.00018n9uis1172fifrc4xqq28xm0f

Zarrella, D. 2013a. "New Data Shows the 7 Most Powerful Calls-To-Actions for More Retweets." *Dan Zarrella*. Retrieved from http://danzarrella.com/new-data-shows-the-7-most-powerful-calls-to-action-for-more-retweets/

Zarrella, D. 2013b. "Tweets between 100–115 Characters Are More Likely to Be Retweeted." *Dan Zarrella*. Retrieved from http://danzarrella.com/new-data-tweets-between-100-and-115-characters-are-more-likely-to-be-retweeted/

Zarrella, D. 2013c. "Use 'Quotes' and #Hashtags to Get More Retweets." *Dan Zarrella*. Retrieved from http://danzarrella.com/new-data-use-quotes-and-hashtags-to-get-more-retweets/

Zarrella, D. 2014. "The Science of Instagram." *Dan Zarrella*. Retrieved from http://danzarrella.com/infographic-the-science-of-instagram/

CHAPTER 7

Social Influence: The Power of Persuasion

Do you remember the famous line from the 1989 movie *Field of Dreams*, starring Kevin Costner? "If you build it, he will come." Many companies have, in the past, and some continue to do so today, assume that social media is a field of dreams—build a social presence and consumers will connect with your company. Unfortunately, that is not the case. Simply having a social presence is not enough. To have overall success in social media and encourage social word of mouth (sWOM), your company needs to apply the powers of persuasion.

One of the best-known and respected scholars on the topic of persuasion, Dr. Robert Cialdini, offers six principles of social influence that can also be applied to social media. Dr. Cialdini, by observing the persuasion tactics of influential people (i.e., religious leaders, salespeople, telemarketers, and so on), followed by experimental studies, developed the persuasion principles of reciprocity, scarcity, authority, consistency, likeability, and consensus. Cialdini outlines these in his book, *Influence: The Psychology of Persuasion* and more recently, *Yes: 50 Scientifically Proven Ways to Be Persuasive*. Both are great reads. How do we apply these principles to social media communication?

Reciprocity

The principle of reciprocity is the idea that people feel obligated to give back when they receive something. And, all of us have felt the influential power of the need to reciprocate. Did you ever get a birthday present from someone and then felt required to return the favor when it was their big day (even if you had not originally planned on it)? Have you made sure you returned a dinner invite after being guests at your friend's home?

There are also numerous examples of how this principle has been applied in commercial settings. Most commonly, it can be seen in business gift giving (e.g., holiday card or gift from a company). It also might be as small as a coupon, calendar, or magnet. A common fundraising tactic that many charities use is giving potential donors personalized address label stickers in their donation request mailing. The idea, of course, is that you if you receive (and use) this gift, you will feel obligated to donate. The impact of this principle is enhanced when the gift is unexpected, personalized, and it ideally should happen *before* you ask them to provide personal information, share the information with others, or make a purchase (Cialdini 2006).

The practice of reciprocity is alive and well in the online arena. Take, for example, Dropbox that offers free storage if you share details of your adoption of the service with friends. Another common practice for companies and bloggers alike is to provide great content via posts, white papers, webinars, and sometimes, e-books in the hopes that you will provide them with your e-mail address. Offering digital free samples, such as the first chapter of an e-books, is another great way to increase the likelihood of a reader purchasing the entire book. So, how can this principle relate to social media? First, social media can be used as the method of distributing great content. Market research company, eMarketer, uses it to distribute articles and reports. They send out e-mail messages and tweets to subscribers of their digital newsletter with a link to new content that their faithful followers can download and then share it with others. Another approach is to provide a small favor or acknowledge the value of your consumers or followers. For example, retweeting or sharing an individual's posts makes them more likely to return the retweet or share. Commenting, liking, @mentions, and tagging are also forms of acknowledgment that may increase your likelihood of having consumers not only engage with your brand, but share your content.

Reciprocity is also at the heart of what has been called "surprise and delight" marketing campaigns. In essence, marketers are connecting with consumers often via social media (or at least finding them when on social monitoring platforms) and providing them with surprise gifts (birthday, holiday, or "just because"), personalized product samples, coupons, or reward discounts. This element of surprise, some would argue, is one of the most powerful marketing tools. It can be addictive, drive behavior change, improve brand perceptions, and magnify emotions. It can also add some needed excitement into not only a personal, but also a commercial relationship (Redick 2013; Harris 2015). It can be used to reward loyal consumers, and "re-engage" consumers that have become rather dormant online (CrowdTwist 2015).

Surprise and delight campaigns can be very effective strategies that are relatively inexpensive. Take, for instance, Kleenex's Feel Good campaign. During winter, Kleenex found 50 consumers in Israel who were discussing their illness on Facebook. They prepared a personalized Kleenex Kit, contacted connected Facebook friends to get a physical address, and sent the package to the ill individuals via a courier within 1–2 hours of the post. Every person who got a kit posted a photo with a positive message on their Facebook wall. The result was over 650,000 impressions and 1,800 interactions (Shaprio 2012). While this had an incredible response rate, getting consumers to share their surprise on social media is not that uncommon (CrowdTwist 2015). One Canadian survey found that women were more likely than men to tell family and friends about a surprise and delight experience (Harris 2015).

Reciprocity commonly blurs the online and offline lines. To illustrate, Bud Light's #UpforWhatever campaign, which culminated in the creation of a fictional city called Whatever, USA (aka Crested Butte, Colorado), became a "content factory" for social media. One thousand consumers were selected out for 200,000 applicants for a weekend filled with random surprises, which included a faux beach, 80s pop star Vanilla Ice, and circus rides. Only 50 of the 37,000 pieces of content that were shared online were created by Bud Light; the rest were all consumer-created (Monllos 2015; Hughes 2014).

Authority

Authority or expert status is a classic method of persuasion used in marketing (Cialdini 2006). From an early age, we have been brought up to listen, respect, and be obedient to those in authority. Therefore, it is not surprising that this principle also works in relationship to making consumption choices. Consumers will often turn to experts, especially if they are not sure about a consumption decision. The idea being—they know better than me. Marketers have long been aware of the importance of communicating authority in marketing material using both explicit and symbolic means in establishing it. Think back to TV commercials that contain a lawyer (or actor) seated at his or her desk surrounded by framed diplomas and leather bound books, or cliché advertising statements like "9 out of 10 doctors recommended [insert product here]." Forewords on books written by experts, a high consumer report rating, and product ownership by a fashionable, well-photographed celebrity are some of the countless examples of how you can convey authority in a consumer culture.

Online, the same principles apply. Amazon highlights positive comments from well-known experts in the book description. Bloggers will often state on their website (using appropriate media logos) newspapers, magazine, and TV shows where they have been featured. Website URL addresses that end in .edu or .gov or also examples of how authority can be quickly and succinctly conveyed online.

Within the cluttered, muddied waters of social media, we could argue that authority and credibility matters even more, and social media platforms have also realized its importance. The most popular social media platforms have devised quick, visual shorthands to indicate whether an account is "officially" from a celebrity or business. Social media platforms have created verifications symbols, often in the form of a checkmark located next to a user's profile information. There are also additional cues to indicate legitimacy—year that the account opened, location, dedicated #hashtag campaign, and simply providing a coherent description void of spelling and grammar mistakes. Also, the careful selection of cover and profile photos, the use of logos, the selection of keywords, and the reporting of accomplishments in your bio or company description can all help convey authority. We will discuss these in greater detail in Chapter 8.

Scarcity

If you spend a view minutes watching the Home Shopping Network (HSN) or QVC, you have seen the scarcity principle in action. Both of these networks include a countdown clock of just how many items and time is left to purchase this shiny, new product that will certainly make your life better. McDonald's owes the success of the McRib and Shamrock Shake to the limited time they are listed on the menu. Yes, there is something extra appealing about a product that seems to be going away in the very near future or is only offered to a "select" group of people.

An increasing number of e-commerce websites are also putting this principle into practice. Consider the value-travel website Expedia. After searching for a hotel, you are not only notified on the price, but also (in red font) told how many rooms are left at this rate. To further punctuate the scarcity principle, the site includes a "Daily Deal" countdown clock, which lets you know how little time you have left to grab this great deal. The site also tells you just how many others are looking at this deal to entice you further into a purchase. In general, e-commerce stores are doing a better job indicating how close an item is to selling out. Scarcity has also been used to launch new services online. In 2004, Gmail began solely through invitations—you could only have an account if someone invited you. Scarcity has also been used in a similar way to launch a new social media platform. This strategy worked for Facebook who at first restricted account membership to Harvard students, before slowly allowing other universities and high schools to join, by which time the rest of us all were eager to have our account. One could also argue the success of Snapchat has largely to do with the limited viewing time of their photos—although the platform has evolved to keep some of these photos under "Memories." Agurably, social media best utilizes the scarcity principle by distributing messages that incorporate access to content for a limited time, offering discount coupons and exclusive deals for a "select" consumer group, and short-duration contests (e.g., best photo with product + Halloween theme posted by the end of today).

Commitment and Consistency

Consumers are generally committed to engaging in future behavior that is consistent with their prior behavior (Cialdini 2006). For example, if a consumer has supported a company in the past, they are more likely to support it in the future. If a consumer likes your post on Facebook, then there is a good chance that he would be willing to share that post with his social network. Sometimes, the consumer just needs to be asked. Think about the number of times you have been asked to make a commitment—"please like," "please retweet," "download," "subscribe here." The key for marketers is to get a consumer to make a small commitment, often referred to as the *foot in the door* technique, which in time, may lead to a larger commitment such as a recommendation or purchase. Commitment can begin with the consumer following your page, followed by liking a post, providing a comment, sharing the post with his network, talking about the brand, and recommending the company or brand to others. This commitment needs to be acknowledged by the company. For instance, when a consumer follows your company Twitter account, respond with a "Thanks @carriemunoz for following, be sure to check out our xxx." In acknowledging the act, you are also reminding the consumer of their commitment. It is highly unlikely that all your consumers will instantly make the leap from following your page to writing long, detailed recommendations. So, you need to help move your consumers through this commitment process by developing social strategies that encourage consumers to follow, like, share, comment, and so on. One popular strategy is to introduce a competition that encourages consumers to engage with the brand and to help spread positive sWOM. A company that has a history of using social media to amplify their message and to attract new business is Jetsetter. Jetsetter (a member of the TripAdvisor group) is a private online community of travelers that provides members with insider knowledge and exclusive deals on travel. To increase sWOM, the company hosts competitions on Pinterest. In one particular competition, consumers were asked to create a Pinterest board that reflected their favorite or ideal vacation in one of the four categories—escape, adventure, style, and competition. Each board was required to have "Jetsetter Curator" in the title and each pin to include the hashtag #JetsetterCurator. A panel of judges selected one winning board from each of the four vacation categories. Winners received a three-night stay at a Jetsetter destination. To encourage consumers to share their boards and pins with their friends, an additional prize of $1,000 in Jetsetter credit was awarded to the board with the largest number of followers. More than 1,100 consumers entered the competition, each posting an average of 40 images. During the two-week competition period, approximately 50,000 images were pinned each containing the hashtag #JetsetterCurator. Traffic from Pinterest to the company's webpage increased 100 percent, page views 150 percent, and the number of Pinterest followers jumped by 165 percent (Drell 2012). Once a consumer has engaged in a behavior that generates a positive response, there is a strong probability of them doing it again.

Social Proof

The persuasion principle of social proof comes down to judging something on the actions of others (Cialdini 2006). If others like it, it must be good! We often refer to this as consensus. For example, would you rather go to an empty restaurant or one with a line out the door? Would you feel more comfortable purchasing a bestseller or a book with only 120 reviews? Social proof is perhaps the most frequently used persuasion principles online and within social media. There are numerous ways to communicate social proof. E-commerce website Zulily and others are quick to point out which products sell well—adding a "popular" icon over specific product images, along with how many of these products have just been sold directly under the price. Other retail websites also provide ample opportunities for consumers to read product reviews, which can dramatically impact whether a consumer purchases a product. Product reviews have also evolved well beyond textual descriptions and now included uploaded images and videos, which only enhance their level of influence (e.g., Remember Rent the Runway from Chapter 1). Outside of product reviews, simple consumer testimonial delivered on a landing page and via social media also serve as powerful examples of social proof.

Social media metrics are not only important for marketers, but consumers and are a form of social proof. Consumers will look at available metrics (e.g., likes, shares, retweets) to determine a message's (and the messenger's) worth. Consumers are more likely to value and share information gleaned from an account with an abundance of followers than they are for accounts that fail to attract the interest of consumers. The same is true with a post that has been liked, shared, retweeted, and favorited hundreds of times. Given that we see these posts from people who we know and like amplifies the effect, making us more likely to share.

Liking

There is a reason that we tend to follow the advice of our friends, family, and the occasional celebrity—it is because we like them (well, most of the time). Not only do we listen to what they say, but we often do what they ask. The secret to successes in word of mouth (WOM) marketing is to be likable. The secret to successes in word of mouth (WOM) marketing is to be likable. So, how can a company get consumers to like them on social media? Success begins at the source of the message, followed by the content of the message. Given that Chapter 6 discussed at length the content of your message, we will focus our discussion here on the source of the message.

If you are fortunate enough to have someone within your company who is well-liked by your consumers, then it may be helpful to have him or her contribute to your social media. Take, for example, Richard Branson, founder of the Virgin Group. When posting to his personal social media accounts, he frequently tags a Virgin company account. The account then retweets or shares the posting with their followers. Branson's Facebook, LinkedIn, and Twitter posts attract hundreds of comments and thousands of shares. In the advertising world, they would say that Branson has social value. His social value originates from his personality and social status. Another factor that also contributes to his social value is his credibility, perceived expertise, objectivity, and trustworthiness. When a communication source has high social value, this can result in a halo effect. A halo effect is a cognitive bias in which the overall positive impression that we have of one person can transfer to another person, product, or unrelated item (Solomon 2017). So, when Branson mentions or recommends a product, service, idea, or another person on social media, the positive feelings that a consumer has about Branson may transfer to the item or person mentioned. But, what if your company does not have a Richard Branson (and let's be honest most companies do not), how do you get consumers to like your brand? Having a famous person posting on your social media can be helpful, but it is not always necessary. Everyday consumers can be just as influential. Have you ever noticed a posting in your Facebook newsfeed that said that one of your friends liked a specific brand? Have you found yourself retweeting or sharing something that a good friend or colleague posted, even if you were not all that familiar with the item or topic they mentioned? If so, the chances are that the person who posted the item is a good friend, someone, who in your eyes, has social value. In Chapter 2, we discussed the power of social consumers and social influencers, everyday people who have the ability to reach and influence a large number of consumers. In the same chapter we examined how companies are using these social influencers to spread positive sWOM. It may be appropriate for your company to solicit the help of influencers to mention your company on social media or to contribute guest posts. We also discussed how your network of followers could be helpful. Each of your followers on social media has the power and potential to introduce your company to a new group of consumers. Tourism Australia offers a great example of how everyday consumers can be influential in spreading sWOM.

Social Sharing at Tourism Australia

Tourism Australia is an Australian government agency founded in 2004, charged with developing strategies to promote Australia as a destination for leisure and business travel. The agency has a website, LinkedIn profile and Twitter account under the name Tourism Australia (www.tourism.australia.com) and a website, Facebook, Twitter, Google+, Instagram, and YouTube account under the name Australia (www.australia.com). Tourism Australia recognized that, perhaps, their greatest asset in spreading the word about Australia was not their social media team of three, but their then 4 million plus Facebook fans (@SeeAustralia.com), 23 million residents, and 6 million international visitors (Jafri 2013). To encourage sWOM, the agency decided to try something that many companies and organizations would shy away from—they turned their Facebook page over to their fans. Fans and followers were responsible for deciding what they wanted to see on Facebook, were allowed submit items for sharing, and empowered to respond to questions posted online. The process began by inviting fans and followers to submit personal photographs of Australia. Fans posted these photographs using a photoboard app and with the understanding that their photographs may be used for promotional purposes. Over 1,000 photographs showcasing iconic landmarks, flora and fauna, and natural scenic beauty were submitted each day and shared on Facebook and Instagram. Whereas many of these photographs showed current day Australia, some dated back as far as 1910. Each week approximately 35 of the photographs were chosen by the Tourism Australia social media team to be published in a digital album—Friday Fan Photos. Every image chosen was designed to tell a story and allow for a story to be told (Tourism Australia 2013). When a picture was posted, other fans would add comments, provide additional details, and add their perspective to create a rich narrative of life in Australia. Fans were even allowed to add their family photos to the timeline. These photographs promoted a series of discussions on traditions and vacations particularly among family and friends who may not, at least at that time been a follower of the Tourism Australia page. This approach allowed Tourism Australia to extend their reach in a more personal less promotional manner. Fans, whose photographs were posted, became experts, actively engaging with other fans and responding to questions about their photograph. Fans were even asked to recommend captions for individual photographs. Many of these consumer-generated photos attracted thousands of likes, shares, and comments. After turning their social media over to their fans, Tourism Australia's Facebook page became the most liked page in Australia and the post popular destination page in the world (Jafri 2013).

So, how do social influence and persuasion apply to this example?

Reciprocity

Tourism Australia posted consumer photographs to the agency's social media account. They hand-selected a small number each week to be published in a digital album. This act alone communicates to consumers that the agency has seen and valued their contribution, which is likely to motivate consumers to continue to participate.

Authority

There is no one more qualified to talk about what it is like to live in Australia than their residents, and no one more qualified to talk about how wonderful a place it is to visit than tourists. It is easy for social media accounts like Tourism Australia's to become just another marketing channel, with professional photographs accompanied with carefully crafted advertising. But, as we know, social media is about communicating. So, by turning the account over to their fans and followers who are the real experts, the account loses that promotional feel and its place something more authentic emerges. Personal photographs and stories from real people help to increase the persuasiveness of the message, particularly when they are shared by someone you know.

Commitment and Consistency

If you posted a photograph on Tourism Australia's Facebook page and that photograph generated likes, comments, and questions, would you feel compelled to jump in, engage with these other consumers, and answer their questions? If your photograph was one of the 35 selected for Fan Photo Fridays, would you want to share that with your social network? When Tourism Australia empowered their fans to answer questions, they were encouraging them to continue to engage with the page.

Social Proof

The more likes, comments, and shares that a posting receives, the more likely it is to appear in a consumer's newsfeed and the potential for greater engagement. We tend to "like" what our network of friends and family like. When this social proof originates from those whom we love, like, admire, or respect, the posting has personal relevance and we are motivated to engage.

Liking

We have no doubt that celebrities like actors Hugh Jackman and Chris Hemsworth are great ambassadors for Australia and that consumers will watch their Tourism Australia commercials on YouTube and Facebook. Indeed, famous faces that we admire and respect are highly successful at capturing our attention. However, beyond the initial "like," we are unlikely to engage any further, and therefore the persuasiveness of the message is limited. But, when your BBF, brother, second cousin twice removed, or friend from kindergarten posts a picture that resonates with you and tells a familiar story, a story that you can and want to contribute to it has more influence. It may be a current photograph or one from yesteryear that evokes feelings of nostalgia. Either way, your desire to engage with it is greater, and because of this, its likely that you will move beyond simply liking the photo to commenting (perhaps repeatedly) and sharing the image with others by either tagging them in your comment or hitting the "Share" button.

So, what can you learn from Tourism Australia that you can apply to your company?

- Let your consumers guide the type of content you post on social media. Ask them what they want to see.

- In some cases, it is your consumers who are the experts, not your employees. Empower your consumers to be the authority figure.

- Consumer-generated content is a great way of sourcing fresh material to share on social media.

- Consumer-generated content may be perceived as more authentic, and therefore may generate higher levels of engagement. Higher engagement can lead to increased visibility.

- Consumer-generated content can help generate sWOM with your existing fan base. It also helps you extend your reach beyond your network and attract new followers.

- Always acknowledge the commitment of your consumers. Thank them for their contribution and effort. Engage them in conversation. This will encourage them to continue to engage with your account.

- Every picture you share on social media should tell a story and allow for a story to be told.

- Allow your consumers to help you tell the story.

References

Cialdini, R. 2006. *Influence: The Psychology of Persuasion*. New York, NY: Harper Business.

CrowdTwist. 2015. *How Surprise and Delight Amplifies Loyalty Marketing Strategies*. Retrieved from http://media.dmnews.com/documents/112/surprise_whitepaper_020415_onl_27880.pdf

Drell, L. 2012. "How Pinterest Boosted Jetsetter's Traffic by 150%." *Mashable*. Retrieved from http://mashable.com/2012/05/23/jetsetter-pinterest/#WITprIiAcl?qf

Harris, R. 2015. "Why Brand Should 'Surprise and Delight' Customers (Survey)." *Marketing*, December.

Hughes, Trevor. 2014. "Bud Light Turns Tiny Ski Town into Whatever, USA." *USA Today*, September.

Jafri, S. 2013. "9 Content Marketing Lessons from Tourism Australia | Search Engine Watch." *Search Engine Watch*. doi:2016-08-11

Monllos, K. 2015. "Whatever, USA: Bud Light's Party Town as 'Content Factory.'" *Adweek*, June.

Redick, Scott. 2013. "Surprise Is Still the Most Powerful Marketing Tool." *Harvard Business Review*, May.

Shaprio, Levi. 2012. "Social Media Campaigns That Achieve the Unthinkable: 100% Response Rates." *The Jerusalem Post*, April.

Solomon, Michael R. 2017. *Consumer Behavior: Buying Having, and Being*. 12th ed. Hoboken, NJ: Pearson.

Tourism Australia. 2013. "The World's Biggest Social Media Team." Retrieved from www.slideshare.net/TourismAustralia/the-worlds-biggest-social-media-team-16545786

CHAPTER 8

sWOM on Popular Platforms

In our final chapter, we offer suggestions on how to encourage positive social word of mouth (sWOM) on popular social media platforms. Our coverage of social platforms is not exhaustive. However, you will see that there are similarities in "best practices" between each platform that you can apply to platforms not covered here. The chapter begins by discussing three important components of a company's social media presence, regardless of the platform you are using; the cover and profile photos and company information. Given that the topic of content is covered in great detail in Chapter 6, in this chapter, we will provide some general comments regarding appropriate content and conclude with some platform-specific recommendations.

Cover Photograph

Where do your eyes first rest when you check out a Facebook, LinkedIn, or Twitter account? Chances are you are looking at the top left-hand corner of the screen. Our eyes quickly scan across the page (left to right) before moving down the screen (Bradley 2011). The same is true of mobile devices (Tam 2012). This eye-scanning pattern suggests that the first thing visitors see when they visit your page is the cover and profile photo. Therefore, you must make a strong, positive impact by selecting the right photo to represent your brand. A cover photo should be professional but unique. It should showcase your brand personality, so we encourage creativity. Companies that have a history of unique and creative cover photos include Old Spice (@oldpsice), Red Bull (@redbull), and Virgin Atlantic (@virginatlantic). The aim is to inspire and motivate the visitor to connect with the company. The cover photo is not a place where you share company information. It is not the place to blatantly advertise products or services. There should be no information about the price of products, discount available, company information, and certainly, no call-to-action (like, share, and so on). In fact, platforms such as Facebook prohibit this practice (Loren 2012). Instead, use your cover photo to communicate one of the following:

Change of season or upcoming holiday: Coke frequently changes their cover photo to coincide with upcoming holidays like Christmas.

Celebrate milestones: Companies such as Ford and Macy's change their cover photo to celebrate anniversaries or key milestones (name changes, acquisitions, and so on). These companies often dig into the company archives to find photos of historical events to post as their cover photo.

Display popular products: The iTunes cover page often includes thumbnails of music and TV shows available on the site.

Showcase new products: Apparel companies such as JCrew frequently post images of new items as a cover photo (without any product information). Music artists have been known to use the cover of their latest CD as their cover photo.

Celebrate and showcase consumers and fans: Many companies including AT&T have added photographs submitted by their fans. Sometimes, they focus on one consumer; other times, they create a mosaic of consumer images.

Highlight your employees: Numerous companies including Telecom New Zealand and the British Army have posted photographs of their employees as a way to humanize the brand.

Show your location or facilities: Telecom New Zealand has also posted photographs that offer consumers a sneak-peek behind the scenes at the company.

Profile Photograph

Your social media account is not the only place consumers will find you. Their first encounter may be from a posting that appears in their newsfeed.

When this occurs, the consumer's eye will is drawn to the company profile photo (typically found to the left of the message's content). The goal of the profile picture is similar to the cover photo; a profile picture needs to communicate your brand'spersonality. Consumers should easily recognize your company from the profile image. One popular strategy is to integrate your profile photo with your cover photo. To illustrate, imagine that your cover photo is a jigsaw puzzle, and your profile photo is one piece of that puzzle. It is clear that they two belong together, but independently, they still effectively communicate who you are. The simplest way to achieve this is by using all or part of the company logo for your profile picture. There are plenty of examples of effective cover and profile photos you can use for inspiration. To begin, review some of the social media accounts of B2B companies mentioned throughout this book (e.g., SAP, Maersk) as well as major consumer brands such as Guinness, Oreo, and Virgin Airlines. If possible and appropriate, try to adopt a similar, if not the same, cover and profile photos for each social media platform to maintain a consistent brand identity.

Company Information

As you know, each social media platform should contain a description of your company in the designated section (e.g., Facebook—About, Twitter—bio). But, what some companies do not realize is that the content and tone of the company description should vary depending on the platform. Recall that consumers use different social media platforms for different reasons. Therefore, consumer expectations for content will also be different for each platform. For instance, a company's presence on LinkedIn should be somewhat formal, sharing the story of the company, mission, and value proposition. In contrast, the informality of Facebook lends itself to an abbreviated and less official sounding description. Twitter only permits a bio of up to 160 characters. On this platform, the company description needs to be not only short and sharp, but also creative. Do not let Twitter's space limitations discourage you. A short bio can still be highly effective at communicating who you are, the purpose of the account, and displaying your brand personality. Check out these examples:

Virgin Atlantic's (@VirginAtlantic) sassy Twitter bio.

"Hello Gorgeous! Follow us for news, banter & assistance 24/7. Visit our blog at ...virg.in/rubyblog or for official concern visit ...virg.in/crel."

Old Spice's bio (@OldSpice) is certainly to the point, but at the same time, conveys the brand's comedic side, which is sure to appeal to their young male consumers.

"MUSCLES.SMELLS.LASERS.COUPONS.GIFS."

Amnesty International is an organization with a more serious agenda, but they still manage to convey the importance of their work in a less somber manner (@amnesty).

"We've been fighting the bad guys since 1961-you can join us! Official Amnesty International USA profile. RT≠endorsements."

If conveying authority and expertise is something that is important, your bio should be rich in authority keywords, official titles, prominent clients served, and highlight achievements (i.e., awards, books, and so on), just like Michael Bloomberg's (@MikeBloomberg).

"Entrepreneur, philanthropist, and three-term mayor of New York City."

To better understand how a company's description is different on each of their platforms, consider the following two examples:

Taco Bell: The fast-food chain's LinkedIn page includes a 295-word company description that includes the company's purpose, the size of their workforce, and number of restaurants worldwide. They also include information on their charitable contributions and community outreach. On Facebook, the company overview is only 79 words and communicates their number of customers and major achievements (e.g., 1 billion burritos served each year). In contrast, their Twitter bio is only two words—Live Más (translation: Live More).

SAP: SAP's 79-word LinkedIn bio describes the company as a market leader and includes their number of customers and the countries where they operate. At 55 words, their Facebook description is an abbreviated version of their LinkedIn description. Their Twitter bio simply communicates that this is their official account and includes the name of the employee responsible for all Twitter postings.

To solidify your authority, you should seek approval to have each of your social media accounts verified. Popular platforms such as Facebook and Twitter will verify social media accounts that are of public interest. A verification symbol, typically in the form of a small icon or badge, will appear on your company's bio and help establish the authenticity of the account.

Content

Throughout this book, we have stressed the importance of posting content that consumers expect and value, but that also reflects your brand. Chapter 6 discussed the importance of storytelling—how to create story content, the creative strategies that marketers can employ, and the importance of textual and visual content. We also discussed that the type and format of the content you post should vary depending upon the platform on which it is shared. Although it is not uncommon to share the same piece of information across social media platforms, it may not always be the best option. Content needs to be calibrated to each platform. When deciding where and what to post, you must ask yourself the following questions (Figure 8.1):

- What is the objective of this account?
- Which consumers are using this platform?
- What is it that my consumers' want to see on this particular platform?
- When (at what time of the day and days of the week) are they most likely to be on this platform?
- In what format do they want to receive this information?

Once you have answered these questions, you then need to take into consideration how social media platforms decide what content makes it into a consumer's news feed and what content becomes digital waste. That is, beyond knowing what it is that your consumers want, you also need to know what content each platform values and will give the greatest visibility. You need to have a basic understanding of newsfeed algorithms. All social media accounts use algorithms to determine which content receives the highest priority and greatest visibility. Algorithms are

Creating Content for Social Media

5 Questions to Answer

1 What is the objective of this account?

E.g. Strengthen brand reputation, share information, improve customer service, recruit new employees, foster pride among employees.

2 Which consumers are on this platform?

E.g. Facebook - Women 18-40 yrs of use.

3 What content do my consumers want to see on this particular account?

E.g. Facebook - fun company photos, LinkedIn - industry news, Blog - company updates.

4 When are they most likely to be on this platform?

E.g. Facebook - daily, early afternoon.

5 In what format do they want to receive this information?

E.g. Videos, infographics, blogs, white papers, photographs

Figure 8.1 Creating content for social media

particularly important on social platforms that have fast moving news-feeds, such as Facebook and Twitter. Not surprisingly, these algorithms are proprietary, but that does not stop marketers from trying to crack the code and use the algorithm to their advantage. The algorithm that receives the most attention and the one that marketers (think) they know the most about is Facebook.

Reports suggest that the variables used in the Facebook algorithm include the type of content, timing of content, interactions, and the relationship between the consumer and the person or company who posted the item (Hutchinson 2016) (Figure 8.2). For the type of content, Facebook appears to give visual posts (photos and videos) higher priority over text posts. This makes complete sense, because as we learned in Chapter 6, consumers are visual learners, we are drawn to and remember visuals more than we do text (Childers and Houston 1984; Paivio, Rogers, and Smythe 1968; Pieters and Wedel 2004). Social posts that include visuals are more engaging and generate higher engagement rates than text posts (Elliott 2015; eMarketer 2014). Engagement refers to the popularity of a post measured by likes, shares, comments, retweets, and so on. Regarding the timing of posts, recency is an important factor. Consumers want to see fresh content whenever they log into their account. So, timing your posts to coincide with the time of day that your consumers are most likely to be checking-in is important. Facebook wants to retain their consumers and the way they encourage repeat visits is by providing them with valuable content. Content popularity is one indicator of value. The more popular a post, measured by the number and type of engagement (e.g., likes, shares, and comments), the greater its perceived value by Facebook. Higher-value posts are more likely to appear in a consumer's

Cracking the Newsfeed Algorithm

# 01	# 02	# 03	# 04
TYPE OF CONTENT	TIMING OF CONTENT	INTERACTIONS	RELATIONSHIPS
Visual posts (photographs and videos) receive higher posting priority over text posts. Try adding a visual element to your post.	Consumers want to see fresh content. Time your posts to coincide with the time of day that they are most likely to login.	Popular or trending content receives high priority. Keep abreast of trending topics and current events. Try to find a way to contribute to the conversation.	Those consumers who interact with your account the most will see your postings in their newsfeed. Find ways to encourage consumers interact with you (like, share, comment, retweet etc.)

Figure 8.2 Cracking the Facebook algorithm

newsfeed than are low-value (unpopular) posts. The final variable, who posted it, refers to the strength of the relationship between the consumer and the company responsible for the post. As we learned in Chapter 1, not all friends are created equal. Facebook gives content posting priority to a consumer's strong ties, those users or company accounts that consumer engages with the most often. It is not uncommon for consumers to become fans of a company, but never interact with the company page or company postings. Reports suggest that as little as 0.07 percent of consumers will engage with a brand after the initial "Like" (Elliott 2015). Your company may have an amazing Facebook page, but if consumers do not visit the page or engage (like, share, comment) with your posts, then the probability that your latest post will make it into their newsfeed is very low (Brown 2016).

Twitter's algorithm is also a carefully guarded secret. However, Twitter does offer some insight stating that the tweets that a user is most interested in will appear first in his or her timeline. Twitter chooses these tweets based on consumer engagement with previous tweets, among other things (Williams 2016). Similar to Facebook, if your followers do not engage with your tweets, then future tweets are given low priority or may not appear in the timeline at all. Even though we do not fully understand how the algorithmic timelines work for other social platforms, it is fair to assume that they use similar variables: type of content, timing of content, interactions, and relationship.

If visual content receives the highest priority on a social media platform, then your posting should incorporate photographs, infographics, and videos. As we discussed in Chapter 6, we know that content that conveys high-arousal emotions increases the likelihood of engagement and more sharing behavior. Therefore, select visual assets that can trigger positive emotions and offer viewers a great story. Even though text postings do not receive the same priority as visuals, they can generate an emotional response, particularly when accompanied by a photograph. When in doubt, use both visual and text in your postings.

As we discussed earlier, there are some strategies you can use to increase content engagement and sharing behavior. Popular tactics include personalizing posts for specific consumers, hosting competitions, consumer polls, distributing coupons only on social media, personalizing content, and asking consumers to create content for your account. It may also include, acknowledging a consumer's engagement, adding hashtags, or politely encouraging consumers to share your content (i.e., please retweet or PLS RT). Remember that your company does not need to be responsible for creating all of the content that you post on social media. A good social media account incorporates a combination of consumer, company, and collaborative content. Just make sure that you choose content that is valued by your consumers, and when sharing or retweeting content created by others, make the content your own—adopt it, place your virtual stamp on it by adding a comment, and encouraging consumers to comment.

Perhaps, the most important piece of advice for increasing engagement and strengthening ties is to remember that social media is a conversation tool. You should be posting content that encourages conversation among consumers and between your company and consumers. Do not forget to thank your consumers for connecting with your account, answer their questions, share their content on your Facebook page (with their permission), retweet their messages, "like" their LinkedIn posts. You can also use social media to distribute exclusive deals and content. As we discussed earlier, creating a sense of scarcity and urgency can be very powerful at persuading consumers to act.

With the foundation created for a professional, persuasive social media pages, the next step is to identify how to create accounts that consumers want to follow and content that they want to share.

LinkedIn: The Concierge

LinkedIn is the ideal platform for allowing existing and potential customers, vendors, investors, and shareholders to learn about your company and your products. It certainly is important for all companies to have a presence on LinkedIn, but it is particularly important for B2B companies. A 2016 report reveals that 94 percent of B2B marketers have a LinkedIn profile. Sixty-six percent of these B2B companies report that LinkedIn is their most effective social media platform, followed by Twitter (55 percent) and YouTube (51 percent) (Content Marketing Institute 2016). These numbers are not surprising, given the benefits of following an individual or company on LinkedIn: to learn more about a company and their products, gain industry insights, find solutions to problems, connect with peers and colleagues, increase company or brand awareness, create a personal brand, and find prospective employees.

When using LinkedIn, you should adopt the mindset that your company is a concierge—your company's LinkedIn page exists to provide information and direction, to connect individuals and companies (Kaplan 2012). Create a page that shares the story of your company; that makes you stand out from the competition, and that includes a variety of forms of shareable content.

To build a network of influencers, you should attempt to attract a diverse selection of followers, including employees, senior management, board members, vendors, customers, shareholders, and industry experts. A simple approach to ensure continuous recruitment of followers is to include a link to the LinkedIn company page at the bottom of company e-mail signatures. Another strategy is to join and participate in existing LinkedIn groups. Identify groups where your targeted audiences might be and actively participate in popular conversation threads. Post helpful comments and questions, but leave out the sales pitch (tell, do not sell) (Kaplan 2012). Instead, you should ask questions, listen and provide guidance. The aim here is to build a rapport and position your company has an expert or opinion leader.

The key to engagement is to provide quality content; content that gives followers a reason to engage, respond, and share. Sixty percent of LinkedIn followers are interested in receiving updates on industry insights, 53 percent in company news, and 43 percent in information on new products and services (Lee 2015). This provides you with the opportunity to post all three forms of content—consumer, company, and collaborative. Consumer content includes links to relevant third-party material, including industry news, expert news, trending news, and media coverage of your company. Just remember to add a comment or post a question to increase engagement. In the area of company-generated content, LinkedIn provides the opportunity to link to a variety of existing company materials, including blogs, interviews, videos, and white papers. Your company's materials may need to be reengineered to make them more palatable—less advertising, more educational. Collaborative content may include guest blogs, case studies, and testimonials. Identify industry influencers for you to interview. Share the interview on your page. Alternatively, invite influencers to post a guest blog or a case study. Ask customers to provide testimonials.

When posting content to LinkedIn, avoid the habit of sharing every post with everyone—the "spray and pray" approach. Ask yourself if there is a specific subset of LinkedIn users that will find this particular post especially valuable. Your posts should be targeted to specific groups, job functions, or industries, so that your updates are reaching the appropriate people. Share and empower your employees to share your posts with their network of followers.

Aim to post one update (consumer, company, or collaborative) each weekday (Lee 2015). Where appropriate, include links. Research reveals that updates that include a link generate upwards of 45 percent more engagement (like, comment, share) than updates that do not include a link (Lee 2015). When you link to these items, it is important to include a comment to draw attention and encourage engagement (social proof in action). Ask followers to comment on the item or pose a question that will hopefully elicit a response. When you receive comments or responses from connections, be sure to reply. A response can be as simple as using the "like" feature to acknowledge that you have seen and read their comment, or you can respond with a new message. Posts that include YouTube videos are also reported to be a great source of engagement on LinkedIn. The inclusion of a YouTube video can attract twice as many likes and comments and 75 percent more shares (Lee 2015). In general, morning updates on LinkedIn receive the highest level of engagement, with a slight increase in the evening. However, it is important to experiment to determine the best time for your followers based on their geographical location (Kaplan 2012). Time your postings to reach the majority of your audience. See Figure 8.3 for a summary.

Facebook: The Personal Face of Your Company

LinkedIn maybe the corporate face of your company, but Facebook is the personal face. Facebook is relevant not only for B2C companies, but it can also be important for B2B companies. It provides your company

LinkedIn

On LinkedIn Your Company is a
CONCIERGE
PROVIDING DIRECTION,
INFORMATION, AND CONNECTING
PEOPLE

Reasons for Connecting

- To learn more about your company and your products
- To gain industry insights
- To find solutions to problems
- To connect with peers and colleagues
- To build their own personal brand

How to Build Connections

- Create a page that shares the story of your company
- Make sure your page stands out from the competition
- Include a variety of forms of shareable content - Consumer, Company, Collaborative
- Aim to attract a diverse selection of followers (employees, vendors, industry experts etc.)
- Identify and join LinkedIn Groups where your target audiences might be
- Actively participate in popular conversations. Post questions and helpful comments
- Avoid the sales pitch
- Provide industry insights, company news, and information on new products
- Target some of your posts to specific groups or subsets of connections
- Share your updates with your employees so that they may share with their network

Figure 8.3 LinkedIn

More Specifically

- Aim to post one update per weekday
- Where appropriate include a link or a video
- When sharing third party content add a comment to make it your own
- When someone connects with you or comments on one of your updates thank them
- Answer questions promptly
- Time your posts to reach the majority of your audience

with the opportunity to humanize and communicate your brand's mission. It is also a great way of reaching potential B2B users and influencers. Forty-four percent of those active social media users surveyed report following brands on Facebook, and 36 percent of Facebook users seek out brand information on social media (Mander 2016). As we discussed in Chapter 2, consumers follow brands on Facebook for many reasons, including as a form of self-expression, to communicate a positive association with a brand, to communicate with the brand, and to receive product information and deals (Lipsman et al. 2012; eMarketer 2015).

When developing content for Facebook, consider two factors, why people love your brand and why people share (Li 2013). The answer to the question of why people love your brand will help you focus on relevant content to post. In Chapter 3, we discussed how Maersk tapped into peoples' love of ships to help determine what to share. The company shared current and historical photos of their ships on Facebook and encouraged fans to share their photographs of Maersk ships from around the globe (Katona and Sarvary 2014). Maersk is a great example of how a B2B company can use Facebook to humanize a brand.

The answer to the second question, why do people share on Facebook, will help you identify the variety of content that you should post. People share content with their network of Facebook friends for numerous reasons, including to make life easier for others, to educate and inspire friends; to help others, to answer questions, to build relationships through conversations and engagement, to craft their identities, to express themselves (Li 2013). As discussed in Chapter 2 and briefly in Chapter 3, when someone decides to follow a brand on social media. that brand becomes a part of their social identity.

Consumers are 40–150 times more likely to consume a brand's content in their newsfeed than they are to take time to visit the brand page. Therefore, it is essential to develop content that will make it into a consumer's newsfeed (Lipsman et al. 2012). Unfortunately, as we discussed earlier, the Facebook algorithm does not favor brands. For this reason, many companies turn to paid advertising on Facebook to reach more consumers. The good news is that Facebook dominates all social media platforms for sharing. Research suggests that approximately 80 percent of the social sharing originates from Facebook, surpassing the number two social sharing platform Pinterest by 10 to 1 (Delzio 2015). The friends of fans audience can be upto 34 times greater than the size of the company's current Facebook fan base (Lipsman et al. 2012).

To maximize the reach of each post, you need to use a variety of content (photos, videos, and so on) from different sources (consumer, company, and collaborative). Images are the most engaging content on Facebook. One study found that the comment rate for images is higher than it is for text (over 90 percent), and linking to YouTube videos also results in a higher "share" rate (75 percent). If you are posting a text update, then you need to consider the wordcount carefully. Text posts of 80+ words are said to garner almost twice the level of engagement than shorter posts (Hussain 2014). One possible reason for this is that short posts often do not provide enough information for people to comment on and can be quickly skimmed. Longer posts provide more information and require a greater level of attention. Sharing can be enhanced further by using simple words. Facebook is not the place to show off your extensive vocabulary. Early research also suggests that the use of verbs in status updates compel people to share (Solis 2010).

Research also suggests that the best days to post to achieve maximum engagement on Facebook are Thursday's and Friday's, with the optimal time to post being early afternoon (1–3 pm) (Bennett 2015). However, you should experiment to identify the best time to reach your audience. Increasing the number of posts per day does not always increase engagement and sharing (Kolowich 2015). It has been suggested that companies should post 5–10 times per week (Hughes 2016). However, companies like the Coca-Cola Company (@TheCocaColaCo), American Red Cross (@redcross), and Maersk (@maerskgroup) all have a history of posting less than once a day and still achieve high levels of engagement. What is more important is the quality of the posts. Well-crafted and strategically timed postings a few times a week can be just as if not more effective than multiple posts each day (Kolowich 2015). See Figure 8.4 for a summary.

Twitter: The New Telephone

The short, concise messaging of Twitter can mimic natural conversations (Dalla Pozza, Wood, and Burkhalter 2015). These conversations can be an effective way of maintaining relationships and spreading positive sWOM. Consumers follow companies on Twitter for entertainment to obtain discounts and deals, hear breaking news, and obtain access to exclusive content and information. Consumers also use Twitter as a customer service channel. When consumers have a problem, concern, or question, they will often reach out to the company on Twitter. Many companies have Twitter accounts dedicated specifically for customer service (e.g.,

Facebook

Reasons for Following

- As a form of self-expression
- To communicate a positive association with the company or brand
- To communicate with the company
- To receive product information
- To obtain discounts and deals

How to Build Connections

- Use Facebook to humanize your brand
- Determine why consumers love your brand and use this to drive your content strategy
- Add content that educates and inspires
- Include a variety of forms of shareable content - Consumer, Company, Collaborative
- Aim to attract a diverse selection of followers (employees, vendors, industry experts etc.)
- Build relationships through conversations with followers

More Specifically

- Aim to post 5-10 times per week. Quality and timing is more important than quantity
- Where appropriate include a photo or a video in your post
- Craft text posts with 80+ words
- Use simple words
- Include verbs in your text posts
- When someone connects with you or comments on one of your updates thank them
- Answer questions promptly
- Time your posts to reach the majority of your audience

80% of Social Sharing Occurs on Facebook

Figure 8.4 Facebook

@virgincare, @microsofthelps) (Jackson 2016). Twitter has, in some ways, become the new telephone (Dalla Pozza, Wood, and Burkhalter 2015).

Twitter can be an effective platform for conveying your brand's personality. The challenge is creating a shareworthy tweet in 140 characters. When compared with Facebook, LinkedIn, and Pinterest, Twitter generates the smallest amount of sharing (Delzio 2015). To encourage engagement in general and social sharing specifically, consider joining multiple tweets together to tell a story, a strategy made popular by journalists reporting on live events. Each tweet provides a new piece of important information, and when the tweets are read in succession, the whole story unfolds. Engagement is also greatly affected by enjoyment. The more a follower enjoys your tweet, the more likely he or she is to engage (e.g., click on the link contained) and the higher level of engagement (e.g., moves from *watching* to *sharing* to *commenting*). Therefore, tweets should be designed to be entertain and engage and avoid excess company or product information (Kwon and Sung 2011). If you are using Twitter as a customer service channels, be sure to respond to questions and comments promptly. If it truly is the telephone of this generation, then consumers do not want to feel like they have been placed on hold.

Tweets that are successful at attracting a large number of retweets possess similar characteristics. An analysis of 1.4 million randomly selected tweets found that tweets of 110–115 characters were 34 percent more likely to be retweeted than tweets that had a shorter or longer character count (Zarrella 2013). Another study examined the tweets of six companies in the tourism industry and found that the inclusion of pictures had a positive impact on retweeting and favoriting (Alboqami et al. 2015), particularly if the image was humorous (Patel 2014). A final study of 1,000 Twitter user accounts found that those tweets that contained images received 128 percent more retweets than the tweets that contained videos. However, consumers were more likely to "favorite" a tweet that contained a video than they were a tweet that contained a photo (Patel 2014). Tweets that contain hyperlinks also gain more attention than those that do not (Alboqami et al. 2015; Solis 2009). These findings can be explained by the Engagement Pyramid (Chapter 2). If your goal is to move consumers up the pyramid, then you need to be aware of the type and format of content that is likely to encourage higher levels of engagement. Excessive use of hashtags or mentions can act as a distraction, making tweets difficult to read. Hashtags should be limited to one or two, particularly if your aim is to encourage retweeting with a comment (Ayres 2015).

Additional research suggests that to encourage sharing, you should tweet like you would talk to a friend. In other words, you should keep the language simple. Talk like a human. Your tweets should be rich with subject pronouns, (e.g., I, you, he, she, it, they, we, what, and do), object pronouns (e.g., me, you, him, her, it, us, them), and imperative verbs (e.g., stop, listen, share, stay tuned) (Kwon and Sung 2011). Punctuation is also important (Solis 2009).

To build your network, identify social influencers to follow. Retweet their content but remember to add your own comment. Tagging social influencers in your tweet may help generate social sharing via retweets (Hughes 2016). Companies should be aiming to tweet 3–5 times per day. B2B companies typically tweet more frequently through the work week than they do on weekends. B2C companies tweet through the entire week, with the highest activity often occurring on Wednesday's and weekends. See Figure 8.5 for a summary.

Tweet Like You Would Talk to a
Friend

🐦 Twitter

Reasons for following

- To learn about products and services
- To stay up to date with company news
- For customer service
- To obtain discounts and deals
- For exclusive content
- To pass the time with entertaining content

How to Build Connections

- Use Twitter as a conversation tool - engage with your followers
- Focus on informing and entertaining your followers
- Avoid excess company or product information - stick with breaking news
- Tag social influencers to encourage retweeting
- Follower influencers and retweet their content adding a comment
- Respond to comments and questions quickly

More Specifically

- Keep tweets under 120 characters
- Post 3-5 times per day
- Join multiple tweets together to tell a story
- Tweet photos
- Include hyperlinks
- Craft tweets that are rich in subject pronouns, object pronouns and imperative verbs
- Include punctuation
- Keep hashtags to a minimum (1-2)

Figure 8.5 Twitter

Instagram: The New Billboard

Instagram is the popular photograph- and video-sharing platform owned by Facebook. The platform allows users to share photographs and videos ranging in length from 3 to 60 seconds with their friends. A lot of the time these are impromptu photographs and videos that show what consumers are doing at that specific moment in time. Recall from Chapter 6, the most frequent types of content posted on Instagram (consisting of almost half of the dataset of photos combined) were friends and selfies (Hu, Manikonda, and Kambhampati 2014).

Consumers follow brands on Instagram because they love the brand, they use the images and videos posted to learn about new products to purchase and to help pass the time (Mander 2016). Across all social media platforms, Instagram boasts the highest rate of engagement (likes, shares, comments combined) (Delzio 2015). A study of major brands revealed that engagement was 58 times higher on Instagram than on Facebook and 120 times higher than on Twitter (LePage 2015). As we discussed earlier, the reason for Instagram's success are that visuals are extremely powerful at evoking emotion and motivating social media users to react. But not all pictures are shareworthy. Many photos end up on the cutting room floor or the digital trashcan. Just because Instagram offers you seemingly, unlimited storage does not mean that you post everything. Be selective. When selecting photos to post, ask yourself "Is this image Instagram-worthy?" Or perhaps an even better question to ask yourself "Is it billboard worthy?" If you think of each image as something to use in a billboard campaign, this should help you identify the images that evoke emotion, and therefore, encourage engagement (likes, comments, and sharing). A good strategy is to select visuals that highlight an experience rather than a product. As we learned from the Tourism Australia example in Chapter 7, one of the strategies to persuade others to engage is to select visuals that tell a story and allow for a story to be told. To illustrate, rather than showing a photo or a video of someone wearing the shoes while running. Your posts should inspire followers to adopt your product as part of their lifestyle. Make sure you include faces. Researchers have found that engagement and higher likes per follower are greater when Instagram photos contained faces (Bakhsi, Shamma, and Gilber 2014; Zarrella 2014).

If a picture is supposed to be worth a thousand words, does that mean that adding text is unnecessary on Instagram? Not at all. On the contrary, including text can be extremely helpful at boosting engagement levels. Instagram permits up to 2,000 characters per post. If you intend to make use of all 2,000 characters, ensure that the text adds value by telling a story. Also, consider tagging your location, and if appropriate, another user's handle. The inclusion of a geotag makes it easier for consumers to find your posts when searching. Posts tagged with a location receive 79 percent more engagement, and those posts that contain another user handle in the caption benefit from 56 percent more engagement. Hashtags can also leverage your social reach by approximately 12.6 percent (LePage 2015). As we discussed in Chapter 6, care should be taken not to include too many hashtags as they may distract from the text component of the post. Use a small number of hashtags that your consumers are likely to search for, that are topically relevant, and that contribute to the message (e.g., #Rio2016, #THATSGOLD). Avoid hashtags that fail to add value, particularly when used in abundance (e.g., #Hastags#Used#In#Ridiculous#Way#lol). You should aim to post once a day every day (Hughes 2016), with the best days to post being Monday through Thursday (Kolowich 2016). But as always, you need to experiment with the best time for your audience. See Figure 8.6 for a summary.

Pinterest: The Digital Scrapbook

Pinterest is an inspiration, planning, and visual bookmarking tool. Pictures and videos are the most commonly pinned items, but consumers and companies can also pin articles, places, and even apps as long as they contain an image. In many ways, Pinterest is a digital scrapbook. Perhaps, not surprisingly, Pinterest's user base skews heavily female. In addition to using Pinterest to discover and pin items that inspire them, women also use Pinterest as a planning tool. For example, before the Internet when planning her wedding, a party, Thanksgiving or Christmas dinner, or preparing to redecorate, women would clip articles, rip pages from magazines, and put them together in a scrapbook or binder. Today, she does this using Pinterest. Some of the most browsed and pinned categories by women include food and drink, home decor, DIY, crafts, holidays,

Instagram

Reasons for following

- Because they love your brand
- To obtain discounts, deals and giveaways
- For shopping
- To pass the time

79% More engagement for posts that include a location

How to Build Connections

- Use Instagram as a visual storytelling tool
- Tag your location to make it easy for consumers to find your posts
- Tag social influencers to encourage retweeting
- Follower influencers and like their content

More Specifically

- Post once per day
- Be selective with what you post - is the image billboard worthy?
- Select visuals that highlight an experience rather than a product
- Include photos of people
- Include text that tells a story
- Use a small number of topically relevant hashtags

*Figure 8.6 **Instagram***

and events. For men, food and drink and DIY are popular categories as are technology, gardening, and humor (Dougherty 2015). Similar to Instagram, when trying to determine what to pin, the aim should be to inspire. Therefore, image quality is important. Once you have motivated a consumer to click through to your website, the last thing you want is to lose them because of a broken link or boring page. Each image should link to a high-quality landing page.

Pinterest allows 500 characters to accompany each posting. Some research suggests that the character count can impact how frequently your pins will be repinned. The optimal length is reported to be 200–300 characters (Dougherty 2015). Descriptions need to be carefully crafted using keywords that consumers are likely to use to research relevant items. You should create a variety of boards to appeal to a wide selection of consumers. For instance, ideas or inspirations, specific occasions, how-to, videos, exclusive deals, new products, behind the scenes, specific themes, or mood boards. Grouping pinned items into common themes can help consumers locate relevant information and may also motivate them to follow the board. Take, for example, the following two Pinterest pages:

Maersk: Maersk's Pinterest page contains 35 different boards. There are boards the include images of specific parts of their ships (e.g., The Nose Job, The Engine Room), boards dedicated to shipping containers (e.g., Container Art, Container Living), and boards that focus on their extensive workforce (e.g., Faces of the Sea, People). The company even has a board dedicated to the Norwich Whale, a whale that was struck and killed by a Maersk ship (In Memory of the Maersk Norwich Whale).

Lowe's: Home improvements store Lowe's Pinterest page contains 66 boards aimed at inspiring and educating their consumers. Some of their boards focus on specific areas of the home (e.g., Bathroom Inspiration, A Kitchen to Dine For, Ultimate Man Caves), others focus on special occasions and days (e.g., Halloween Fun, Holiday Home Ready, Father's Day Gift Ideas). There are also boards that offer advice and tips for DIY projects (e.g., How You-How To, Helpful Hints, Lowe's Fix in Six).

When adding boards to your Pinterest page, placement is important. Place your best boards in the first two rows as these are what consumers will see first when using a computer. If the first two rows of boards are not appealing, consumers may not take time to explore the remainder of your page.

Most consumers use Pinterest during the evenings and on weekends, particularly Saturday (Kolowich 2016). Companies should make an effort to pin all three forms of content—consumer, company, and collaborative. It is important to engage your consumers on Pinterest just as you would on other social platforms. For example, be sure to like and comment on content pinned by your consumers. The majority of clicks (70 percent) are likely to occur within the first day of an item being pinned, so posting every day is important (Hughes 2016). Research offers conflicting results on the optimal number of items a company should be pinning each day. It could be as little five to as many as 30 (Hughes 2016; Kolowich 2016;

Dougherty 2015). If you plan to pin a large number of items, it is advisable to spread these pins out throughout the entire day. Dumping a large number of pins in a short period can result in your account being flagged for spamming. This may result in you being temporarily locked out of your account—being put in "Pinterest Jail," or being banned completely. When you account has been put in "Pinterest Jail," only you can see your pins. It may be a while before you even realize that your account is suspended. One tell-tale sign is that people have stopped repinning your pins because they cannot see them. If this happens, you will need to wait to be released or contact Pinterest support and politely ask to be released. Frequent offenders can expect lengthy sentences or even "life incarceration"—banned completely ("Don't Land in Pinterest Jail" 2015). See Figure 8.7 for a summary.

YouTube: The One-Stop Shop for Entertainment, Inspiration, and Education

The most-watched YouTube video of all time, with more than 2.5 billion views, is the music video Gangnam Style by Korean pop star Psy. In fact, the top ten most watched YouTube videos of all time are all music related (Heisler 2016). Obviously, YouTube entertains, but consumers also turn to YouTube to be inspired. Do you remember the video "Achieving Your Childhood Dreams" or as it was more commonly known as, "The Last Lecture" by Carnegie Mellon Professor Randy Pausch? Professor Pausch, who was diagnosed with terminal cancer, spoke about finding ways to celebrate and enjoy life. Over 18 million people logged on and tuned in to be inspired. Consumers also readily turn to YouTube to learn and for instruction. For example, millions of teenagers rely on YouTube star Michelle Phan for lessons on how to apply makeup. Finally, YouTube videos help consumers decide what to buy (Jarski 2016).

Video is the perfect platform for generating awareness, creating interest, making an emotional connection, and encouraging consumer advocacy. Given that consumers turn to YouTube for entertainment, inspiration, and education, your videos should offer a combination of emotion and intellect. One of the best ways to make a connection with

Pinterest

70% of clicks are likely to occur in the first day of an item being pinned

Reasons for Pinning

- To be inspired
- To assist with planning
- To bookmark for future reference
- Wish or task fulfilment list (to-do, to-buy, to-make)

How to Build Connections

- Use Pinterest to inspire
- Pin Company, Consumer and Collaborative content
- Use high-quality images
- Add comments to Pins
- Tag influencers and like their content
- Create a variety of boards

More Specifically

- Post every day of the week
- Pin 5-30 images a day
- Spread pins throughout the day
- Make sure some items are pinned in the evening when consumers typically use Pinterest
- Keep text to 200-300 characters
- Choose words that consumers are likely to search for
- Ensure that each item links to a high-quality landing page
- Create a variety of boards (e.g. new products, deals, themes, videos)
- Place your best boards in the first two rows

Figure 8.7 Pinterest

your consumers via video is to tell a story (see Chapter 6). Like every good novel, or movie, each story has a beginning, middle, and end, or if you prefer, three acts:

- Act One is the setup where you set the scene, and the characters are introduced. The first ten seconds of the video are very important. After this, engagement drops off significantly. Therefore, the opening of the video needs to have a strong hook, something that pulls the viewer in and holds his or her attention (Uganec 2012).

- Act Two is where conflict is introduced. Typically, this where something goes wrong, where you present the problem or opportunity. The second act is where bad goes to worse, where funny turns to funnier, and the emotional element intensifies.

- Act Three is the resolution where the climax and conclusion are presented. Regardless of whether your video is inspiring, shocking, moving, or controversial, whether it makes people happy, sad, angry or delighted, the goal is to stimulate high-arousal emotions. Evoking emotions will increase the likelihood of your video being shared (Uganec 2012). Research reveals that high-arousal videos generate twice as much sharing, then do low-arousal videos (Karen Nelson-Field, Riebe, and Sharp 2013).

There is no perfect video length, although the prevailing wisdom is that shorter is better (Smith 2015). To help determine the optimum length, consider where the video will be posted and potentially shared. Short-form videos are more successful on Facebook, LinkedIn, Twitter, Pinterest, and Instagram, long-form videos are more successful on You-Tube (Sahakians 2015; Pedersen 2015; Smith 2015). Keep in mind that 30 seconds into the video, you probably have lost at least a third of your audience and at the two-minute mark over 60 percent have stopped watching (Pedersen 2015). If you find yourself wondering "is this too long?," then generally speaking, "yes" it is. Your video should be just long enough to achieve its goal. If your video is too long, consider breaking it up into multiple short videos—nonlinear chapters or vignettes. Making them nonlinear allows consumers to watch them out of order, which may help with engagement and sharing (Uganec 2012).

Video creation is a time-consuming activity, so to maximize value, create videos that will have a long lifespan. Unlike other social media platforms, where engagement peaks a short time after the initial post, it can sometimes take months for a YouTube video to attract high viewership numbers. Your company should view YouTube as a medium to long-term strategy for sWOM. To attempt to accelerate the number of views and sWOM, your company should create a YouTube channel that reflects your brand. You may want to consider creating multiple playlists to appeal to a variety of consumers. For example, you could create a playlist of new product videos, another for tutorials, demonstrations, product reviews, and behind the scenes. Take, for example, the following three YouTube channels:

TOMS shoes: TOMS YouTube channel contains 450+ videos categorized into 24 different playlists. There is a playlist for their products (e.g., Product Details: TOMS shoes), a playlists that contains videos that answer questions (e.g., Frequently Asked Questions), and another playlist of videos that highlights their philanthropic relationships (e.g., TOMS Partnerships).

SAP: The software company has 1800+ videos categorized into 39 playlists. There are playlists for existing customers (e.g., Run Live Executive Series), potential customers (e.g., The Future of Work with SAP), the media (e.g., SAP for Media), and potential employees (e.g., Careers), to name a few.

GoPro: Action camera manufacturer GoPro's YouTube channel contains 1600+ videos categorized in 29 playlists. There are playlists for different sports and interests (e.g., Surfing, Auto), playlists for GoPro award-worthy and award-winning videos (e.g., GoPro Awards: Offical Selections). There is also a playlist of the most popular videos (e.g., Liked Videos) and one promoting specific causes (e.g., GoPro for a Cause).

As always, remember that the quality of your video is more important than the number of videos that you post. Top performers on YouTube all have a schedule for posting new videos. Create a manageable schedule for creating and posting new videos and stick to it.

To ensure your video's high visibility in search engine results, carefully select a title for each video. The title of a video is the main source of information in the YouTube search algorithm. Use keywords that your consumers would use to search. For example, tutorial, review, how-to, what is. Place these keywords once in the title, once or twice in the description, and if appropriate in the tags (Patel 2016).

Companies often create videos hoping that they will go viral—that the video will spread like a virus throughout the social web—attracting downloads, likes, comments, and shares of epic proportion. Do not start out with the goal of making a viral video. Your goal should be to make a good video, post links in the appropriate locations (blogs, website, and so on) at the right time and then use your social network in general and social influencers specifically to help spread the word (Khan and Vong 2014). Remember that who shares and views your video is just as, if not more, important than how many people share and view (Uganec 2012). This may also help at attracting subscribers (Nanji 2013).

Additional strategies for increasing engagement is to promote your videos on other social media platforms (e.g., Facebook and LinkedIn),

YouTube

Reasons for Watching

- To be entertained
- To be inspired
- To Learn
- To find instructions
- To help them decide what to buy

96% Click Thru Rate

For videos that are embedded in emails

How to Build Connections

- Create a YouTube channels that reflects your brand
- Create a variety of playlists to appeal to different consumers
- Produce videos that tell stories and are a combination of emotion and intellect
- Devise a manageable schedule for creating and posting videos
- Quality of video is more important the quantity
- Don't try to make a viral video, make a good video

More Specifically

- Aim for short videos
- Cross promote your videos on other social platforms (e.g. Facebook, LinkedIn)
- Embed videos in emails and provide links in email signatures
- Use keywords in titles, descriptions and if appropriate tags
- Time posting to reach the majority of your audience, or during the hours of 12-5pm

Figure 8.8 YouTube

include video links in your e-mail signature and embed videos in an e-mail. Researchers report that videos embedded in an e-mail have a click-through rate of approximately 96 percent (Jarski 2016). You should find other YouTube channels to follow and invite influencers to subscribe to your channel. Time your postings to reach the majority of your audience or alternative post between the hours of 12–5 pm when viewership is greatest on all devices except for TV (Jarski 2016). See Figure 8.8 for a summary.

Conclusion

When we decided to write this book, it was not our intention to provide a comprehensive guide to sWOM. If that were the case, this book would be titled "The Complete Guide to Social Word of Mouth (sWOM)." The reality is that social media is a moving target. As social media grows and evolves and social consumers change the way in which they use social, so too will your strategies. The fluid nature of social media makes it challenging to write a book that will stand the test of time, at least for a few years. Instead, we wrote this book to provide you an understanding of sWOM and how you can use it within your company. We included examples of how other companies have embraced social media and sWOM to make connections, enhance their relationships with consumers, create their brand voice, and build their brand identity. We provided, guidelines, checklists, and resources to help you apply what you have learned here to your company. Although this is the end of our book, it certainly is not the end of your education on sWOM. Indeed, this is only the start of what is sure to be an interesting, and hopefully, rewarding direction for your company. We hope that this book has provided you with a sound foundation on sWOM and the motivation to begin this important journey. If it has, we encourage you to spread the word. #Share.

References

Alboqami, H., W. Al Karaghouli, Y. Baeshen, I. Erkan, C. Evans, and A. Ghoneim. 2015. "Electronic Word of Mouth in Social Media: The Common Characteristics of Retweeted and Favourited Marketer-Generated

Content Posted on Twitter." *International Journal of Internet Marketing and Advertising* 9, no. 4, pp. 338–58. doi:10.1504/IJIMA.2015.072886

Ayres, S. 2015. "Tips from 13 Experts on How to Use Hashtags on Facebook." *Post Planner.* Retrieved from www.postplanner.com/how-to-use-hashtags-on-facebook/

Bennett, S. 2015. "What Are the Best Times to Post on #Facebook, #Twitter and #Instagram?" *SocialTimes.* Retrieved from www.adweek.com/socialtimes/best-time-to-post-social-media/504222

Bradley, S. 2011. "3 Design Layouts: Gutenberg Diagram, Z-Pattern, and F-Pattern." *Vanseo Design.* Retrieved from http://vanseodesign.com/web-design/3-design-layouts/

Brown, E. 2016. "Will Facebook's New Algorithm Destroy Its Relationships with Brands? | ZDNet." *ZDNet.* Retrieved from www.zdnet.com/article/will-facebooks-new-algorithm-destroy-relationships-with-brands/

Childers, T.L, and M.J. Houston. 1984. "Conditions for a Picture-Superiority Effect on Consumer Memory." *Journal of Consumer Research* 11, no. 2, pp. 643–53.

Content Marketing Institute. 2016. *B2B Content Marketing—2016 Benchmarks, Budgets and Trends—North America.* Retrieved from www.slideshare.net/CMI/b2b-content-marketing-2016-benchmarks-budgets-and-trends-north-america/1

Dalla Pozza, I., N.T. Wood, and J.N. Burkhalter. 2015. "Tweeting for Service: Twitter as a Communication Channel for Customer Service." In *Maximizing Commerce and Marketing Strategies through Micro-Blogging,* eds. J.N. Burkhalter and N.T. Wood, 111–29. IGI Global. doi:10.4018/978-1-4666-8408-9

Delzio, S. 2015. "Social Sharing Habits: New Research Reveals What People Like to Share: Social Media Examiner." *SocialMedia Examiner.* Retrieved from www.socialmediaexaminer.com/social-sharing-habits-new-research/

"Don't Land in Pinterest Jail." 2015. *Writer Access.* Retrieved from www.writeraccess.com/blog/dont-land-in-pinterest-jail/

Dougherty, J. 2015. "25 Pinterest Stats, Facts & PR Best Practices | Cision." *Cision.* Retrieved from www.cision.com/us/2015/01/25-pinterest-facts-and-pr-best-practices/

Elliott, N. 2015. "Instagram Is The King of Social Engagement." *Forrester.* Retrieved from http://blogs.forrester.com/nate_elliott/14-04-29-instagram_is_the_king_of_social_engagement

eMarketer. 2014. "Photos Cluttering Your Facebook Feed? Here's Why." *eMarketer.* Retrieved from www.emarketer.com/Article/Photos-Cluttering-Your-Facebook-Feed-Heresquos-Why/1010777

eMarketer. 2015. "Social Promoters More Likely Than Sharers to Actively Engage Directly with Brands." Retrieved from www.emarketer.com/Article/Social-Promoters-Power-Brand-Engagement/1012758

Heisler, Y. 2016. "Most Popular YouTube Videos of All-Time." *BGR*. Retrieved from http://bgr.com/2016/01/17/most-popular-youtube-videos-all-time/

Hu, Y., L. Manikonda, and S. Kambhampati. 2014. "What We Instagram: A First Analysis of Instagram Photo Content and User Types." In *Proceedings of the 8th International AAAI Conference on Weblogs and Social Media*.

Hughes, B. 2016. "How to Optimize Your Social Media Posting Frequency—Social Media Week." *Social Media Week*. Retrieved from https://socialmediaweek. org/blog/2016/03/optimize-social-media-time/

Hussain, A. 2014. "How to Craft Perfect Posts for Facebook, LinkedIn & Twitter [SlideShare]." *Hubspot*. Retrieved from http://blog.hubspot.com/marketing/ create-perfect-social-media-posts-slideshare#sm.00000k25m12ca6cnzqc7bv oco5n0b

Hutchinson, A. 2016. "How Facebook's News Feed Works—As Explained by Facebook | Social Media Today." *SocialMedia Today*. Retrieved from www. socialmediatoday.com/social-networks/how-facebooks-news-feed-works-explained-facebook

Jackson, D. 2016. "10 Tips for the Best Twitter Customer Service." *Sprout Social*. Retrieved from http://sproutsocial.com/insights/twitter-customer-service/

Jarski, V. 2016. "YouTube Engagement, 5 Notable Ways to Increase Engagement." *MarketingProfs*. Retrieved from www.marketingprofs.com/ chirp/2016/29939/five-noteworthy-ways-to-increase-engagement-on-youtube-infographic

Kaplan, A. 2012. *How to Build Relationships That Drive Business: A Best Practice Guide to LinkedIn Company Pages*. Hootsuite University. Retrieved from https://learn.hootsuite.com

Katona, Z., and M. Sarvary. 2014. "Maersk Line: B2B Social Media—'It's Communication, Not Marketing.'" *California Management Review* 56, no. 3, pp. 142–56. doi:10.1525/cmr.2014.56.3.142

Khan, G.F., and S. Vong. 2014. "Virality over YouTube: An Empirical Analysis." *Internet Research* 24, no. 5, pp. 629–47. doi:10.1108/IntR-05-2013-0085

Kolowich, L. 2015. "How Often Should You Post on Facebook? [New Benchmark Data]." *Hubspot*. Retrieved from http://blog.hubspot.com/marketing/facebook-post-frequency-benchmarks#sm.00000k25m12ca6cnzqc7bvoco5n0b

Kolowich, L. 2016. "The Best Times to Post on Facebook, Twitter, LinkedIn & Other Social Media Sites [Infographic]." *Hubspot*. Retrieved from http:// blog.hubspot.com/marketing/best-times-post-pin-tweet-social-media-infogr aphic#sm.00000k25m12ca6cnzqc7bvoco5n0b

Kwon, E.S., and Y. Sung. 2011. "Follow Me! Global Marketers' Twitter Use." *Journal of Interactive Advertising* 12, no. 1, pp. 4–16. doi:10.1080/1525201 9.2011.10722187

Lee, K. 2015. "LinkedIn Marketing: The All-in-One Guide to Content and Scheduling." *Buffer Social*. Retrieved from https://blog.bufferapp.com/linkedin-marketing

LePage, E. 2015. "A Long List of Instagram Statistics and Facts That Prove Its Importance." *Hootsuite*. Retrieved from https://blog.hootsuite.com/instagram-statistics-for-business/

Li, J. 2013. *Facebook Brand Pages: Rules of Engagement*. Hootsuite. Retrieved from https://learn.hootsuite.com.

Lipsman, A., G. Mudd, M. Rich, and S. Bruich. 2012. "The Power of 'like': How Brands Reach (and Influence) Fans through Social-Media Marketing." *Journal of Advertising Research* 52, no. 1, pp. 40–52. doi:10.2501/JAR-52-1-040-052

Loren, T. 2012. *5 Best Practices for New Facebook Pages with Hootsuite*. Hootsuite University. Retrieved from https://learn.hootsuite.com

Mander, J. 2016. "Half of Instagrammers Follow Brands." *Globalwebindex*. Retrieved from www.globalwebindex.net/blog/half-of-instagrammers-follow-brands

Nanji, A. 2013. "Social Media—Successful Brands on YouTube: Best-Practices and Metrics." *Marketing Profs*. Retrieved from www.marketingprofs.com/charts/2013/11358/successful-brands-on-youtube-best-practices-and-metrics

Nelson-Field, K., E. Riebe, and B. Sharp. 2013. "Emotions and Sharing." In *Viral Marketing: The Science of Sharing*, eds. K. Nelson-Field and B. Sharp. First, 13–32. South Melbourne, Australia: Oxford University Press.

Paivio, A., T.B. Rogers, and P. Smythe. 1968. "Why Are Pictures Easier to Recall Than Words?" *Psychonomic Science* 11, no. 4, pp. 137–38.

Patel, N. 2014. "What Type of Content Gets Shared the Most on Twitter." *Quicksprout*. Retrieved from http://blog.hubspot.com/marketing/content-social-media-popularity#sm.00000k25m12ca6cnzqc7bvoco5n0b

Patel, N. 2016. "The Complete Guide to Building a Successful YouTube Channel." *Quick Sprout*. Retrieved from www.quicksprout.com/2016/01/22/the-complete-guide-to-building-a-successful-youtube-channel/

Pedersen, M. 2015. "Best Practices: What Is the Optimal Length for Online Video? | DigitalNext—AdAge." *Advertising Age*. Retrieved from http://adage.com/article/digitalnext/optimal-length-video-content/299386/

Pieters, R., and M. Wedel. 2004. "Attention Capture and Transfer in Advertising: Brand, Pictorial, and Text-Size Effects." *Journal of Marketing* 68, no. 2, pp. 36–50.

Sahakians, S. 2015. "Twitter Video: The Marketing Advantage No One Is Using Yet." *Buffer Social*. Retrieved from https://blog.bufferapp.com/twitter-video

Smith, A. 2015. "What Is the Optimal Video Length for YouTube and Facebook Videos?" *Tubularinsights*. Retrieved from http://tubularinsights.com/optimal-video-length-youtube-facebook/

Solis, B. 2009. "The Science of Retweets on Twitter—Brian Solis." Retrieved from www.briansolis.com/2009/10/the-science-of-retweets-on-twitter/

Solis, B. 2010. "7 Scientific Ways to Promote Sharing on Facebook—Brian Solis." Retrieved from www.briansolis.com/2010/05/facebook-sharing-driven-by-simplicity/

Tam, D. 2012. "What Facebook (and Every Other Site) Can Learn from Eye Tracking—CNET." *CNET*. Retrieved from www.cnet.com/news/what-facebook-and-every-other-site-can-learn-from-eye-tracking/

Uganec, C. 2012. *How to Use Social Video to Drive Results*. Hootsuite University. Retrieved from https://learn.hootsuite.com

Williams, O. 2016. "Twitter's New Algorithm Is Now on for Everyone." *The Next Web*. Retrieved from http://thenextweb.com/twitter/2016/03/17/twitter-quietly-turned-new-algorithmic-timeline-everyone/#gref

Zarrella, D. 2013. "Tweets between 100–115 Characters Are More Likely to Be Retweeted." Retrieved from http://danzarrella.com/new-data-tweets-between-100-and-115-characters-are-more-likely-to-be-retweeted/

Zarrella, D. 2014. "The Science of Instagram." *Dan Zarrella*. Retrieved from http://danzarrella.com/infographic-the-science-of-instagram/

APPENDIX

List of Resources

Sample Social Media Policies

Adidas	https://goo.gl/0yW5bV
Air Force	https://goo.gl/6bjWRr
Best Buy	https://goo.gl/1FO5Gw
Coca-Cola	https://goo.gl/0vX6tP
Dell	https://goo.gl/wV5G5Q
EPA	https://goo.gl/aG3MyU
Ford Motor Company	https://goo.gl/ERKE36
IBM	https://goo.gl/pl9E3d
Intel	https://goo.gl/UvMo9h
SAP	https://goo.gl/6qYBGK
Target	https://goo.gl/CBTSRe
The Social Media Governance Website	http://socialmediagovernance.com/policies

Applications for Creating Shareable Content

Photographs

Afterlight   **afterlight.us**

Afterlight is an image editing application. Users can choose from a large selection of filters, textures, frames, and cropping tools.

BeFunky   **befunky.com**

BeFunky is a photoediting, graphic design, and collage-making website. It is also available as an app for iOS and Android devices. It boasts an easy to use interface, quick load time, and the ability for easy sharing on a wide selection of social media platforms.

EMV Headline Analyzer   Aminstitute.com/headline/

The emotional marketing value headline analyzer allows a user to analyze and rate the amount of emotion in a headline. The EMV score will let you know if the headline applies more to intellectual, empathic, or spiritual appeals.

Flare   flareapp.com

Flare is a photo editing app for Mac. The app boasts a wide selection of artistic filters. Photographs can be shared with your social networks directly from the application.

Fused   easytigerapps.com

Fused is an app that allows you to blend photos, videos, or a combination of both to create one of a kind image.

Pablo   pablo.buffer.com

Pablo is a web application that allows you to use stock images or upload your photographs to make engaging social media posts. The application offers filters and allows marketers to overlay their photographs with logos and text. Images are created in the correct size and format to share on Facebook, Twitter, Instagram, and Pinterest.

Pixabay   pixabay.com

Pixabay offers 700,000 royalty-free stock photos, vectors, illustrations, and videos.

PicFlow   redact.us

PicFlow is a slideshow maker for Instagram. Users can choose from over 18 transitions to create timed slideshows. Music can be added from your iPod library.

PicLab   museworks.co/piclab

PicLab is an iOS photo editor and collage maker. It offers a wide selection of features, including photo filters, photo effects, drawing tools, overlays, stickers, and artwork.

Phonto   **phon.to**

Phonto is an app for the iOS, which lets you add text to photographs. The app offers text in over 200 decorative fonts. Text can be added on placards, badges, and inside thought bubbles.

Priime   **prime.com**

Priime for iOS offers professional-grade photo filters and editing tools. Prime analyzes each photos properties and suggests a style of photo filter to apply.

Stencil   **getstencil.com**

Stencil is a web app for creating text-based images. The application offers 50+ design templates, 200,000+ graphics and icons, and 700,000+ royalty-free photographs and backgrounds. Images are available in 34+ sizes, allowing you to create images for all social networks.

GIFS

Reaction GIFs   **reactiongifs.com**

Reaction GIFs allows users to search for GIFs by popular tags and specific feelings.

GIFS from Last Night   **gifsfln.tumblr.com**

A source for funny GIFs related to TV, movies, news, and pop culture.

Giphy   **giphy.com**

Giphy is one of the largest resources for GIFs.

Gifbin   **gifbin.com**

Gifbin is a good resource for unique and yet-to-be-discovered GIFs.

Reddit   **Reddit.com**

Reddit offers multiple subreddits dedicated to GIFs.

Cinemagraphs

Cinemagra.am   Cineagra.am

An iPhone app that creates living photos to share on social media.

Flixel   flixel.com

Flixel creates professional HD-quality living images for the Web and social networks.

fotodanz   fotodanz.com

Fotodanz is a simple-to-use app for the Android.

Video

Vont   phon.to/vont

Created by the makers of Phonto, Vont is an app for iOS for adding text to videos. Users can select from over 400 fonts. Text is rotatable, and the size, color, gradient are all changeable.

Quik   quik.gopro.com

Quik is a video app for iOS. The app analyzes your videos and photos to find the best moments. Users choose from 28 video styles. Text overlays can be added, transitions altered, focal points on photos changed, and your video synced to 70+ free songs. Alternatively, you can add your own music. Video can be downloaded or shared instantly on social media.

Magisto   magisto.com

Magisto is an effortless video maker that takes your visuals and turns them into videos that tell stories. Users load their photos and videos and Magisto's automatic editor reviews each item, selects the best, adds music, themes, and effects. Videos can be easily shared on social media.

Hyperlapse   hyperlapse.instagram.com

Hyperlapse by Instagram allows users to create time-lapsed videos, which can be instantly shared on Facebook and Instagram or downloaded and shared on other platforms.

Infographics

Canva   **canva.com**

Canva is an easy-to-use application for graphic design. Using the drag and drop feature, users can create great images and infographics for social media. Canva is available on the Web and as an iOS app.

Easelly   **easel.ly**

Easelly is, as the name suggests, an easy-to-use drag and drop website for creating infographics. Users can select from one of the thousands of templates, or they can start fresh. Infographics can include text, charts, drawings, photos, and videos.

Piktochart   **Piktochart.com**

Piktochart allows users to create photographs and infographics for sharing on social media. Users can select from a variety of customizable templates. Piktochart also allows users to create posters, presentations, and reports.

Venngage   **Venngage.com**

Vennage is a web application for creating infographics. The website offers a variety of templates base on your needs. It offers both basic and advanced tools to cater to all skills levels. Infographics can be published directly to social media, embedded on a website, or downloaded as a pdf.

Quotes

Instaquote   **redcact.us**

Instaquote is an app for iOS that adds text captions to photograph. Users can customize font size, color, alignment, position, and line spacing. Photographs can be shared on Instragram, Twitter, and Facebook.

Recite   **recite.com**

Recite is a super-easy website for creating shareable quotes. Users type a quote or statement into the textbook, which is then posted into a wide selection of templates. Images can be shared instantly to Facebook, Pinterest, Twitter, and Tumblr.

Newsletters and Stories

Curated

Curated.co

Curated is a website that allows you to create an online newsletter comprised of content from around the Web. Newsletters are published as a website with fully searchable back issues. Reader analytics and audience management features are included.

Elink

elink.io

Elink allows you to curate a wide selection of web content, including videos, webinars, podcasts, articles, pictures, infographics, pdfs, Google Docs, and much more. Content can be curated and edited on any device (phone, tablet, and computer) and shared as a webpage, newsletter, or website embed. You can also share your elink on Twitter, Facebook, Pinterest, LinkedIn, and Reddit.

Paper.li

Paper.li

Paper.li enables you to publish newspapers comprised of content from anywhere on the Web. Your newsletter can be embedded on your website, shared on social media, or they can be delivered to e-mail accounts.

Roojoom

roojoom.com

Roojoom allows users to create MiniSites, online magazines, and e-newsletters with personalized content for the consumers.

Storify

storify.com

Storify allows users to create stories by importing content from social media platforms, such as YouTube, Twitter, Instagram, and Facebook. Users identify a topic of interest, search for information on social media platforms, and then drag this content into Storify. The published story can be shared with your social networks.

Scoop.It

scoop.it

The Scoop-It website allows you to search the Web for content on a desired topic. Users select the content that is the most relevant and appealing, add their comments, and publish it. The curated topic page can then be shared on social media.

Lists

List.ly

List.ly

List.ly is a collaborative list building tool popular with bloggers. Bloggers create a list for a given topic and embed it into their blog. Subscribers to the blog can add to the list, vote items up or down, and share it on social media.

Apps for Content Curation

Addict-o-matic   Addictomatic.com

Addict-o-matic searches the Web for the trending news, blog posts, videos, and images.

Bundlr   Bundlr.com

Bundlr allows you to create bundles with photos, videos, tweets, and documents. These bundles can be shared privately or publically on social media.

BuzzSumo   Buzzsumo.com

BuzzSumo is a content discovery, content analytics, and influencer insights service. The website will help identify the most shared content across all main social networking sites. It will also provide analytics for content, which will allow you to identify the content that resonates the strongest with your consumers. BuzzSumo will also help you identify influencers by location or topic.

ContentGems   contentgems.com

ContentGems is a content discovery search engine. Users can search for content using a selection of filters. Relevant content can then be shared on social media, e-mail newsletters, websites, intranets, Web, and mobile apps.

Curata   curate.com

Curata allows users to create, curate, organize, annotate, and share content with consumers on social media.

LinkWithin linkwithin.com

LinkWithin is a blog widget that allows your consumers to identify additional content they find interesting. The widget is placed under or beside each post and provides links to relevant stories from your blog archive. Stories are chosen based on tags, content, and titles or headlines.

Repost for Instagram repostapp.com

Repost is an iOS app that lets you favorite photos and videos on Instagram while giving credit to the original Instagramer.

Rock The Deadline rockthedeadline.com

Rock the Deadline lets you discover the latest news and trends in your industry, share and discuss these items with your colleagues, add your comments to the news, and share it with your social networks.

The Tweeted Times tweetedtimes.com

The Tweeted Times finds, curates, and shares niche Twitter news content into a visually appealing online newspaper to share with your followers.

UpContent Upcontent.com

UpContent is a content discovery tool. Users create a topic using keywords and phrases to identify relevant information. Results can be filtered by relevance, recency, shareability, and influence. Content can be shared with your social network directly from the application.

Trap!t Trap.It

Trap!t is a popular curation tool used by sales representatives. The application allows a company to search for news, insights, trends, and analysis with employees, sales representative executives, and consumers. Once relevant information has been identified, it can be distributed to specific members of your workforce (e.g., sales), who can then share this information on social media with your consumers.

Waywire Enterprise enterprise.waywire.com

Waywire is video curation portal consisting of dozens of standalone channels, each devoted to a niche topic.

Apps to Make Your Content Shareable

Click to Tweet   **clicktotweet.com**

Click to Tweet makes it easy for your consumers to tweet valuable content from your company, blog, website, e-books, and so on. Marketers identify the most tweetable sentences (quotes, statistics, and so on) and using the application, create a custom hyperlink. When consumers click on the "Click to Tweet" button next to the sentence, it is automatically shared with their Twitter network. The tweet includes a link back to the source. When selecting sentences to tweet, leave enough room for consumers to RT and add a comment.

Hashtagify   **hashtagify.me**

Hashtagify, a fee-based service, allows you to quickly search for hashtags related to your desired topic on Twitter and Instagram.

SumoMe Highlighter   **sumome.com/app/highlighter**

SumoMe Highlighter is an application that allows readers to select sections of your articles, blogs, and so on, and share them with their network. Unlike Click to Tweet, which requires the marketer to identify tweetable content in advance, SumoMe gives the consumer the autonomy to select the content they find the most relevant and shareworthy. Consumers highlight the text, just like they do in real life, and share it on Twitter and Facebook.

Social Analytics, Sentiment, and Identifying Social Influencers

Brandwatch   **Brandwatch.com**

A social media listening system. It offers analytics, competitor benchmarking, influencer identification and outreach, market research, and reputation management.

BuzzSumo   **BuzzSumo.com**

BuzzSumo will also help you identify influencers by location or topic.

Hootsuite

Hootsuite.com

A social media management dashboard that allows you to not only keep track and manage your company's social media posts, but also monitor (and respond) to brand-related conversations.

Howsocialable

Howsociable.com

Howsociable measures a brand's impact on social media. They calculate a magnitude score that provides a level of online activity around a brand.

Influential

Influential.co

An agency that specializes in pairing brands with social influencers.

Keyhole.co

Keyhole.co

Keyhole tracks #hashtags, @account, keywords, @mentions, and URLs on both Twitter and Instagram.

Klear

Klear.com

A social intelligence platform that helps brands find influencers based on skill and location. Klear also allows marketers to analyze social user profiles and offers listening and analytics tools.

Little Bird

GetLittleBird.com

Little Bird helps businesses discover social media influencers.

Mention

Mention.com

Mention helps you identify the most important people talking about your company.

Salesforce

Salesforce.com

An enterprise solution cloud-based CRM platform. Within the platform, is a social media dashboard (Social Studio) that allows for planning, distribution, and analytics.

Social Mention

Socialmention.com

A social media search and analysis platform. It allows you to track your brand's performance on social media and identify individuals who are discussing your brand.

Social Rank   **Socialrank.com**

SocialRank lets you arrange your Twitter and Instagram followers based on value or engagement.

Sysomos   **Sysomos.com**

Sysomos provides social analytics software.

Tribe   **Tribegroup.co**

A word-of-mouth agency for brands seeking social influencers.

Triberr   **Tribber.com**

Triberr is a social network for bloggers. Companies can use Triberr to identify, connect, and hire with influential bloggers to be part of the social media marketing initiatives.

Viral Heat   **Viralheat.com**

Viral heat is a social media management platform that allows you to engage and publish with consumers, as well as providing monitoring and analysis.

Visual Intelligence and Analytics Firms

Beautifeye   **Beautifeye.co/**

Beautifeye is a visual intelligence platform that allows you to find and analyze images within Twitter, Facebook, Instagram, and Pinterest with your desired hashtag. It also analyzes specific image attributes (e.g., faces) and identifies influencers. Users have access to photos through a user-friendly visual dashboard.

Ditto   **Dittolabs.io/**

Ditto analyzes the contents of images. Specifically, they recognize brand logos and contextual image elements within most major visually orientated social media platforms. They are able to calculate a brand's visual impression and engagement and compare its performance against competitors. They can identify and engage with influential advocates.

LogoGrab

Logograb.com

LogoGrab has visual recognition software that finds logos within photos, videos, GIFs, and Vines. They are able to provide quantitative analysis of the logos through a customizable dashboard.

Visual e-Commerce Solutions

The following software types offer your brand e-commerce solutions that are attached to visual platforms and images:

like2buy	www.curalate.com/product/like2buy/
Tapshop	www.olapic.com/tap-shop/
Have2havit	https://have2have.it/

Social Media News Websites

Mashable	http://mashable.com/social-media
Social Media Examiner	www.socialmediaexaminer.com
The Next Web	http://thenextweb.com
Readwrite	http://readwrite.com
Re/Code	http://recode.net
Cnet	www.cnet.com
Business Insider	www.businessinsider.com
TechCrunch	http://techcrunch.com
Social Media Today	www.socialmediatoday.com/
Forbes	www.forbes.com/social-media/
Huffington Post	www.huffingtonpost.com/news/social-media/
Business Week	www.businessweek.com/companies-and-industries/social-media

Social Media Statistics and Insights

Pew Internet Research Project   www.pewinternet.org

McKinsey & Company
(Insights: Marketing and Sales)   www.mckinsey.com

Nielsen Insights   www.nielsen.com

eMarketer   www.emarketer.com

Statista   www.statista.com

Ethical and Legal Resources and Guidelines

Word of Mouth Association   www.womma.org/resources/online-resources

Offers a selection of online resources, including whitepapers, guidebooks, and code of ethics. Some resources are free, others require a membership.

Federal Trade Commission (News-Events)   www.ftc.gov

Truth in advertising (including guidelines for endorsements via social media).

Protecting consumer privacy and mobile technology issues.

Federal Drug Administration   www.fda.gov

Industry guides for using social media.

Securities Exchange Commission   www.sec.gov

Provides guidance on the use of social to announce key information to financial investors.

Financial Industry Regulation Authority   www.finra.org

FINRA issues guidance to firms and brokers on how to use social networking sites to communicate with the public.

American Medical Association   www.ama-assn.org

Guidelines on professionalism in the use of social media (ethics).

Social Media Thought Leaders to Follow

Brian Solis	www.briansolis.com
Seth Godin	http://sethgodin.typepad.com
Jeff Bullas	www.jeffbullas.com
Guy Kawasaki	www.guykawasaki.com

Index

OTHER TITLES IN OUR DIGITAL AND SOCIAL MEDIA MARKETING AND ADVERTISING COLLECTION

Victoria L. Crittenden, Babson College, Editor

- *Presentation Skills: Educate, Inspire and Engage Your Audience* by Michael Weiss
- *The Connected Consumer* by Dinesh Kumar
- *Mobile Commerce: How It Contrasts, Challenges and Enhances Electronic Commerce* by Esther Swilley
- *Email Marketing in a Digital World: The Basics and Beyond* by Richard C. Hanna, Scott Swain, and Jason Smith
- *R U #SoLoMo Ready?: Consumers and Brands in the Digital Era* by Stavros Papakonstantinidis, Athanasios Poulis, and Prokopis Theodoridis
- *Social Media Marketing: Strategies in Utilizing Consumer-Generated Content* by Emi E. Moriuchi
- *Fostering Brand Community Through Social Media* by William F. Humphrey, Jr., Debra A. Laverie, and Shannon B. Rinaldo

Announcing the Business Expert Press Digital Library

Concise e-books business students need for classroom and research

This book can also be purchased in an e-book collection by your library as

- a one-time purchase,
- that is owned forever,
- allows for simultaneous readers,
- has no restrictions on printing, and
- can be downloaded as PDFs from within the library community.

Our digital library collections are a great solution to beat the rising cost of textbooks. E-books can be loaded into their course management systems or onto students' e-book readers. The **Business Expert Press** digital libraries are very affordable, with no obligation to buy in future years. For more information, please visit **www.businessexpertpress.com/librarians.** To set up a trial in the United States, please email **sales@businessexpertpress.com.**